Identity Poetics

Race, Class, and the Lesbian-Feminist Roots of Queer Theory

Linda Garber

COLUMBIA UNIVERSITY PRESS

NEW YORK

Columbia University Press

Publishers Since 1893

New York   Chichester, West Sussex

Library of Congress Cataloging-in-Publication Data

Garber, Linda.

Identity poetics : race, class, and the lesbian-feminist roots of queer
theory / Linda Garber.

p. cm. — (Between men—between women)

Includes bibliographical references and index.

ISBN 0-231-11032-4 (cloth : alk. paper) — ISBN 0-231-11033-2 (pbk. : alk. paper)

1. Lesbian feminist theory. 2. Lesbians—Identity. 3. Lesbians—Poetry. 4.
Lesbianism—Philosophy. I. Title. II. Series.

HQ75.5 G373 2001

305.48'9664—dc21

2001025747

∞

Casebound editions of Columbia University Press books are printed
on permanent and durable acid-free paper.

Printed in the United States of America

c 10 9 8 7 6 5 4 3 2 1

p 10 9 8 7 6 5 4 3 2 1

To Barbara, of course

Contents

Acknowledgments

A number of people aided me in concrete ways while I worked on *Identity Poetics.* My thanks to the many librarians and archivists who provided assistance, especially the reference team at Stanford's Green Library, the staff and volunteers of the Lesbian Herstory Archives in New York (special thanks to Maxine Wolfe and Polly Thistlewaite), the June Mazer Collection in West Hollywood, and the Gay and Lesbian Historical Society of Northern California. Josie Saldaña provided crucial assistance with translation of Gloria Anzaldúa's poems. My former student and research assistant Rain Healer performed valuable cataloging and indexing. Third World Newsreel generously loaned me a copy of *A Litany for Survival,* Michelle Parkerson's documentary about Audre Lorde, for research purposes. The Provost and the College of Social Sciences at California State University, Fresno provided travel grants and periodic reductions from a heavy teaching load to make research and writing possible.

Kind words and constructive criticism were invaluable along the way. My thanks to Vilashini Cooppan, Peg Cruikshank, Kathryn Forbes, Barbara Gelpi, Judy Grahn, Diane Middlebrook, Ann Pellegrini, and Bonnie Zimmerman for sharing their opinions and advice on various parts of the manuscript. I am grateful to Merrill Schleier for inviting me to present my ideas about Audre Lorde's work to a large audience at the University of the Pacific.

Lillian Faderman supported the project all along and believed in me as a scholar before it was begun, when I saw myself as only a student compiling a large bibliography. For her body of work, her friendship, and her faith, there will never be adequate words to express my gratitude.

Barbara Blinick endured the entire research and writing process, and, although she would probably disagree, in many ways *Identity Poetics* is our collaborative effort. For her vital contributions, her love, and her unwavering support, I am deeply grateful.

Identity Poetics

Introduction: Race, Class, and Generations

Identity Poetics examines the works of five influential poet-activist-theorists to demonstrate the links between two schools of thought that are frequently pitched as opponents in ideological battle—often figured as a generation gap between lesbian thinkers—and to restore to their central place in the story the works of working-class/lesbians of color whose marginalization is foundational to the misbegotten construction of the debate itself.[1] The debate between lesbian feminism and queer theory (or, as it is often more broadly labeled, postmodernism) presents a simplistic either/or choice between two terms that are mutually implicated. Queer theory labels lesbian feminism essentialist (an academic code word for unsophisticated if not stupid), but even a cursory reading of foundational texts makes clear that lesbian feminism is a basically social constructionist project. Queer theory's "purists," to borrow Marilyn Farwell's term, assert the death of the subject (if not the subject position), but again and again find the need for strategically "'deploying' or 'activating' essentialism."[2] I propose the term *identity poetics,* a sort of postmodern identity politics, to bridge this gap that is not one: first, to account for the simultaneity of staunchly grounded identity politics and fluid positionality, particularly evident in the work of lesbians of color, as early as 1970; second, to highlight the ideas of working-class/lesbians of color, who exist as the third term—alternately marginalized, appropriated, and silenced—in the current arguments over lesbian politics and theory raging among (primarily) white lesbian academics.

I am not the first to suggest that the lesbian feminism/queer theory polarization is overwrought and unproductive—though I think that many of us began to suspect it at about the same time. By around 1993, I seemed to find myself in the following scenario quite often: a conference panel, or book release party, where the topic is related to lesbian politics and/or queer theory. I am in my late twenties, not quite "Gen X," but not a Baby Boomer either. A white lesbian academic or political activist who is older than I am begins to discuss the "generation gap" in lesbian theory, bemoaning the derision and/or erasure of lesbian feminism in queer theory. I raise my hand and say, "Excuse me, but I'm part of the 'younger generation,' and I know a lot about lesbian feminism. I've read a great deal of queer theory, but I agree with much of what you've said. We should be talking to each other, not fighting, and we definitely shouldn't be blaming this all on a generational difference." Or, at another variety of conference panel, or book release party, where the topic is related to lesbian politics and/or queer theory, someone around my age is deriding lesbian feminism, promoting queer theory, and insinuating (or outright stating) that our "generation" has seen the light and is no longer mired in the essentialisms of lesbian feminism and identity politics. I raise my hand and remind my peer that she doesn't speak for all "twenty-something" queers, many of whom still prefer to call ourselves lesbians.

Proposing my dissertation in 1992, this is what I wrote about the lesbian feminism/queer theory debate:

Contemporary theory adores a vacuum. Its practitioners are particularly adept at erasing the history of their ideas as they have evolved out of social movements, activist polemics, and literature. In many cases, "queer theorists" currently engaged in essentialist-vs.-constructionist debates over lesbian identity do little more than employ a different language to cover political ground familiar to the student of 1970s lesbian feminism. One side argues that homosexuality is innate, an "essential" identity; the other counters that social and historical circumstances shape and define, or "construct" identity. A third discourse denounces the either/or nature of the argument.

If, as I argue, the "third discourse" requires placing working-class/lesbians of color on center stage, then what am I, a white middle-class academic, doing as the author of this text? Poststructuralist theory would have it that my identity doesn't matter, but of course it does. To suggest otherwise is either callous or naive. To suggest otherwise is, once again, to blithely appropriate the texts and ideas of working-class/lesbians of color.

My race and class obviously mattered to an undergraduate in one of my classes who accused me of speaking from a "white, middle-class bias." He was a young, male, African American ROTC officer hostile to feminism, lesbians and gays, the analysis of social problems in general (preferring a "just work hard and shut up about it" approach)—and, as the old joke goes, he probably didn't like *me* much, either. I replied that yes, of course, without any escaping it, my own bias is white and middle class. It didn't matter that I had foregrounded this fact, prioritized women of color in the syllabus, and was dismantling racist arguments against affirmative action when the accusation was made. He was right. No matter what, my perspective is white and middle class.

That perspective, proscribed as it necessarily is, is the same one I bring to this book. I refuse the notion that this means that I cannot or should not write about lesbians of color, their work, and the impact of their work on me, on the lesbian-feminist and queer movements, and on feminist and LGBT studies.[3] I refuse the notion that my race and class privilege give me the right to, or, worse yet, require that I, ignore all of that. I learned this most directly from Audre Lorde, who wrote,

> And where the words of women are crying to be heard, we must each of us recognize our responsibility to seek those words out, to read them and share them and examine them in their pertinence to our lives. That we not hide behind the separations that have been imposed upon us and which so often we accept as our own. For instance, "I can't possibly teach Black women's writing—their experience is so different from mine." Yet how many years have you spent teaching Plato and Shakespeare and Proust? (Lorde, "Transformation," 43–44)

Lorde also had a lot to say about privilege. Ten years ago, when I was a graduate student, I was fortunate to hear her speak at Stanford University, where that topic has particular resonance. She reminded us (and I paraphrase here) that privilege is not neutral. If you do not pick it up and use it in the service of justice, if you leave it lying in the street, someone will pick it up and use it against you.

If there is a generation gap among white lesbian academics—for let's be clear that that is primarily whom we are discussing when the subject turns to the defending of academic or other institutional turf in this context—I don't think it is so much a chronological split between lesbian feminism and queer theory as a difference in the influence of the monumentally important work of lesbians of color, Audre Lorde and Gloria Anzaldúa paramount among them. Certainly, their works had a profound effect on many white lesbian academics who are older than I (who am thirty-five years old at this writing), and just as certainly there are white lesbian academics of my own generation who are aware of but are who are not, it seems, meaningfully or centrally cognizant of their importance. But the point is still worth making, I think, that I am of a generation of lesbian scholars whose "higher education," both inside and outside the academy, included Lorde, Anzaldúa, *This Bridge Called My Back, Home Girls,* and a variety of other work by women of color in the 1980s. It was not something added on later. They—not only Adrienne Rich (I refer to her work from the 1970s), not yet Judith Butler (who would be required reading in graduate school in the 1990s)—were the leading voices of feminist and lesbian theory. From our privileged positions in a mostly white academy and a white-dominated movement, my peers and I *could choose* to ignore them, but many of us didn't. Their critiques of racism within feminism were widely accepted as true by the time I heard about them. (That is, I wasn't one of the white feminists who heard Lorde's "The Master's Tools Will Never Dismantle the Master's House" at an almost entirely straight white conference that I had organized or attended; I read it when I was a college student— though probably not as a class assignment, given the paucity of women's studies offerings in my undergraduate education.)

What remained for my generation, then, was a choice of what to do with this work. We could: 1) quote it, footnote it, acknowledge its existence but remain fundamentally unchanged by it (the option of white privilege, of both the power and pressure of the academy), or 2) take it to heart. The option of ignoring it outright, or of refusing to really "get it," was not something aided and assisted by years of academic training and activist practice, as was true for many older white critics—some, but not enough of whom, of course, refused and resisted their racist educations and have produced vital work about women of color, white privilege, and racism. (Peggy McIntosh, Minnie Bruce Pratt, Adrienne Rich, Mab Segrest, and Elizabeth Spelman come to mind as prominent examples.)

I worry about the cohort of scholars and activist thinkers coming after me—educated through and by queer theory and the absence or derision of its predecessors and alternatives—a "generation" that includes some of my chronological peers and elders. (And, as Bonnie Zimmerman once quipped, in academia a "generation" is "about eight years" ["History"].) Does the institutionalization of queer theory, such as it is, mean that the impact of Lorde, Anzaldúa, and others will be a blip on the screen?

The question, it seems to me, is whether queer theory comprises a set of "master's tools" as it straps on the master's theories, whether or not (or to what extent) queer theory opposes "the master's house"—and at what point queer theory itself becomes the house that screams for dismantling. (My friend Elisabeth Bentley, whom I met at Harvard, used to call that venerable old institution "the dick factory": "If you don't have one when you get there, you have one by the time you leave.") Sure, in a little while, the need for another "generation" of LGBT/queer scholars to make their mark will result in opposition to queer theory—but I'm not certain that it needs to. I want to resist, kicking and screaming, the oedipal story of generational over-throw—the baby with the bath water—that is the heart and twisted soul of the academic conference circuit and the dissertation proposal process.

Much as I know that *Identity Poetics* has the potential to anger some peo-ple, I actually intend it to be a gesture of reconciliation—though one that looks like the kid who pointed a finger at the naked man, while the grownups were ooh-ing and aah-ing, and shouted, "The emperor wears no clothes!" The "emperor" in this case, is the by now axiomatic generation gap between lesbian feminists (sometimes more simply called "lesbian scholars" or "lesbian studies") and queer theory. I argue, first, that the divide, such as it is, is not, nor does it need to be, generational; second, that the divide, in certain ways, is *not* a divide but rather something like a failure to communi-cate, coupled with the coercive, divisive pressure of the academy to smash our forerunners—even if it means misreading and/or misrepresenting their work—to establish our own careers, which others will later take apart; third, that the defensiveness on the part of the "older" generation, which amounts to a rejection of new ideas, isn't real productive either; and, fourth, and cen-trally, that the creation and sustenance of the debate relies upon the margin-alization of working-class/lesbians of color.

It is also worthwhile to step back and wonder whether this "debate" is implicated in the old saw that academic fights are so vicious because so little is at stake. To whom is this fight important? Does it resonate outside the pages of journals and conference rooms at the MLA? As Barbara Christian noted over a decade ago, "Theory has become a commodity which helps determine whether we are hired or promoted in academic institutions—worse, whether we are heard at all." And so she asked pointedly, "For whom are we doing what we are doing?" ("Race," 335, 343). I am reminded of Adri-enne Rich's response to a harsh critique of her work by Helen Vendler: "Who owns poetry? . . . Is poetry owned by academic critics, or is it owned, in the largest sense, by people, by its readers, and by those who love it and write it?" ("Adrienne Rich"). Posed more broadly by Zimmerman, "So what is the responsibility of the critic to the writer, to the text, and to the community of readers?" ("Lesbians," 13). Who, finally, owns or defines lesbian identity, or queer politics? How does—Does?—this "debate" play in Peoria?

Clearly, within the academy—which, let us not forget, means among the mostly white, educated elite—the stakes are high. They include who gets hired in a desperate job market, but they have further implications for "the construction of knowledge," a knowledge we reproduce for an audience of students—so that, at least for the college educated, while they're in college (they stay roughly five years; we stay, if we're professionally successful, much longer), the stories we tell, the theories we espouse and that shape our work do affect others, some of whom will go on to become professional academics. And so the cycle continues.

Identity Poetics joins a small but encouraging body of work that refuses the either/or choice of lesbian feminism versus queer theory, in favor of a both/and option that reserves the right to healthy skepticism in both directions. A number of authors grapple with the issue in two important collections of essays: Dana Heller, ed., *Cross Purposes: Lesbians, Feminists, and the Limits of Alliance* (1997) and Bonnie Zimmerman and Toni A. H. McNaron, eds., *The New Lesbian Studies: Into the Twenty-First Century* (1996). Zimmerman, whose work appears in both collections, explains that the debate is created in part by an oversimplification of second-wave feminism, whose many strains were "largely boiled down" by nineties critics "to two binary oppositions: cultural feminism [standing in for lesbian feminism] and poststructuralist feminism [for queer theory]" ("'Confessions,'" 159). This left Zimmerman, a critic of cultural feminism, accused of being a cultural feminist because she does not wholeheartedly embrace poststructuralism. McNaron and Zimmerman explain that differences between lesbian feminists and queer theorists, and charges of essentialism and inaccessibility (respectively), are "hardened too often and too quickly in public fora, creat[ing] a dangerous gulf between scholars and activists who can ill afford to be divided" (xv).

Performance theorist Sue-Ellen Case, in her *Cross Purposes* essay, "Toward a Butch-Feminist Retro-Future," flippantly describes both her disenchantment with the drift of queer theory in the mid nineties and her nostalgia for an attitude common to both early lesbian feminism and early queer theory: "Early on, before its assimilation by postsomething or other's positioning of the discourses constructing sexuality, 'queer' theorizing still emulated the sense of taking back the insult—inhabiting the 'bad girl'—playing the monster—as 1970s lesbian feminism had taught some of us to do" (207). Like Case, political scientist Shane Phelan reaches back to some basic tenets of 1970s lesbian politics. Phelan claims the usefulness of a "deessentialized identity politics" straight out of the 1977 Combahee River Collective Statement, in combination with poststructuralism's resistance to global theories (Phelan, *Getting Specific*, 146). While naming herself a postmodern theorist and at times taking the familiar queer step of overgeneralizing about lesbian feminism (see, especially, *Getting Specific*, xvi), Phelan nevertheless overwhelmingly rejects the temptation of false dichotomies. "Within the confines of theory and politics in the United States, we are pressed to choose: individual or collective? liberal or communitarian (of whatever stripe)? These choices are as false as those of modern/postmodern and same/different" (xvii).

The queer theory/lesbian feminism dichotomy is often described as, among other things, a difference of emphasis: queer theory on sexuality, lesbian feminism on gender. Colleen Lamos sums up her skepticism in the title of her *Cross Purposes* essay, "Sexuality Versus Gender: A Kind of Mistake?" in which she describes the debate as "tiresome" (91). Michèle Aina Barale calls for a queer feminist theory (or, arguably, a feminist queer theory) when she asserts, simply, "Gender and sexuality cannot be experienced separately" ("When," 100).

While critics such as Zimmerman and McNaron can be, indeed have been, dismissed as lesbian feminists opposed to poststructuralist theory, Case, Barale, and other are less easily disregarded by a self-appointed queer avant-garde. The point is not that one is right and the other wrong, nor that one type of theory is smarter or more sophisticated than the other, but that either taken alone leaves great patches of the theoretical canvas bare. As in the case of emphasizing sexuality versus gender, both positions make the same mistake of insisting on a primary axis in a multiple reality, insisting that a theory must focus on one of only two conceivable alternatives. *Identity Poetics,* then, is not a nostalgic argument for a "fundamentalist" lesbian feminism (as no doubt its critics will charge), but an acknowledgment of the nuanced genealogy of lesbian and queer theories.

Marilyn Farwell skillfully negotiates the lesbian feminism/queer theory divide in her book *Heterosexual Plots and Lesbian Narratives,* a study of the heterosexual narrative convention and the resistance offered by "romantic," "heroic," and "postmodern" lesbian texts. Before elucidating her taxonomy of genres, Farwell first must return to one of lesbian literary criticism's persistent questions, What is lesbian literature? This leads her to the more contemporary concern, What constitutes a lesbian subject? embroiling her in lesbian-feminist and queer theory squabbles over the boundaries—even the very existence—of lesbian identity. Farwell refuses to take the bait dangled by either side, preferring "to refuse the either/or gambit" (14) and "to let the two positions remain problematically intertwined" (97):

Formulating a theory of the lesbian narrative that addresses both sides of this issue is one step toward healing this fractious dispute which refuses to see the continuity between yesterday's lesbian thinking and today's. That kind of separation for women and lesbians has always meant disaster, for which we must usually wait another generation or two to heal. The alternative is not to erase all difference between two seemingly opposed philosophical positions but to explore the similarities and connections that have been heretofore ignored. (24–25)

While Farwell is critical of "the story" of the lesbian subject told in the twentieth century, while she sees the similarities between lesbian feminism and queer theory, like many white lesbian theorists she leaves out the third figure, the move by working-class/lesbians of color that I see as a postmodern identity politics. In other words, Farwell can't account for the position of women of color, as described by Chela Sandoval, both "within and outside" the movement—because finally, for Farwell as for so many others, "the movement"—political, literary, academic—is white. In both the putative divide between lesbian feminism and queer theory and some attempts to heal it, working-class/lesbians of color exist as the third term that moves between the two others, a major force in both, yet centrally present in the story of neither. What would the story sound like if it were the story of women of color's identity poetics, with lesbian feminism and queer theory as white middle-class bit players, sideshows, or as mere interpretive structures in its narrative? Would the rise of queer theory, then, be proof positive that Audre Lorde was right, as opposed to Lorde being used as what my friend Vilashini Cooppan once referred to as queer theory's "retroactive poster child"?

A central contention of *Identity Poetics* is that the "heretofore ignored" connections are most clearly seen when looking at the pivotal writings of working-class/lesbians of color whose articulations of multiple, simultaneous identity positions and activist politics both belong to lesbian feminism and presage queer theory. For, in the words of Black British cultural studies critic Stuart Hall, "What the discourse of the postmodern has produced is not something new but a kind of recognition of where identity always was at" (115).[4] I raise this central point not merely in the name of fairness or inclusion but rather in what I think is a kindred spirit to a challenge issued by Sharon P. Holland in her essay "(White) Lesbian Studies":

I am not arguing solely for an inclusion of black lesbian writing in lesbian theories of the self, but rather, arguing for another revolutionary space:

one that begins to ask a 'how' question, rather than a 'why' question; one that seeks to extrapolate a position on the nebulous inclusion of women of color in lesbian studies as caused by a much larger problem in the emerging field than mere in/exclusiveness implies. (251–52)

I conceive of *Identity Poetics* as having three parts: a critical overview of recent historical writing about the women's and lesbian-feminist movements of the 1970s, one chapter each on the writing of Judy Grahn, Pat Parker, Audre Lorde, Adrienne Rich, and Gloria Anzaldúa, and a final chapter on the rise and hegemony of queer theory within LGBT studies. My intention is to place the work of key lesbian poet-theorists at the center of the tug of war over lesbian subjectivity—or, put less combatively, to frame their work with salient historical and theoretical conversations about lesbian identity and politics. I consciously chose not to write a book about theory alone, since that choice of genre performs the exclusions that I seek to undo. If this book "dotes" on poetry to the exclusion of other forms, as Farwell considers to be the case of too much lesbian criticism (*Heterosexual Plots*, 5), it is because of the central role of lesbian poets as theorists of lesbian identity and activism, the subject with which I begin my study.

Chapter One

The Social Construction of Lesbian Feminism

At least since the early twentieth century, when the medical profession in Europe and the United States both pathologized and popularized the concept of homosexuality, poetry has been central to the self-conscious construction of European American lesbian identity and community.[1] The self-reflective possibilities of the lyric and the mythmaking potential of the epic surely play a role here, but the importance of poetry for white lesbians rests largely in the historical figure of Sappho, poet of Lesbos. While Radclyffe Hall adopted the sexologists' terminology to plead for acceptance in her novel *The Well of Loneliness*, Renée Vivien and Natalie Clifford Barney, Hall's contemporaries in the lesbian literary subculture of 1920s Paris, translated and rewrote Sappho.[2] Vivien and Barney even attempted to create a community of women on the isle of Lesbos, geographically and symbolically linking lesbians and lesbian writing to the central figure of lesbian mythmaking. The idea of Sappho, whether or not the actual woman was what we would call a lesbian today, has been central to white lesbian identity and community because her presence in history provides a foundation on which lesbians could build a lineage: connection to the past (both mythic and historical), connection to others, and the possibility of surviving into the future.[3] Some lesbians of color also look to Sappho as an ancestor, although many rely on the history and spiritual traditions of their own ethnic heritages. For example, Audre Lorde incorporates the West African Yoruba tradition and names herself "zami," a Carriacou name for women who work together as friends and lovers in her mother's homeland of Grenada. Gloria Anzaldúa writes about indigenous Mexican figures from Coatlicue to Malintzín/La Chingada and names herself the "new mestiza." The dominant white culture's name for all women-loving women comes, not surprisingly, from classical Western culture rather than from any of the many cultures of people of color now living in Europe and the Americas.

In *The Gay and Lesbian Liberation Movement,* Margaret Cruikshank explains that the desire to create a tenable lesbian/gay history is linked to "self-esteem. . . . Lesbians [throughout history] took great pride in the sixth-century poet Sappho" (28). In 1955, Daughters of Bilitis, which would later become the first national lesbian organization, took its name from Pierre Louys's *Songs of Bilitis* (*Chansons de Bilitis,* 1895), a book of poems about an explicitly lesbian, fictional character named Bilitis, supposed to have been a student of Sappho of Lesbos.[4] In the 1970s, when lesbian culture flourished publicly on a large scale for the first time, Sappho's name was everywhere. In *Sappho Was a Right-On Woman,* Sidney Abbott and Barbara Love presented "A Liberated View of Lesbianism." A short-lived newspaper in Brooklyn was titled *Echo of Sappho;* another was, simply, *Sappho.* Suggestive or creatively reconstructed fragments of Sappho's poems were printed on posters for sale at women's bookstores. A political button proclaimed, "Sappho Is Coming." In the mid 1980s, Judy Grahn traced a lineage of lesbian poets back to Sappho in *The Highest Apple: Sappho and the Lesbian Poetic Tradition.* Grahn names Sappho, Emily Dickinson, Amy Lowell, H.D., and Gertrude Stein as "historic foremothers of today's Lesbian poets," a multicultural group including contemporary writers Adrienne Rich, Audre Lorde, Olga Broumas, Paula Gunn Allen, and Grahn herself (xix).

Through poetry as a vital locus of cultural meaning, lesbians have self-consciously created lineage, history, and identity. In this sense lesbian-feminist poetry is a social constructionist project. While some lesbian feminists, especially in the late 1970s, undeniably tended to essentialism, early radical writers questioned the institution of heterosexuality and self-consciously worked to create lesbian identity and community. Diana Fuss's explanation of the extent to which constructionism and essentialism are interdependent provides a key to understanding my contention. Particularly in the context of political movement, Fuss explains that all essences are constructs of historically and politically situated language. All essentialisms are therefore what the philosopher John Locke termed "nominal essences . . . not 'discovered' so much as assigned or produced—produced specifically by language" (Fuss, *Essentially Speaking,* 5).

In lesbian-feminist writing it is clear that "lesbian" is a nominal essence in this sense; that is to say, lesbian is a socially constructed category. However, over time this construct became more rigidified in practice, in some communities leading to censure of certain lesbian behaviors and ideologies. As a result, many queer theorists in the 1990s dismissed lesbian feminism wholesale as an unsophisticated, essentialist politics. Chapters 2 through 6 of this volume trace the construction of lesbian in the work of five lesbian-feminist poet-theorists—Judy Grahn, Pat Parker, Audre Lorde, Adrienne Rich, and Gloria Anzaldúa—pursuing what Fuss suggests ought to be the central question asked by students of identity politics: "not 'is this text essentialist (and therefore "bad")?' but rather, 'if this text is essentialist, *what motivates its deployment?*'" (xi). Following Gayatri Spivak, Fuss validates the strategic use of essentialisms "by the dispossessed themselves," as having the potential to be "powerfully displacing and disruptive" (32). If essentialism itself is a social construct, if in that sense we can only speak of essentialisms (plural), then, following Fuss, one must acknowledge the possibility of "deploying" an essentialism in a politically progressive sense rather than "lapsing into" essentialism in a purely reactionary stance (Fuss 20).

Lesbian feminists have both deployed and lapsed into use of identity categories, however, and it is for the latter that they are most well known today. Consequently, Fuss (and many others) have "some serious reservations" about the provisional deployment of essentialisms, since "there is always a danger" that a strategic wielding of an essentialism "may, in fact, lead once again to a re-entrenchment of a more reactionary form of essentialism" (32). As Shane Phelan notes, "The radical critique [of heterosexuality] notwithstanding, the drive for self-justificatory explanation [i.e., unrepentant essentialism] has also operated freely within lesbian feminism" (Phelan, "(Be)Coming," 771). Pitfalls aside, Phelan and Fuss both conclude, with Spivak, "that the 'risk' is worth taking" (Fuss 32). As I argue throughout *Identity Poetics,* that "risk," as taken by a variety of lesbian-feminist writers, laid the groundwork for the poststructuralist theories of lesbian subjectivity that came to dominate academic lesbian discourse by the 1990s.

In *Odd Girls and Twilight Lovers: A History of Lesbian Life in Twentieth Century America,* Lillian Faderman explains that lesbian feminists in the 1970s created community by building cultural institutions based on what seemed to be "a consensus . . . about what the broad configuration of the Lesbian Nation would finally look like: a utopia for women, an Amazon dream" (218). Much of the early theorizing of lesbian feminism took place in literature and performance no less than in political essay-writing. "Lesbian-feminists believed in the beginning of their movement that the commonality of committed lesbianism would be sufficient to help them build a unified lesbian community," and for all types of theorists—literary, activist, academic—"language became important . . . as an indication of political awareness and as a tool to raise consciousness" (Faderman, *Odd Girls,* 218, 219). Critic Harriet Malinowitz acknowledges that despite the often enormous differences she sees between lesbian feminism and queer theory, it must be conceded that being "selective or inventive about the language systems and discursive rules within which we compose ourselves"—a seemingly postmodern goal, on the face of it—"*has* been a major endeavor of lesbian feminist work" ("Lesbian Studies," 267). Lesbian-feminist writers, artists, and performers self-consciously created lesbian community—a social constructionist project—based upon readily available definitions of women and lesbians. At times lesbian-feminist theories seem to strategically deploy the identity categories; elsewhere they rely on what Faderman terms a "unity [that] seemed easy to attain" (*Odd Girls*, 218).

Farwell reminds readers, however, that lesbian-feminist identity constructions "refuse any simple essentialism" as they consciously reposition "the subject in relation to other women, a repositioning which connects the lesbian subject to the categories of gender and, simultaneously, disturbs them" (Farwell, *Heterosexual Plots*, 90). Using contemporary theoretical language, Farwell explains that "the lesbian-feminist construction of the lesbian subject concentrates on positionality, on the 'between' space and the direction that is revamped when one woman faces another instead of a man" (92). Just as she explains the social construction of lesbian feminism's seeming essentialism, Farwell points out that "the fluidity of lesbian sexuality described in many postmodern theories has become its own essentialist construct" (101).

Paramount in the construction of lesbian-feminist theory and culture in the 1970s was the establishment of periodicals and publishing houses, which were able to distribute lesbian-feminist literature and political theory to women living outside major urban centers (Faderman, *Odd Girls*, 224–26). Among the first books published were collections of poetry, and nearly every grassroots newspaper published poems as well. Carol Seajay, editor of *Feminist Bookstore News* and a founder of the Women in Print movement in the mid 1970s, recalls that because of the proliferation of women's newspapers, "I got to read [Grahn's poem] 'Edward the Dyke' sitting in my own living room in Kalamazoo, Michigan in 1973" (Seajay, "Women-in-Print Movement," 54). In the late 1960s and early 1970s, cutting-edge lesbian-feminist "ideas were very much in poetry . . . and poetry was published in the magazines and newspapers" (Seajay, "Women-in-Print Movement," 42). The first lesbian press on the West Coast, the Women's Press Collective in Oakland, was cofounded in 1970 by Grahn and later included other poets as well. Seajay and Grahn recall that "the poetry and the grassroots organizations" came first, followed by a few newspapers, and then the boom in women's publishing generated by the establishment of women's presses and bookstores (Seajay, "Women-in-Print Movement," 56–57). Cruikshank emphasizes "the crucial importance of writing in gay culture" and notes the role of small lesbian- or gay-owned presses (*Gay and Lesbian,* 128–29).

Within the lesbian literary and cultural boom of the early 1970s, poetry was particularly important. In "Culture Making: Lesbian Classics in the Year 2000?" Melanie Kaye(/Kantrowitz) compares "women's poetry in the early seventies" to "shakespeare [*sic*] in his own time" or "the audience for rock in the late sixties"; in their own context each was "extremely popular, the best . . . exploding with mass energy and creativity" (24). Cruikshank agrees, "Women's poetry readings have held a special place" in lesbian culture; she cites Audre Lorde, Adrienne Rich, and Judy Grahn as "among the most respected figures" (136). In her 1993 study of the political uses and institutionalization of lesbian poetry, Sagri Dhairyam elaborates on the poets' participatory role in the creation of communal lesbian identity: "[The lesbian] poet is not only the person who creates a literary text, but overlaps with the person who reads, who participates in a ritual for identity. . . . Poetry is an integral mode of willing communal identity in women's gatherings (Dhairyam, "House," 47, 57).

Grahn herself has called poets the "map makers" of lesbian feminism, "going out first and laying down the dimensions of the terrain and what the landscape (and the future) could possibly look like" (Seajay, "Women-in-Print Movement," 61). Lorde makes a similar point in her essay "Poetry Is Not a Luxury": "[Poetry] lays the foundations for a future of change, a bridge across our fears of what has never been before. . . . In the forefront of our move toward change, there is only poetry to hint at possibility made real" (Lorde 38, 39). Grahn reports that "masses of women" attended lesbian-feminist poetry readings in the early days of the movement, and that "fifteen years later . . . 'the movement' still keeps one ear to the ground to hear what else its poets may be telling." According to Grahn, "The leadership exerted by Lesbian and feminist poets as the mass movements of women developed during the 1970s cannot be exaggerated" (Grahn, *Highest,* xviii, 71).

Grahn's and Lorde's assessments are not self-aggrandizement. Critics— from academic journals to feminist newspapers—attest to the importance of lesbian-feminist poets in defining lesbian identity and lesbian community, that is, as I have contended, in self-consciously constructing and politically deploying the identity categories lesbian and woman. Estella Casto, in her study of Sexton, Rich, Lorde, and Broumas, concurs that feminist and lesbian poetry "demonstrates how poetry can be a means of political agency" ("Reading Feminist Poetry," 17). In 1981, Jan Clausen went so far as to call feminism—including, but not limited to, lesbian feminism—"a movement of poets." Clausen questions what she sees as the pervasive, sometimes counterproductive, strategies of feminist and lesbian poets in the 1970s in her pamphlet-essay, "A Movement of Poets," the most comprehensive treatment so far of lesbian-feminist poetics. Clausen considers lesbian poetry to be the driving force behind the larger phenomenon of "feminist poetry," which is the subject of her study. She begins with the proposition that not only has feminism made feminist literature possible but that the reverse is also true:

> Any serious investigation of the development of contemporary feminism must take into account the catalytic role of poets and poetry; that there is some sense in which it can be said that poets have made possible the movement.
>
> It might even be claimed, at the risk of some exaggeration, that poets *are* the movement. Certainly poets are some of feminism's most influential activists, theorists, and spokeswomen; at the same time, poetry has become a favorite means of self-expression, consciousness-raising, and communication among large numbers of women not publicly known as poets (3).

The feminist poets of whom Clausen writes are similar in that they name themselves feminist, and they "confirm that identification through the radicalism of their vision, and frequently their activism." She explains that most of the poets she considers "feminist" in this sense are "lesbians of color, non-lesbian women of color, white lesbians"; only "a few are straight white women. . . . Few are academics; fewer still are academically respectable" (5).

Clausen provides a brief history of poetry in the movement, illustrating its widespread publication both in journals and underground presses, and charting its development from the "I am a woman" theme of the early 1970s to "I am a lesbian" by mid decade (15). Despite her appreciation of the transformative power of politically motivated feminist poetry, Clausen laments the relative lack of serious criticism, which she sees as a failure to scrutinize what Adrienne Rich in another context called "the assumptions in which we are drenched" (15). Clausen sees several feminist imperatives that she fears trivialize poets and their work, to the point of being responsible for a diminished vitality of and audience for feminist poetry by the early 1980s (31). She draws "a caricature of feminist poetic practice" to highlight the expectations that she thinks induce self-censorship in politically active, aspiring poets (17). Ironically, Clausen's caricature amounts to a typology of the strengths of early lesbian-feminist poetry, articulating characteristics that had perhaps gone stale by the beginning of the 1980s:

> Feminist poetry is useful.
>
> Feminist poetry is accessible.
>
> Feminist poetry is "about" specific subject-matter: oppression, woman-identification, identity. It avoids both traditional forms and distancing techniques. . . . It is a statement of personal experience or feeling, with the poet a first-person presence in the poem.
>
> Feminist poetry is a collective product or process.
>
> Where feminist poetry is concerned, criticism is politically suspect—or irrelevant.
>
> The world of feminist literature is sufficient unto itself; the feminist poet need look no further for inspiration, audience, or support. (17, 22, 24, 25, 27, 29)

By the time this caricature came to seem like an actual repressive (or "politically correct") code, feminists of color, among others, were raising explosive, productive challenges to movement orthodoxies and hierarchies with increasing frequency and visibility. Clausen's essay was originally published the same year as *This Bridge Called My Back: Writings by Radical Women of Color,* a collection she sees as signaling "the most significant development for feminist poetry in the past few years . . . the emergence into public voice of a large group of feminist poets of color" who were "creating a movement-within-a-movement of great power and vitality" (31).

In "The Re-Vision of the Muse," Mary J. Carruthers draws a definition of lesbian poetry from her readings of Rich's *The Dream of a Common Language,* Lorde's *The Black Unicorn,* Grahn's *The Work of a Common Woman,* and Olga Broumas's *Beginning with O.* Carruthers writes that "among them, these volumes articulate a distinctive movement in American poetry. . . . I call this movement 'Lesbian poetry,' because the 'naming and defining' of this phrase is its central poetic preoccupation" (Carruthers 293). Carruthers views lesbian poets, of all the poetry movements of the 1970s, as having "the moral passion of seer and prophet" (299), which they bring to the task of establishing "a new *civitas*" (302) through the reinvention of mythologies in the creation of a new lesbian epic (300). Carruthers's "new *civitas*" is "predicated upon familiarity and likenesses, rather than oppositions"; it is troubling "to the general public" in its "use of the lesbian bond to signify that wholeness, health, and integrity which are minimized or negated by the death-devoted sickness of male-inspired civilization" (304). Both in "The Re-Vision of the Muse" and her earlier essay "Imagining Women: Notes Towards a Feminist Poetic," Carruthers opposes the antiromantic imagery and diction of much lesbian love poetry to the physically "alienated," "confessional" style of earlier woman poets like Sylvia Plath and Anne Sexton.

In her poststructuralist psychoanalytic look at "Lesbian Poetry and the Reading of Difference," Liz Yorke locates the poetic articulation of lesbian identity particularly in the erotic ("Primary Intensities"). She argues that "the language of poetry especially lends itself to the lesbian-feminist poet's strategic and combative project," which is to displace and rename images of sexual otherness pervasive in dominant culture (158), that is, "writing and theorising the female body as a positivity rather than a lack" (165). Yorke sees lesbian erotic poetry as offering a positive subjectivity with which lesbian readers can "identify" (158) in both a political and a Lacanian-psychological sense. "The lesbian [learns] to love and identify with herself in the affirming field of meaning of the lesbian Other. . . . [It] is, at deepest levels, the mirroring discourse of the lesbian *lover* which enables the lesbian subject to *make* herself, to identify herself" (192). For Yorke this psychological development is no mysterious process of the unconscious but rather "a crucial strategy for a lesbian poetics" (165).

Existential or Essential? Lesbian Identity Theory in the 1970s

The pejorative tag *essentialist* has stuck to lesbian feminism despite the decades-old preoccupation of lesbian poets and critics with definitions and constructions of lesbian identity, and despite more recent postmodern understandings of the strategic deployment of provisional essentialisms. Within LGBT studies the essentialism/constructionism debate has been claimed by "queer theory," which tends to characterize 1970s lesbian feminism as unreflectively essentialist, when it is addressed at all. In fact, early lesbian-feminist writers were not only participants in the social construction of lesbian identity, they were actively engaged in a version of the essentialism/constructionism debate itself. Faderman explains that in the late 1960s and early 1970s there were two strains of lesbian-rights activism, essentialist and existentialist. "Essentialists," who were likely to refer to themselves as "gay women," believed they were born homosexual and that their problems came from society's attitudes toward homosexuality; they were more likely to be aligned with the gay liberation movement than the women's liberation movement. Lesbian feminists, who "believed they 'existentially' chose to be lesbians," argued that the problem was society's attitudes toward women, and that lesbians suffered the extreme of that sexism (Faderman, *Odd Girls*, 189). The lesbian-feminist writer Carol Anne Douglas goes so far as to state that the "essentialist" position that sexual orientation is genetically determined "is more commonly held by gay men than by lesbians." Her assessment goes beyond Faderman's assertion, but Douglas does agree that "lesbians who see their lesbianism as predetermined . . . more often . . . identify as gay women than as lesbian feminists, and they are more likely to belong to gay groups, if they belong to any political groups, than to radical feminist or lesbian feminist groups" (Douglas, *Love*, 138). Just as essentialist lesbians earlier in the century had been boosted by sexology's claims that they were "born that way," lesbian feminists' existential argument was bolstered by the mental health profession's "minimalist definition of mental health," which depathologized homosexuality (Faderman, *Odd Girls*, 202).

In the 1990s, the political Right appropriated the radical idea that homosexuality is a "chosen lifestyle" in order to vilify those who would make the choice, ignoring the corollary critique of heterosexuality as less than natural itself. LGBT academics tend to espouse more complex and politically progressive constructionist theories than those forwarded by political conservatives; however, in response to the Right the predominant view now voiced outside the academy in many LGBT communities (and in the media) is the essentialist position. Much like Radclyffe Hall in the 1920s, these contemporary essentialists argue for civil rights based on the minority status that is their due because they were born gay. Their political strategy ignores the history of invasive and even violent psychiatric "cures" foisted upon homosexuals earlier this century.[5]

In the 1970s, lesbian feminists confronted the heterosexism of the women's movement and the essentialism (and sexism) of the gay liberation movement with the declaration that any woman could choose to be a lesbian. Writing in the 1990s, when "homophobia" became a household word, Cruikshank reminds readers that in the 1970s "simply naming heterosexuality and considering it as an institution was liberating. . . . The next step was to conceive of lesbianism as . . . a possible choice for large numbers of women. . . . Lesbianism could then be viewed as more than a personal preference; it was a stand against male domination" (*Gay and Lesbian*, 150). Faderman argues that lesbian feminists "took a revisionist approach to essentialism. It was true, they said, that lesbians were born 'that way.' But actually *all* women were born 'that way,' all had the capacity to be lesbians, but male supremacy destroyed that part of most women before they could understand what was happening." Lesbian feminism did not deny "primary" or "essentialist" lesbians but rather encouraged all women to become "elective, existentialist lesbians" (Faderman, *Odd Girls*, 206–7).

The early lesbian-feminist manifesto "The Woman-Identified Woman" asked, "What is a lesbian?" and answered with a rhetorical flourish illustrative of both Faderman's point and Fuss's explanation of the deployment of essence: "A lesbian is the rage of all women condensed to the point of explosion" (Radicalesbians 240). According to Douglas, "The Woman-Identified Woman" was the first expression of lesbianism as political strategy (Douglas, *Love*, 144).[6] A small but vocal number of heterosexual feminists followed the Radicalesbians's lead, going so far as to declare themselves "political lesbians." Best known for this stance is the radical feminist writer-activist Ti-Grace Atkinson, whom Douglas calls "the first non-lesbian radical feminist to acknowledge the political importance of lesbianism in the [women's liberation] movement." Douglas notes that in the early 1970s Atkinson "called herself a political lesbian until lesbians told her they felt the term did not recognize the specificity of their experience" (Douglas, *Love*, 143).[7] Once heterosexuality was understood as an oppressive institution, lesbianism could be construed as a conscious, political choice—"feminist theory in action" (Abbott and Love, *Sappho*, 136)—revolutionary both in its rejection of men and, more important, in the central value it placed on women. "In this respect," Faderman explains, "the 1970s offer a prime example of sexuality as a social construct" (*Odd Girls*, 207–8). Zimmerman concurs. Commenting on "Lesbians in Revolt" (1972) by Charlotte Bunch, one of the architects of lesbian-feminist theory as a member of the separatist Furies collective, she points out that "Bunch is positing a constructionist, not essentialist, argument. Feminists are not essentially lesbians, any more than lesbians are necessarily feminists. To state that feminists must become lesbians assumes that lesbianism is a matter of choice and conviction, not biological conditioning or sexual behavior" (Zimmerman, "'Confessions,'" 162).

The commonality of "lesbian experience" was assumed by too many white lesbians in the seventies, but by the end of the decade any easy sense of sisterhood in the women's and lesbian-feminist movements was straining under the massive weight of differences among feminists in particular and among women in general. The radical-feminist tenet that all oppression stems from sexism simply did not match the experiences of many women; after a decade of the women's liberation movement, they made it clear that focusing on sexism alone would not solve the problems of racism, classism, and homophobia in the world at large or in the movement itself. While white middle-class women continued to hold most positions of feminist institutional power in the 1980s, lesbian feminism and the wider women's movement became largely focused on the agendas of women of color and sex radicals. The two watershed events in this gradual progression were the publication in 1981 of *This Bridge Called My Back* and the Barnard College sexuality conference in 1982. *This Bridge* was the first book of writings by and about women of color primarily addressed to each other rather than to the white women's movement. The Barnard conference was the originary moment for the "sex wars" raging around pornography and sadomasochism.

According to Phelan, by the time the sex wars and organizing by women of color were in full swing, the early radical/constructionist focus of lesbian feminism had largely slipped into essentialist interrogations of the true meaning of lesbianism. Widespread belief among lesbian feminists that lesbians are the best feminists, that no one but a lesbian can be trusted as an ally, that all systems of discrimination derive from sexism, and that therefore racism and sexism are less of a problem for lesbians than for others "served as the basis for codes of authentic lesbian existence and identity. . . . Whether explicitly separatist or not, these theories have worked to turn our communities inward rather than to propel us toward alliances and coalition with others" (Phelan, "(Be)Coming," 766). In other words, narrowing definitions of "lesbian" generated from some quarters of lesbian feminism have left out many lesbians who feel disenfranchised (or merely affronted or repulsed) by rigid definitions of lesbian identity and politics. Simply stated, "While the second wave of feminism in the 1960s originally provided a powerful discourse for lesbians, that discourse eventually manifested its limits" (Phelan, "(Be)Coming," 779). In her attempt to negotiate between experiential specificity and postmodern strategic posturing (which reads somewhat like a plea for a truce among warring factions), Phelan makes clear that contesting ideas of lesbian identity remained a problem in the nineties: "Lesbians should not refuse the specificity and reality of lesbian experience; neither should we reify our experience into an identity and history so stable that no one can speak to it besides other lesbians who agree on that particular description of their existence" (786).

Faderman attributes the factionalization of the lesbian community in the 1980s on the one hand to the movement's successful creation of social space, in which less radical (or merely different) lesbians felt safe to come out and join the political fray, and on the other to infighting born of some lesbian feminists' intolerance of anything less than strict adherence to unofficial but widespread rules governing behavior, appearance, and politics. The utopic dream of Lesbian Nation "was doomed finally to failure,"

> because of youthful inexperience and inability to compromise unbridled enthusiasms, but nevertheless it helped to change the meaning and the image of lesbianism by giving love between women greater visibility and by presenting visions of self-affirmation through lesbian-feminist music and literature (*Odd Girls*, 220).

Faderman identifies class, race, separatism, and sexual behavior as the main focuses of "factions and battles" that had developed within the lesbian community by the 1980s. All were issues that could not be resolved by lesbian feminists' "excessive idealism," "unrealistic notions," and "little capacity for compromise" (*Odd Girls*, 236–40, 231–32, 243–44). Oddly, Faderman spends an entire chapter discussing the sex wars, squeezing a discussion of the remaining disputes (along with several others) into a single chapter.

Whereas Faderman singles out the sex wars, Linnea Stenson argues that "despite other problems in Lesbian Nation . . . the difficulties for lesbians of color who were expected to integrate a primarily white lesbian-feminist movement played a large part in the failure of that experiment" (Stenson 186). Chela Sandoval agrees, explaining that although *This Bridge Called My Back* "made the presence of U.S. third world feminism impossible to ignore on the same terms as it had been throughout the 1970s," lesbian feminism did not instantly become multicultural and antiracist; rather, the increased presence of lesbians of color led to new strategies for the marginalization of women of color in feminist discourse ("U.S.," 5).

"Problems of Exclusion" in Lesbian History

Despite the evidence that lesbian feminism in the 1970s proved unable to cope with the diversity of its own constituents, there is a more complex history to be told about the movement than a straightforward narrative of intolerance and utopianism would suggest. The "official stories by which the white women's movement understands itself and its interventions in history" (Sandoval, "U.S.," 5) provide only part of the picture, serving to erase the history of lesbians of color while vilifying all white lesbian feminists for a particular type of narrow vision. The current trend in LBGT studies and activism is to elevate queer theory and politics to a privileged position from which to sneer at lesbian feminism, which is seen as outdated, rigid, and intolerant. This bias might be appropriate if by now "the movement" had entirely repudiated the aims and ideas of the 1970s; then one could argue that contemporary activists and academics need only learn what was bad about lesbian feminism so as to avoid repeating history. But many of the same radical ideas are still circulating—sometimes in more or less their original forms, sometimes only in part or reformulated in poststructuralist language.

In her 1992 essay, "Sisters and Queers: The Decentering of Lesbian Feminism," sociologist Arlene Stein typifies 1990s queer avant-gardism. She calls for looking at "the process by which movements remake identities" (36), seemingly unaware of how her own essay remakes 1970s lesbian feminism. She begins with the premise that lesbian feminism was ideologically, if not geographically, a centralized movement, operating upon a "fundamental hegemonic logic" (35). That is, despite the utter lack of organization on a national scale, according to Stein lesbian feminism somehow had unified, definable goals and methods. It is perhaps because of this assumption that Stein is able to declare the "end" (36) of lesbian feminism, out of whose ashes she thinks a more sophisticated notion of lesbian identity has arisen. And perhaps because her research was conducted "primarily in the San Francisco Bay Area" (35), Stein ignores the continuing influence of (sometimes separatist or cultural feminist) lesbian feminism throughout the United States, Canada, and beyond. She implies that as goes San Francisco, so goes the lesbian world, and all for the better. Her bias is against those lesbian feminists in the hinterlands, "nonurban areas, where the pace of change may be slower," that is, where lesbian feminism is still firmly entrenched (35). By Stein's own admission, then, it seems that stodgy old lesbian feminism is alive and well all over the place.

Sisters, Sexperts, Queers: Beyond the Lesbian Nation, a 1993 anthology edited by Stein, labors so diligently to dethrone lesbian feminism that the movement's continuing influence is apparent. While a few excellent essays provide insight into the intersections of race, class, and sexuality,[8] the dominant theme of the collection is hostility toward a stereotyped version of 1970s lesbian feminism. Declarations of the rigidity of lesbian-feminist ideology are repeated so frequently that they take on an air of accepted truth, but what is missing from Stein's and most of her contributors' perspectives is in-depth analysis and historical substantiation. If lesbian feminism has fallen into disfavor with so many (especially younger) lesbians, how and why has this happened? By the middle of the book, statements like this one, from Stein's "Androgyny Goes Pop: But Is It Lesbian Music?" are merely redundant: "Lesbian feminists attempted to universalize the possibility of lesbian experience by removing its grounding in biology, but in its place they often created rigid ideological prescriptions about who belongs to the lesbian community" (108). Had Stein detailed what she means by "the lesbian community," or specifically which lesbian feminists create what ideological prescriptions and the means by which these rules are enforced, she would have provided a much needed analysis of the current state of lesbian affairs. As reviewer Sarah Schulman points out, Stein instead offers a collection nearly obsessed with "disassociat[ing] from seventies feminism. And for all [the contributors'] combined credentials in academia and on the street, none are able to step back far enough to ask why" (24). (Apparently chastened by critiques like Schulman's, Stein repudiated her blanket antilesbian-feminist stance in her next book, *Sex and Sensibility.* "In retrospect, my book, among others, appears overly critical of lesbian feminists' excesses and insufficiently appreciative of some of their contributions. It also tended to homogenize the legacy of lesbian feminism, which was far from seamless and monolithic" [4].)

Faderman's tone is more moderate than Stein's critique in *Sisters, Sexperts, Queers,* and she provides ample historical evidence and analysis to support her claims. But Faderman, too, seems relieved that lesbian feminism—seen as a "revisionist essentialism" (Freedman 16)—appears to be dead. Faderman writes,

> The women-identified-women who hoped to create Lesbian Nation in the 1970s failed in their main goal . . . a goal born of excessive idealism. . . .
> Their failure was inevitable not only because of their unrealistic notions, but also because, like most true believers, they had little capacity to compromise their individual visions (*Odd Girls,* 243–44).

Faderman implies that few, if any, lesbian feminists (or separatists) were left after 1979—and curiously, she fails to place herself in this history, although she came out in the mid 1950s and started doing lesbian academic work in the mid 1970s.[9] However, she does note the successes and contributions of lesbian feminism—chief among them the raising of consciousness toward more widespread lesbian self-acceptance, the identification of gay liberation as sexist and women's liberation as homophobic, and the creation of "women's culture" (*Odd Girls,* 244).

Two other recent works of lesbian history appear to represent those lesbian feminists whom many scholars and much popular gossip consider obsolete. Margaret Cruikshank's *The Gay and Lesbian Liberation Movement* discusses "Lesbian Feminism from the 1970s to the 1990s," indicating the author's sense that the movement is still vital, if in a different form or forms than it took in the 1970s (154–60). Contrary to Stein's narrative of the decline of radical lesbianism in the 1980s, Cruikshank asserts that "the broad lesbian feminist movement gained momentum" during the 1980s and diversified, serving it well in the face of a massive right-wing backlash (157). Where Stein and Faderman see a new political movement, Cruikshank sees an evolution of lesbian feminism. Similarly, Carol Anne Douglas assumes the importance of radical and lesbian feminisms. She presents a veritable primer on their multiple strains of thought in her book *Love and Politics: Radical Feminist and Lesbian Theories.* As opposed to the historians, Douglas uses present-tense verbs to lay out a body of political theory that she describes as current and thriving.

Despite their different assessments of lesbian feminism's continuing impact, all the recent histories of 1970s lesbian feminism generalize from the separatist, white (downwardly mobile) middle-class aspects of the movement. Most accounts claim that lesbian feminism died of its own political correctness around 1980, giving way to pluralistic coalition politics. The division by decade seems too neat, however. Historical shifts are rarely so abrupt.[10] While criticisms of militant lesbian-feminist didacticism are often well-founded, they are usually also based on generalization, if not outright stereotype. Claiming that lesbian politics belonged to white women in the 1970s and to women of color in the eighties denies the persistence of lesbian feminism in the 1980s (and nineties) and ignores white women's continuing privilege; it also overlooks the participation and leadership of women of color in lesbian politics and culture in the 1970s. Historians of lesbian feminism have so far failed to tell stories centered on the many working-class lesbians/lesbians of color who were in fact instrumental to the movement— from the beginning, and increasingly by the late 1970s.

Most representations of lesbian feminism suffer from what white feminist philosopher Elizabeth Spelman has termed "Problems of Exclusion in Feminist Thought" (*Inessential Woman*). Spelman explains that in order to discuss women "as women" feminism has ignored "the heterogeneity of women" (*Inessential Woman,* ix) and/or added race and class as categories of analysis separate from gender. Thus what social constructionists have called gender essentialism Spelman recognizes as a racist, classist focus on white, middle-class women, as if their experience were somehow about gender alone. This leads to the phenomenon Spelman names, in the subtitle to a chapter of her book *Inessential Woman,* "The Ampersand Problem in Feminist Thought," the addition of "race & class" (and I would add, "& sexuality") to the analytical category of gender. The ampersand problem implies that gender & race & class & sexuality are separate categories that can be "piled upon each other" (123). Spelman demonstrates that categories of identity and/or oppression "must be seen as interlocking" (123) since, for example, "sexism and racism do not have different 'objects' in the case of Black women" (122)—calling to mind the title of the breakthrough anthology of black women's studies, *All the Women Are White, All the Blacks Are Men, But Some Of Us Are Brave.*

Gender essentialism and the ampersand problem obscure the fact that white women experience sexism in the context of white skin privilege, whereas women of color experience sexism in the context of racism (and vice versa). In this sense, then, there are sexisms, plural. Spelman explains,

> We cannot automatically conclude that the sexism all women experience is the same. We have to understand what one's oppression "as a woman" means in each case. . . . Moreover, we cannot describe what it is to be subject to several forms of oppression, say, sexism and racism and classism, by adding together their separate accounts (14).

Because gender is constructed and experienced differently in conjunction with various races/classes/ethnicities/sexualities, in an important sense there exist a variety of genders. Hence, à la Fuss, gender essentialism must be seen as a specific—racist, classist—construction of gender.

Spelman lambastes white feminist attempts to deal with "the problem of difference," pointing out that the "problem" is really one of privilege (162). She examines three typical, well-intentioned statements that inadvertently serve to reinscribe white, straight women as the central topic of feminist inquiry:

1. Feminist theory must take differences among women into consideration.
2. We need to hear the many voices of women.
3. Feminist theory must include more of the experiences of women of different races and classes (162–63).

Statement number 1 preserves the division between feminist theorists and women from whom they differ, making clear that feminist theory as currently constituted does not include women who are "different" from the presumed white, heterosexual, middle-class norm. "Take . . . into consideration" is echoed in the "we" of statement number 2. Who are "we"? Or, as African American poet Lorraine Bethel so clearly puts it in the title to her 1979 essay "What Chou Mean *We,* White Girl?" Statement number 3 reveals the power of those who might (or might not) choose to "include" women somehow different from themselves. "Welcoming someone into one's own home doesn't represent an attempt to undermine privilege," Spelman explains, "it expresses it" (*Inessential Woman,* 163).

When "inclusion" is the goal of a feminist and/or lesbian study, the ampersand problem is often the result. Typically, a chapter about a given topic as it relates to "women" (of the essentialized variety) concludes with a section describing how the same topic affects women of color, working-class women, and/or lesbians. That issues of race, class, and/or sexuality appear at all is of course an improvement over earlier (or sometimes contemporary but merely worse) renditions of topics in women's studies. But this is akin to saying that sitting in the back of the bus is better than having to walk; the Montgomery Bus Boycott demonstrated otherwise. The fact remains that most accounts of women in relation to whatever particular topic take women to include only white, straight, and middle-class women, unless the explicit focus of the work is women of color, working-class women, lesbians, or some combination of these categories. But the problem is rarely solved there either.

Although Spelman's ideas on some level may seem obvious, much historical writing about lesbian-feminism replicates earlier models, now perpetrating "problems of exclusion" in *lesbian* thought—despite, and sometimes because of, white historians' attempts to be inclusive. For example, Faderman discusses "lesbians"—and then lesbians of color. Reviewing *Odd Girls and Twilight Lovers,* Estelle Freedman points out that Faderman is particularly attentive to class distinctions but tends to subsume "race . . . under class in her discussion." Freedman further suggests that because of the availability of sources Faderman mistakenly considers "white, educated, professional women [to be] the vanguard of the emergence of modern lesbianism" (16).

Few white lesbian historians ignore outright the "problems of exclusion" of race and class, although most perpetuate them in some way. In her first chapter, Carol Anne Douglas calls attention to racism and her own white skin privilege, listing the names of white women whom she discusses throughout her book, "so that whiteness will not be seen as the norm." She adds, "I am white, as well" (Douglas, *Love,* 18). An admirable attempt, perhaps, but from there the book persists mainly in ampersand mode (with the exception of the chapter on separatism, where the critique of lesbians of color is fully integrated). Cruikshank's narrative of modern lesbianism is peppered with isolated references to well-known lesbians of color, includes a thoughtful section on the challenge to lesbian-feminist conformity by lesbians of color in the 1980s, and ultimately focuses on "lesbians" (quote/ unquote). That is, back to square one. Faderman makes passing mention of lesbians of color who were politically active in the 1970s (*Odd Girls*, 220, 235, 242), but she only takes up their stories in a brief section about racism in the predominantly white movement of the 1970s (240–43) and in another about the "Validation of Diversity" in the 1980s (284–92). In "Sisters and Queers," Stein argues that lesbian-feminist ideology suppressed differences to such an extent that relatively few lesbians of color identified as "lesbian feminists" (45). Despite this insight, the essay focuses on women who according to Stein did identify as lesbian feminists, implying that what she considers important about the 1970s is the political activism of white women. While these accounts all deal in some ways with white lesbian-feminist racism, none take seriously the study of the lives and politics of lesbians of color before the publication of *This Bridge Called My Back* in 1981. All imply that lesbian feminism was created and sustained by white, middle-class women alone.

In their revaluation of the political agency of working-class lesbian bar culture in the 1940s and fifties, historians Elizabeth Lapovsky Kennedy and Madeline D. Davis explain,

> Joan Nestle, Audre Lorde, and Judy Grahn, all of whom related to some aspect of working-class lesbian communities in the 1950s, give us the beginnings of a new tradition, one that portrays working-class lesbians as creating lesbian culture and resisting oppression in the context of a severely oppressive environment. (*Boots of Leather*, 14)

These three working-class-identified lesbians—one of whom is African American, another Jewish—continued to be instrumental to the creation of lesbian-feminist culture in the 1970s. At a time when historians see a white, Protestant, middle-class movement, Nestle, Lorde, and Grahn were drawing on their diverse racial and ethnic identities and on the working-class lesbian culture of an earlier era while simultaneously laying the groundwork for the diversity typically associated with the 1980s and nineties.

Ample evidence shows that working-class/lesbians of color were active in lesbian feminism and the women's liberation movement in the 1970s. Chela Sandoval explains that women of color were both active within and "at odds with" white feminism "from the beginning of what has been known as the second wave of the women's movement" ("U.S.," 4). Among the early lesbian, bisexual, and heterosexual feminists of color she cites are African Americans Francis Beal and Toni Morrison, Asian Americans Mitsuye Yamada and Nellie Wong, Native American Paula Gunn Allen, and Chicana Velia Hancock (4, 9). Similarly, Judy Grahn describes the diversity of the women involved in the women's and lesbian-feminist movements on the West Coast as early as 1969, including black lesbians, Asian American lesbians, "Jewish radical Lesbians," and women "from the European folk 'marginal culture' known variously as lower class, working class, white trash" (Seajay, "Women-in-Print Movement," 25; Grahn, *Highest*, xviii). Discussing "class oppression" in 1970, activist Robin Morgan wrote in the introduction to *Sisterhood Is Powerful* that "a large percentage of the movement comes from working-class backgrounds" (xxxl).[11]

The "Combahee River Collective Statement," issued in 1977 by a group of black feminists and lesbians who had been meeting and organizing since 1974, points out that the National Black Feminist Organization was formed in 1973 as a result of racism and elitism in the women's liberation movement: "Black, other Third World, and working women have been involved in the feminist movement from its start, but both outside reactionary forces and racism and elitism within the movement itself have served to obscure our participation" (272–73). In "Toward a Black Feminist Criticism" collective member Barbara Smith notes the existence in 1977 of "at least one Black lesbian writers' collective, Jemima," as well as a handful of groundbreaking black lesbian writers and critics, despite the predominance of white feminists' literature and criticism in print (175, 172–73). *Azalea*, a literary magazine for Third World lesbians, was launched the same year that the "Combahee River Collective Statement" and Smith's essay were published (Morse and Larkin, "Introduction," xxi). At least seventeen other periodicals by and for women of color were publishing in the 1970s.[12]

Asian American poet Willyce Kim recalls that it was difficult to find other lesbian feminists of color in the early 1970s in the San Francisco Bay Area, although she did work with African American poet Pat Parker and knew at least one other Asian American lesbian writer. Parker herself, in "Have You Ever Tried to Hide?" her often quoted poem first published in 1973 about racism in the women's movement, describes not only white racism but also the "pain" and "silent rage" she encounters in "the other Blacks" present at a feminist political meeting (Parker, *Movement in Black*, 47). Tiana Arruda remembers the 1970s as the time when she first connected with "many women of color," including other Latina lesbians, through her participation in a variety of feminist organizations in California. Darlene Pagano, a white working-class-identified women's bookstore activist, insists on recognition of the many working-class women involved in the women's movement and lesbian feminism from the late 1960s on. The "Lesbian Feminist Declaration of 1976" presents a movement vitally concerned with race, class, age, imperialism, and the environment. Its authors, "representatives of the Dykes for an Amerikan Revolution," call for "social and economic revolution," claiming "full power to levy war against sexism, racism, classism and all other oppressions. We declare solidarity with all who struggle for liberation."

Diversity is where you look for it, and as the Combahee River Collective pointed out, white middle-class historians seem to be looking the other way. Intent on telling the story of lesbians "as lesbians" in the 1970s, they give short shrift to the many working-class/lesbians of color active within and around lesbian feminism, missing the story behind the multicultural lesbian and feminist explosion of the 1980s. Sandoval argues that women of color are erased by typologies of "white hegemonic feminism" because women of color often have operated "between and among" the organizations and strategies of resistance commonly associated with the white feminist movement.

> This unusual affiliation with the movement was variously interpreted as disloyalty, betrayal, absence or lack: "When they *were* there, they were rarely there for long" went the usual complaint, or "they seemed to shift from one type of women's group to another." They were the mobile (yet ever present in their "absence") members of this particular liberation movement. It is precisely the significance of this mobility which most inventories of oppositional ideology cannot register ("U.S.," 13–14).

Sandoval outlines the "typology" that "comprises the mental map of . . . the U.S. white women's movement" and argues persuasively that the accepted discourse of that movement "sets limits on how the history of feminist activity can be conceptualized, while obstructing what can be perceived or even imagined by agents thinking within its constraints" ("U.S.," 10). Yolanda Chávez Leyva concurs in her essay "Breaking the Silence: Putting Latina Lesbian History at the Center," explaining that "Latina lesbian history challenges a number of . . . aspects of the Anglo-lesbian paradigm of the emergence of modern lesbian identity," such as urbanization, economic opportunities, "a public culture that allows lesbians to find each other; and finally, the eroticization of individuals by intellectuals who view sexuality as central to a person's identity. These factors take on difference meanings and nuances, not yet fully understood, when we look at Latina lesbian experiences in the United States" (149). In short, "Latina lesbian history puts Latina lesbians at the center" (151). We might say, conversely, that white lesbian history, which just about every- one simply calls, "lesbian history," puts white lesbians at the center, acting as if lesbians of color did not attend the party, fight at the barricades, or form lesbian identities until the 1980s. Taxonomies of lesbian and queer theory sim- ilarly exclude working-class/lesbians of color, relegating their work to other domains. As Sharon Holland explains, "The 'colored girls' do all the soul work of the discipline, and the white women shell out the theories that decide how this soul work is going to be read, disseminated, and taught in juxtaposition to already canonized white lesbian authors" ("(White) Lesbian Studies," 250). Tiana Arruda sums up the problem of exclusion in lesbian-feminist thought when she recalls that the 1981 publication of *This Bridge Called My Back* was "the end" result of years of activism by working-class/lesbians of color, "not the beginning."

Chapter Two

Putting the Word Dyke *on the Map: Judy Grahn*

Judy Grahn's paean to Sappho, *The Highest Apple: Sappho and the Lesbian Poetic Tradition,* traces the influence on twentieth-century lesbians of the seventh-century B.C.E. poet who gave modern Western culture "two of our most important names . . . Lesbian and Sapphic" (xxi). For her part, the working-class-identified Grahn has said that she wants to follow in Sappho's footsteps, "to be remembered as someone who helped put the word *dyke* on the map."[1] Grahn writes that Mary Carruthers's essay "The Re-Vision of the Muse: Adrienne Rich, Audre Lorde, Judy Grahn, Olga Broumas," published in 1983, "positively influenced" *The Highest Apple* (Grahn, *Highest Apple,* xix); however, Carruthers's genealogy of lesbian-feminist poetry contradicts both Grahn's account of recent lesbian history and evidence of foundational writing and activism by working-class/lesbians of color early in the movement.

Carruthers begins her definitional study of "Lesbian poetry" with Adrienne Rich because, she writes, "it is impossible not to. Adrienne Rich was an active influence in some way on all the other three writers" ("Re-Vision," 296). Certainly, by the early 1980s Rich was central to lesbian-feminist poetry and to lesbian feminism in general, but in the late 1960s and early 1970s—when Grahn wrote, performed, and originally published *Edward the Dyke and Other Poems, The Common Woman, She Who,* and *A Woman Is Talking to Death*—Rich was an influential feminist poet who had not yet published explicitly lesbian work. Judy Grahn was to lesbian feminism in the late 1960s and early 1970s what Rich became in the late 1970s and early 1980s.

Grahn was a member of the Gay Women's Liberation Group, the first lesbian-feminist collective on the West Coast, founded around 1969. The collective established the first women's bookstore, A Woman's Place, and the first all-woman press, the Women's Press Collective (Case, "Judy Grahn's," 49), which "devoted itself exclusively to work by lesbians disfranchised by race or class" (Harris, "Introduction," xxxi). Grahn's poems, circulated in

periodicals, performances, chapbooks, and by word of mouth, were foundational documents of lesbian feminism. Her work enjoyed a wide underground readership before 1975 (Larkin, "Taking Risks," 92), although it did
not reach commercial audiences until the late 1970s. Collected as *The Work
of a Common Woman* in 1978, the poems were published first by Diana Press
(a small lesbian-feminist press into which the Women's Press Collective was
incorporated in the early 1970s), then the New York publishing house St.
Martin's Press, and finally by Crossing Press. According to Carl Morse and
Joan Larkin, "Grahn's work, both as legendary poet and independent publisher, fueled the explosion of lesbian poetry that began in the 70s" (Morse
and Larkin, *Gay and Lesbian*, 140).

Carruthers cites Rich's introduction to Grahn's collection, *The Work of a
Common Woman*, as evidence of Rich's influence on Grahn's poetry, and
Grahn herself has acknowledged Rich, among others, as important to the
development of her work. What Carruthers fails to note, however, is that
Rich was moved to write the introduction to *The Work of a Common Woman*
because of the impact of Grahn's work on her own poetry years earlier. In
Rich's introduction, "Power and Danger: *The Work of a Common Woman* by
Judy Grahn," Rich describes weeping when she first read Grahn's "A Woman
Is Talking to Death" in 1974: "I knew in an exhausted kind of way that what
had happened to me was irreversible. All I could do with it at that point was
lie down and sleep, let . . . the knowledge that was accumulating in my life,
the poem I had just read, go on circulating in my bloodstream" (9). The most
clear evidence that Grahn influenced Rich's later work is Rich's adoption of
the term "common" from Grahn's widely circulated chapbook of poems, *The
Common Woman* (1969), in *The Dream of a Common Language: Poems,
1974–1977* (1978) "where it was greatly broadened by new phrases" (Grahn,
Highest Apple, 73).

Carruthers's beginning with Rich reflects contemporary assessments of
lesbian poetry and politics and is inconsistent with the history of lesbian-
feminist publishing and literary influences. In *The Highest Apple*, Grahn
"credit[s] as influences" Rich, Olga Broumas, Paula Gunn Allen, and Audre
Lorde—"*beginning about 1977*, except for Lorde, whose work I was beginning to know and utterly love by 1971" (emphasis added). The point here is
not to suggest that Grahn is somehow "better" or "more lesbian-feminist"
than Rich because her prominence within lesbian feminism preceded Rich's.
However, the starting point for a study of lesbian feminism greatly deter-
mines the themes of that study. When the movement, or even only its poetry,
is seen as beginning with or centering on Adrienne Rich, then the movement

and its poetry are likely to reflect a white middle-class bias. Focusing on Grahn trains the spotlight onto the working-class materialist politics that were more prevalent among white women in the lesbian-feminist and women's liberation movements in the late 1960s and early 1970s than in the predominantly white cultural feminism of the late 1970s and early 1980s.

Early on, the women's movement and lesbian feminism were informed by the class consciousness and materialist analysis inherited from prevailing left-ist movements of the 1960s. One dominant strain of feminism followed Marxist socialism and defined women's struggle in terms of class oppression.[2] Various writings by working-class-identified lesbians, not necessarily associated with socialist-feminist publications and organizations, were widely circulated among lesbians in the early 1970s, mostly in feminist and lesbian newspapers such as *Furies,* the *Lesbian Tide, Spectre,* and *Focus.*[3] Diana Press published the anthology *Class and Feminism* in 1974 and a collection of Rita Mae Brown's essays, *A Plain Brown Rapper,* in 1976; the Women's Press Collective published working-class-identified books such as Sharon Isabell's *Yesterday's Lessons* in the early 1970s. In an interview conducted in 1984, Grahn commented on the "heavy materialism of political consciousness" in the 1960s and seventies, noting that "as a longtime movement activist" she "was very materially oriented" (Abbott, "Judy Grahn," 47).

While the rhetoric of class consciousness was prominent in white lesbian writing of the early 1970s, by the late 1970s liberal and cultural feminism had subsumed the more radically leftist voice. Class issues reemerged in the radical writing of women of color, which began to be published frequently in the early and mid 1980s. Joan Gibbs and Sara Bennett's self-published *Top Ranking: A Collection of Articles on Racism and Classism in the Lesbian Community* (1980) marks the transition from white socialist feminism to a feminism of women of color that focuses on classism and racism as well as sexism and homophobia. *This Bridge Called My Back* (1981) includes a section "On Culture, Class, and Homophobia," *Home Girls: A Black Feminist Anthology* (1983) reprints the black socialist feminist statement of the Combahee River Collective, and Audre Lorde's 1984 *Sister Outsider* reprints her essay "Age, Race, Class, and Sex," among others that touch on classism as well as racism, sexism, and homophobia. Presumably egged on by the radical writing of women of color, white lesbians once again took up the topic of class in the pages of newspapers and journals in the late 1980s. *Lesbian Ethics* and *Sinister Wisdom* both published special issues on class in the early 1990s, and working-class-identified writers such as Joan Nestle and Dorothy Allison were much more prominent in the 1990s than they had been in the early 1980s.

A Poem Before Its Time: "The Psychoanalysis of Edward the Dyke"

Judy's Grahn's well-known cycle of love poems to the working-class woman, *The Common Woman,* was written in one night in 1969, during a time when Grahn was in a consciousness-raising group and "the early women's libera- tion movement had already caught us in its mind-changing net" (Grahn, "Red," 543). As such, *The Common Woman* belongs in the context of a bud- ding feminist and lesbian political community. But Grahn wrote her first working-class-identified lesbian work, "The Psychoanalysis of Edward the Dyke," in 1964 and 1965,[4] before the women's liberation movement had gained widespread participation or national attention. She considered her "little satire about a woman and her psychiatrist" to be "unpublishable," not only because of its lesbian content, but because of its working-class empha- sis as well ("Judy Grahn," 1983, 96; Seajay, "Women-in-Print Movement," 20; Grahn, *Work,* 24). The *Ladder,* published by the lesbian social and polit- ical group Daughters of Bilitis, was the only regularly publishing lesbian magazine at the time, and DOB's politics were decidedly middle class. In a 1990 interview Grahn reported that she "was pretty sure *The Ladder* wouldn't take ["Edward the Dyke"] so I didn't even try" (Seajay, "Women-in-Print Movement," 20). Grahn had read the *Ladder* often enough to know that the magazine regularly published articles and short stories that vilified the sort of working-class dyke personified by Edward and exhorted readers to conform to feminine societal norms.

DOB was very much concerned with winning over the psychiatric estab- lishment that "Edward" viciously satirizes. In this regard DOB was similar to its male counterpart, the Mattachine Society, which after an initial period of political radicalism was "primarily interested in winning acceptance on the mainstream's own terms. . . . They preferred to rely on 'experts' rather than on political organizing to plead their cause." While Mattachine and DOB were too conservative for early radicals, they nonetheless remained too radical for most lesbians and gay men in the late 1950s and early 1960s, when "only the most intrepid would consider joining" either group, as historian Martin Duberman notes (*Stonewall,* 77–78). Despite the groups' small mem- berships, however, Duberman points out that gay and lesbian "resistance to oppression did not begin at Stonewall in 1969" (99). Grahn herself was among some fifteen conservatively dressed protesters picketing in front of the White House with Mattachine in 1965 (Lunde, "Judy Grahn," 237).

Radical as DOB and Mattachine seemed at the time, the *Ladder* had never published anything like the satiric, antiestablishment humor of "The

Psychoanalysis of Edward the Dyke," a parody of a butch dyke's visit to her sadistic psychiatrist. As a misfit six-foot-four-inch lesbian, Edward seeks help assimilating into straight society. Dr. Merlin Knox proposes surgery, hormone therapy, and violent behavior modification—the therapeutic wizardry of the mid twentieth century—to turn Edward into "exactly the little girl we've always wanted you to be" (*Work,* 27). Edward is awash in sentimental, nearly incoherent images of loving women: "Love flowers pearl. . . . Lips chewing oysters without grimy sand or whiskers. Pastry. Gingerbread. Warm, sweet bread. Cinnamon toast poetry" (*Work,* 27). Dr. Knox counters her images of "strawberries" and "lemon cream pie" with institutional accusations of "Narcissism," "Masochism, Sadism. Admit you want to kill your mother. . . . Admit you want to possess your father. . . . Admit you have a smegmatic personality." By the end of the session Edward is overcome and pronounces herself "vile"; she leaves the psychiatrist's office "tonguing" a phallic lollipop he has given to her (*Work,* 30). Dr. Knox is cruel, professional, and mainly concerned with his large bank account (as in Fort Knox); Edward is vulnerable, hard-working, and willing to pay for the help she has been convinced that she needs. Neither Edward nor Dr. Knox knows how to make Edward into a well-adjusted lesbian—the goal that DOB hoped to achieve with the cooperation of mainstream institutions such as psychoanalysis—because no role models or community exist in the world of the poem to support such an identity.

As a working-class, butch "dyke," Edward does not fit into the middle-class world of the professional psychiatrist, and as a lesbian she fails to fit his heterosexual paradigm of mental health. When Edward describes her "real date"—which Dr. Knox calls "our experiment we arranged for you"—it becomes clear, in the terms of the old saw, that you can dress Edward up, but you can't take her anywhere. Edward's description of preparing for the date is characteristically wry: "Well I bought a dress and a wig and a girdle and a squeezy bodice. I did unspeakable things to my armpits with a razor. I had my hair done and my face done and my nails done. My roast done. My bellybutton done" (*Work,* 28–29). Until commanded to buy them by Dr. Knox, Edward does not own any of the trappings of conventional femininity (either heterosexual or lesbian femme). To Dr. Knox's assumption, "And then you felt truly feminine," Edward rejoins, "I felt truly immobilized. I could no longer run, walk bend stoop move my arms or spread my feet apart" (*Work,* 29). Edward requires her body to be useful, to work, while Dr. Knox demands that it be grotesquely ornamental. The psychiatrist's prescription results in both physical injury and psychological torment when

Edward's weight drives her three-inch spiked heels "all the way into the thick carpet and [I] could no longer move. . . . you must understand that my underwear was terribly binding and the room was hot. . . . So I fainted. I didn't *mean* to, I just did. That's how I got my ankles broken" (*Work,* 29). Dr. Knox interprets Edward's failed date as "Penis Envy, which showed when you deliberately castrated your date by publicly embarrassing him" (*Work,* 30).

As Adrienne Rich explains in the introduction to *The Work of a Common Woman,* Edward is a victim of her own isolation and romanticism, which leave her vulnerable to the brutality of the psychoanalyst.

> Because Edward has no sense of her love for women as anything but utopian, individual and personal, she has no resistance to "treatment," in fact seeks it out; she is easily turned against herself. The warning of "Edward the Dyke" (and it is a serious one, couched in an apparently witty and lighthearted fable) is that if you unquestioningly accept one piece of the culture that despises and fears you, you are vulnerable to other pieces. ("Power and Danger," 13–14)

Unlike Edward, Grahn of course understands this; she has a sense of community and identity defined by the word *dyke,* of which Edward seems only vaguely aware. Edward is cognizant of her sexual orientation, and she also knows its name. The narrator of the poem calls the protagonist "Edward the Dyke" in the opening of the poem; in the sixth paragraph Edward refers to herself as "really only a harmless dyke" when she is accosted in "the powder room of a department store [by] three middle-aged housewives [who] thought I was a man" (*Work,* 26). Edward's claiming of the derogatory term is ineffective as a political stance, however, because she performs it in isolation—a situation analogous, perhaps, to Grahn's inability to publish the poem before the advent of lesbian feminism. Edward has a protorevolutionary sense of her sexuality, but no way to act upon it. In addition to "cinnamon toast poetry," Edward tells Dr. Knox that homosexuality means "justice equality higher wages. Independent angel song. It means I can do what I want" (*Work,* 27). That is, it would mean those things if she weren't vulnerable to her psychoanalyst, who stands in for society's homophobia.

Although Edward is at the mercy of her psychiatrist, Grahn and her readers were openly rebelling against the institutionalized sexism and homophobia he represents. When the Women's Press Collective published "Edward the Dyke" in 1971, in *Edward the Dyke and Other Poems,* it was enthusiastically received by lesbian feminists who were then forming identity and community with the help of writers and activists like Grahn. The poem was a first, riotously humorous, and feminist literary challenge to the power that the psychiatric establishment had wielded for so many years.

In 1964, "Edward the Dyke" was unpublishable in the straight world because of its lesbianism and seemed to Grahn unpublishable in the lesbian magazine the *Ladder* because of its working-class challenge to the medical establishment. Grahn writes in *The Work of a Common Woman* that she chose the title of the poem so that "people had to say the word *dyke*" (*Work,* 24). *Edward the Dyke and Other Poems* forms a bridge between the working-class lesbian culture in which Grahn came out in the 1950s and the lesbian-feminist political culture she worked to create, which attracted many middle-class women in the 1970s. Grahn published the book for a lesbian audience in the context of a separatist movement she played a part in establishing ("Judy Grahn," 1983, 98). It was not the straight world she was forcing to say the word *dyke*; it was the lesbian community. Historians Elizabeth Lapovsky Kennedy and Madeline D. Davis explain that working-class lesbians in the 1950s did not refer to themselves as "dykes." *Dyke* was a derogatory term used against them by straight people and "by more upwardly mobile lesbians to indicate the crudeness of rough bar lesbians" (*Boots of Leather,* 68). In the mid sixties, then, the title "Edward the Dyke" was, among other things, a response to class oppression perpetrated by other lesbians.

By the early 1970s, when "Edward the Dyke" was published and performed, a poem about a "dyke" was empowering to a nascent movement of lesbian feminists, both working and middle class. Grahn explains, "Lesbians had never heard the word *dyke* used in a performance, in any kind of legitimate way. They'd only heard it used as an underground or as a cuss word used to make them feel bad. So to hear it said out loud by someone who was standing up in front with a microphone was just *thrilling* to them" (Aal, "Judy Grahn on Women's Poetry," 73). *Edward the Dyke* "was not the first time the word "Lesbian" had appeared in poetry, but probably no poetry book ever had 'dyke' in it." Grahn calls the term a "magical underground taboo word" (Grahn, *Highest Apple,* 30). Like *queer,* reclaimed on a mass-movement scale in the nineties, *dyke* was taken up by lesbians in the seventies.

Joan Larkin points out the irony of discussing Grahn's poetry in "academic language," since Grahn herself is so thoroughly "committed to writing of and to 'The Common Woman'" (92). "The Psychoanalysis of Edward the Dyke" hardly fits conventional definitions of poetry at all; it is, by most standards, a (very) short story. Grahn comments on the form of the poem in the preface to "Edward" that appears in *The Work of a Common Woman:* "By insisting that

'Edward' was a poem, I was telling myself that women must define what our poetry is. I believe this about every other aspect of our lives also" (*Work,* 24). Insisting that a story is a poem reinforces the parallel move of insisting that material not typically deemed suitable for poetry (and certainly not for publication) makes a new kind of poetry, if a community of women says it does.

By the early 1970s, that community existed, in part called forth by the performances of poets like Grahn. *The Common Woman* poems literally became part of community institutions and lesbian-feminist culture, as Grahn reports: "They were reprinted hundreds of thousands of times, were put to music, danced, used to name various women's projects, quoted and then misquoted in a watered-down fashion for use on posters and T-shirts" (*Work,* 60). In 1980, Grahn told interviewer John Felstiner that "*The Common Woman* poems spread: the last time I counted them was about eight years ago, and they had been reprinted half a million times from Canada to Australia and to Germany" ("Judy Grahn," 1983, 97). Sue-Ellen Case explains that the development of lesbian and feminist publishers and bookstores created "a place for lesbians to find their own literature and to meet informally" as well as "a performance site for readings of the works":

> a site where the community began to form around this literature which shared its values and its metaphors. In this way, the voice of the lesbian feminist poet helped to produce as well as to be produced by the growing sense of a "common voice" or communal voice. The voice was marked by its own history and created a history for the grass roots community. . . . To some extent, these authors [such as Grahn] become characters or *personae* of their community. The readings become communal celebrations. ("Judy Grahn's Gynopoetics," 50)

Diane Lunde and Liana Borghi agree with Case's assessment of the importance of Grahn's (and other poets') work to the formation of lesbian community. Lunde writes that Grahn's poetry creates "communal bonding" ("Judy Grahn," 241), and Borghi describes how the community, in turn, grants "authority" to its poets ("Between," 68). The interchange between poet and community is related to Carruthers's concept of lesbian-feminist poets' creation of a "Lesbian *civitas*" (Carruthers, "Re-Vision," 304), which Grahn takes up in *The Highest Apple,* asserting the paramount importance of lesbian poetry to the movement (xviii, xxi, 56, 71).

Margot Gayle Backus interprets Grahn's long elegiac poem, "A Woman Is Talking to Death," as a calling "into being [of] a unified human *communi-*

tas, a 'we' capable of containing and healing the divisions between subject positions that the capitalist appropriation of human labor, emotions, time, and lives has represented as natural and desirable. Grahn invokes a living, intersubjective community" ("Grahn and the Lesbian Invocational," 835). Grahn herself writes that poets build community by "making cross connections and healing the torn places in the social fabric of myth we have all inherited, but that the outcast especially inherits" (*Highest Apple,* 84). (As a committed activist in the 1970s, Grahn clearly also believed that poets build community by founding and contributing to various grassroots institutions and political actions.) Grahn conceives of herself as a poet in a community of lesbians and of other lesbian poets developing "a new voice . . . a new women's literature" (Aal, "Judy Grahn on Women's Poetry," 76).

Before this community emerged, Grahn and her character Edward the Dyke appeared to number among "the Nat Turners of the world," in Duberman's phrase:

> Resistance to oppression takes on the confident form of political organizing only after a certain critical mass of collective awareness of oppression, and a determination to end it, has been reached. There are always isolated individuals who prefigure that awareness, who openly rebel before the oppressed community of which they are a part can offer them significant support and sustenance. These individuals—the Nat Turners of the world—are in some sense transhistorical: They have somehow never been fully socialized into the dominant ideology, into its prescriptions and limitations; they exist apart, a form of genius. (*Stonewall,* 75)

Humorless Lesbians and Other Misrepresentations

By the early 1970s, a growing community of lesbian feminists, which included Judy Grahn, was in dead earnest about fomenting revolution. Far from the stereotypical "humorless" feminist or lesbian, however, Grahn is among the funniest of contemporary American poets. Her broad use of humor—described in turns as "raucous," "macabre" (Martinez, "Poetry," 49), anarchic (Backus, "Grahn and the Lesbian Invocational," 816), "witty and lighthearted" (Rich, "Power and Danger," 14)—itself redefines what is appropriate to serious poetry. Inez Martinez writes that "the dominant tone and voice of [Grahn's] poems consists of deflating male supremacy through humor, and of taking her place among the imperfect" (49). But despite the prevalence of wit in Grahn's poetry, critical writing about her work tends to focus on her long, weighty poem, "A Woman Is Talking to Death." (Martinez sees "grim and desperately puzzled" humor in the poem's parodic elements [49]. In addition, the narrator not only talks to but in the end defiantly laughs at death—"Hey you death / ho and ho poor death" [ll. 466–67]—but humor in the common sense is hardly the dominant tone of the elegiac poem.)

In "Judy Grahn and the Lesbian Invocational Elegy," Margot Gayle Backus paraphrases Celeste Schenck's argument that "the elegy has functioned in the European tradition as the form that best signals a writer's serious career aspirations as a poet" ("Grahn and the Lesbian Invocational," 817).[5] Perhaps critics are drawn to "A Woman Is Talking to Death" because of the lofty status of the elegist; the poem helps place lesbian-feminist poetry on the cultural and academic map. Carruthers, similarly, emphasizes the "unaccustomed voice, that of epic" taken on by some lesbian poets in the 1970s ("Re-Vision," 299–300). The allure of lesbian elegy or epic for academics schooled in canonical forms and approaches to literature may be intensified by the conscious eschewing of traditional forms by many lesbian-feminist poets. According to Elly Bulkin's introduction to the 1981 anthology, *Lesbian Poetry,* only those lesbian poets "who began to write long before the existence of the women's movement . . . worked in a world of traditional (white bourgeois male) academic values relating to every facet of poetry—its style, its structure, its subject, its audience" (xxiii–xxiv).[6] Bulkin categorizes early seventies lesbian poetry as "deliberately, perhaps even defiantly, 'anti-poetic'" (xxvii), citing Grahn's *Common Woman* poems as an example of poetry that was part of a new "tradition that was anti-literary, anti-intellectual, anti-hierarchical" (xxvi). Backus justifies her focus on the decidedly poetic, carefully structured "A Woman Is Talking to Death" in political terms, by stating that the poem "has had an electrifying theoretical and practical impact on many of its readers and listeners" ("Grahn and the Lesbian Invocational," 816).

Less appreciative reviewers than Backus have dismissed Grahn's work either on the grounds that it is too polemical or too frivolous, or sometimes because it is both. Clayton Eshleman, reviewing *The Work of a Common Woman* in the *Los Angeles Times Book Review,* deems Grahn's work predictable, limited by what he considers Grahn's refusal to "allow contradiction or confusion." At the same time that he accuses Grahn of taking her feminism too seriously, Eshleman delivers the backhanded compliment that Grahn's "best writing in this collection [is] in the genre of the Spoon River

Anthology"—at once equating Grahn's work with relatively unimportant "genre" writing (compared to the cultural significance of great elegy or epic, for example) and asserting that the genre is made to bear a ponderously weighty subject matter. Not surprisingly, Eshleman entirely ignores "A Woman Is Talking to Death," and he also neglects to mention—perhaps because he cannot understand?—Grahn's pointedly humorous writing. (This suggests one derivation of the humorless feminist stereotype: misogynists simply do not get the joke.) Eshleman makes clear that he wishes he could like Grahn's writing, as testified by his self-conscious presentation of liberal feminist sympathies early in the review; but he is unable to take her work on its own terms, and it fails to match up to the traditional standards he implies but fails to reveal.

Eshleman's review, published in 1985, projects an attitude oddly similar to more recent queer hostility toward so-called politically correct lesbian feminism. While self-defined "queer" women of the 1990s presumably know better than to think that all lesbians or all feminists are humorless, the prevalent assumption that all *lesbian feminists* take themselves too seriously ignores the humor and joie de vivre of sensibilities like Grahn's. This is not to say that a "typical" queer theorist would be dismissive of Grahn's work per se; rather, queer writing that pointedly stereotypes and denigrates lesbian feminism necessarily ignores important lesbian-feminist work in order to construct derogatory generalizations. Where some only want to see rigidity against which to define their own postmodern playfulness, many feminist commentators have looked to Grahn (among others) and seen movement.

Again and again, appreciative critics and reviewers refer to the power of Grahn's poetry to "transform." Rich writes that the word *transformation* best describes the goal of feminism and feminist poetry like hers and Grahn's; unlike " 'revolution' [which] has become not only a dead relic of Leftism, but a key to the dead-endedness of male politics," transformation is "a process which will leave neither surfaces nor depths unchanged, which enters society at the most essential level of the subjugation of women and nature by men. We begin to conceive a planet on which both women and nature might coexist as the She Who we encounter in Judy Grahn's poems" (Rich, "Power and Danger," 7–8). Lunde considers Grahn's "feminist vision of personal and social transformation" to be one of her basic themes, which are "inseparable" from "her transformation of language" ("Judy Grahn," 238). Carruthers writes that the "energy" of lesbian-feminist poetry "springs . . . from the perception that women together and in themselves have a power which is transformative." She sees a special role for lesbian-feminist poets in this transformation because "in order to recover their power women need to move psychically and through metaphor to a place beyond the well-traveled routes of patriarchy and all its institutions, especially its linguistic and rhetorical ones" ("Re-Vision," 294).

As an architect of lesbian feminism, Grahn indeed played a key role in transforming earlier conceptions of "the lesbian" and the language used to pathologize her. Close attention to Grahn's work should also transform current stereotypes of "the lesbian feminist"; the poetry presents a much more diverse community of lesbians than is presumed to have been active and/or represented in the 1970s. Grahn transforms the pejorative words *dyke* and *queer* by recontextualizing them (twenty years before the rise of queer theory and the invention of the annual Dyke March on the eve of Gay Pride), expands and undoes the meaning of "common" as it relates to class, and reevaluates what love means for women—by inverting language and seemingly predictable situations, by laughing in the face of adversity, by inventing new fables and myths.

Grahn frequently works her transformations of meaning by humorously presenting the unexpected; both the joke and the political impact of some of her funnier poems turn on a punch line. As Rich writes in her introduction to *The Work of a Common Woman,* "Language is the key" ("Power and Danger," 14). A succinct example of Grahn's use of humor is this brief poem from *She Who:*

> parting on the left,
> parting on the right,
> braiding. (*Work,* 82)

Grahn wittily turns the fraught political divisiveness implied by the first two lines into an intimate, usually female activity, braiding. At the same time she suggests a metaphor for conceiving a way out of political disarray. If a woman's hair is unruly, or mussed, she might braid it to smooth it out and keep it in place; an adult might braid the hair of a young girl for the same reason. In African American women's literature in particular, women braiding each other's hair has figured as an intimate, sometimes homoerotic act (e.g., *The Color Purple, Beloved*). Grahn is suggesting that the complex problem of political factionalization might be solved by learning a simple lesson from the domestic world of women, so often infantilized by allegedly sophisticated men operating in the public sector. The poem can be read as a gentle reminder to political women to draw on the lessons and connections of all the parts of their lives, and perhaps as an assertion to misogynist political men of the superiority of women's quotidian expertise at solving knotty problems.

"If you lose your lover," from *Edward the Dyke and Other Poems,* also relies on a punch line, as it wittily continues the antiromantic reappraisal of love begun in the book's title poem (*Work,* 43). Whereas Edward describes the sensations and emotions of being in love, this poem describes the loss of love with similarly overwrought images:

> If you lose your lover
> rain hurt you. blackbirds
> brood over the sky trees
> burn down everywhere brown
> rabbits run under
> car wheels. should your
> body cry? . . . (ll. 1–7)

The narrator answers the self-indulgent, romanticized first half of the poem with a pragmatism calling for self-esteem, self-reliance, and a rejection of the debilitating version of love (won and lost) that plays a part in subjugating women:

> . . . to feel such
> blue and empty bed dont
> bother. if you lose your
> lover comb hair go here
> or there get another (ll. 7–11)

The narrator of this poem advocates a course of action far removed from the helpless isolation of Edward in "The Psychoanalysis of Edward the Dyke." In advising the lesbian reader to "get another" lover, the narrator assumes the existence of a lesbian community in which to find one.

The transformation of love from a purely personal, emotional experience to a politicized concept runs throughout *The Work of a Common Woman,* starting with "The Psychoanalysis of Edward the Dyke," reappearing at various points in *Edward the Dyke* and *She Who,* receiving extended treatment in "A Woman Is Talking to Death," and culminating in *Confrontations With the Devil in the Form of Love,* in which Love is a character rather than an emotional state. More than one commentator has pointed out that Grahn's love poetry and political poetry are inseparable (e.g., Montefiore, *Feminism and Poetry*, 74; Ostriker, *Stealing*, 177; Rich, "Power and Danger," 12–13). From a lesbian-feminist perspective, love poetry about lesbians in itself qualifies as political, particularly so if written, performed, or published in the virulently homophobic 1960s and seventies.

In her introduction to "A Woman Is Talking to Death," in *The Work of a Common Woman,* Grahn explains that when she wrote the poem she was unaware that she "would begin a redefinition for [her]self of the subject of love" (112). And indeed, by figuring love as responsibility, considering as lovers all people she meets who are in need, Grahn explodes the boundaries of the conventional love lyric written to the one-and-only beloved of the poetic persona. By section 9 of "A Woman Is Talking to Death," when the narrator states "to my lovers I bequeath / the rest of my life" (ll. 481–82), Grahn has established an expansive definition of "lover" that includes her lesbian lover, Wendy; an African American man brutalized by police, for whom the narrator is too afraid to be a witness because she is a lesbian; the lesbians in the military who "drowned" with the narrator when she was kicked out of the service and forced to sign "the confession of what we / had done together" (ll. 242–44); her junior high school classmate who became pregnant, whom she loved "because nothing like her trouble / would ever happen to me, because I hated it that she was / pregnant and unhappy and an outcast" (ll. 303–5); friends with whom she has been drinking at a bar; and a fifty-five-year-old Asian woman she happens upon, who has been beaten, raped, and left bleeding in the snow. Thus, in "A Woman Is Talking to Death," Grahn most clearly illustrates her sense of herself, like Sappho, writing "*from* the context of a women's community . . . *into* the context of her society at large" (*Highest Apple,* 50). On one important level the poem is "about" the narrator's particularly lesbian perspective on society at large; in this sense the poem could be read as a poem by and for lesbians primarily. But Grahn's inclusive conception of love and her focus on various forms of oppression—classism, sexism, racism as well as homophobia—belie such a simplistic reading of her lesbian-feminist politics and poetic themes.

When Grahn intentionally takes up the topic of love in *Confrontations with the Devil in the Form of Love,* she states that she was clear before writing the poems that she "wanted to be accurate, provocative, full of intellect rather than dazzled or dreamy-eyed" (*Work,* 134). The poems reject the sentimental language of love, except to mock it, to point out the poison in stereotyped, disempowering models of love. Commenting on "the quest for identity" in women's poetry, critic Alicia Ostriker explains that "the twentieth-century poet continues to live in a society which first of all discourages the possibility of an autonomous female identity by defining womanliness primarily in terms of love—selfless connubial love, ecstatic romantic love, nurturing maternal love" (*Stealing*, 60). Grahn rejects the equation of female with self-abnegation; the first poem in *Confrontations* makes clear the disempowerment and bitterness that result from buying into traditional ideas of romantic love (*Work*, 136):

> Love came along and saved me saved me
> Love came along and
> after that I did not feel like fighting for
> anything anymore after all (ll. 1–4)
>
> but didn't I have
> company in my nothing? (ll. 8–9)

Ostriker sees in this "sardonic" poem a summary of "many a parallel story of romantic loss" in which a woman poet shows how loss of love is socially construed to equal loss of identity. Ostriker places the poem in a tradition that "begins to appear as far back as Maria Osgood and Emily Dickinson" ("I'm Nobody! Who are you?") (*Stealing*, 60–61). The punch line to Grahn's poem is not humorous, but devastating:

> & then one day Love left to go save someone else.
> Love ran off with all my self-esteem my sense of being
> wonderful and all my nothing.
> now I am in the hole. (ll. 12–15)

The lilting, singsong rhythm of the poem's first two lines, when the narrator is wrapped up in the fantasy of romantic love as salvation, rapidly degenerates into a disjointed, arrhythmic pattern. By the end of the poem the narrator's voice is straightforward, almost conversational, until the deadpan declaration of the last line: "now I am in the hole." On the surface, the last line clearly indicates a sense of indebtedness, of having been robbed of and left destitute by love experienced, entrusted, and lost.

The word *hole* appears in two earlier poems in *The Work of a Common Woman*, with more pejorative connotations. In the first poem of the book, Grahn writes, "I'm not a girl / I'm a hatchet / I'm not a hole / I'm a whole mountain" (ll. 1–4, *Work*, 25). Grahn counters the psychoanalytic interpretation of woman as lack and the derogatory sexual reducing of woman to "hole" with a pun on the word, turning perceived lack into awesome presence: "a whole mountain." The word *hole* appears five times in "The enemies of She Who call her various names" (*Work*, 84–85), the first half of which is an example of how men use derogatory language to stereotype and oppress women, for example, "a hole a slut a cunt a slit a cut / a slash a hole a slit a piece / of shit, a piece of shit, a piece of shit" (ll. 13–15). Similar to the call and response structure of "I'm not a girl," the second half of "The enemies of She Who" shows how the mythical everywoman, "She Who bears it," just as she has borne the labor of childbirth:

> all over the world
> the waters are breaking everywhere
> everywhere the waters are breaking
> the labor of She Who carries and bears
> and raises and rears is the first labor,
> there is no other first labor. (ll. 23–28)

In *Confrontations*, Grahn's narrator rescues herself, and by implication all women willing to give up on the dead end of romantic love, from the "hole" by interrogating and redefining love. In Grahn's words, "Love is being named, personified, and confronted with the limitations that have been placed on her, is being asked to become more, much much more. . . . She is being asked to transform her functions now, to include protection, provision and power, and to be out in the world with us, as our partner" (*Highest Apple*, 121). By the opening of the fifth poem in the collection, "Love came along and saved / no one" (ll. 1–2, *Work*, 145). The enjambment of the lines raises traditional expectations, set up in part by the first poem, only to dash them in the second line. (The enjambment works as a sort of ironic pun through poetics; it was the Romantic poets who revived the use of enjambment after it "fell into disrepute" among the neoclassical British poets of the eighteenth century [Preminger, *Princeton*, 241].) The fourth from last poem in the collection echoes the utter antiromanticism expressed in "If you lose your lover" (from *Edward the Dyke*), this time without naming "love" at all (*Work*, 154):

> I only have one reason for living
> and that's you
> And if I didn't have you as a

reason for living,
I would think of something else.

By the last poem of *Confrontations* (*Work,* 157–58), Grahn invokes her own responsibility in remaking love, by personifying herself in the same manner in which she has personified Love:

My name is Judith, meaning
She Who Is Praised
I do not want to be called praised
I want to be called the Power of Love. (ll. 1–4)

In the second stanza, Grahn posits love as protection, rebirth, and provision, and asks "why," if she cannot provide those three necessities, "would you call my name Love?" (l. 13). In the final stanza, the first- and second-person singular give way to the first-person plural, as the responsibility to transform love is transferred to Grahn's predominantly lesbian-feminist community of readers:

not until we have ground we call our own
to stand on
& weapons of our own in hand
& some kind of friends around us
will anyone ever call our name Love,
& then when we do we will all call ourselves
grand, muscley names:
the Protection of Love
the Provision of Love & the
Power of Love. (ll. 28–37)

Not until the lesbian-feminist revolution has been engaged and realized "will anyone ever call our name Love," and, by then, the revolution will have transformed the disempowering meaning of love into something "grand, muscley." After the climactic three-part naming of Love, Grahn ends the poem with a sobering denouement, which can be read as a subtle provocation:

until then, my sweethearts,
let us speak simply of

romance, which is so much
easier and so much less
than any of us deserve. (ll. 38–42)

Grahn, of course, rarely speaks "simply of romance," except to mock it, to criticize its hold on women. Throughout *Confrontations*, she speaks complexly of romance, contrasting it to her political vision of love as active responsibility.

Contrary to Grahn's observation that she first began to redefine love in "A Woman Is Talking to Death," love and romance appear as subjects of her poems as early as the mid 1960s. Perhaps less self-consciously than in *Confrontations*, Grahn interrogates the role of love in women's lives in a variety of short poems, in addition to the better known, and longer, "The Psychoanalysis of Edward the Dyke," "A Woman Is Talking to Death," and *Confrontations with the Devil in the Form of Love*. In the shorter poems, Grahn often explores love and romance in relation to perceptions of women's beauty. As in all else, Grahn has the capacity to be humorous when approaching "the problem for a lesbian feminist of writing about women's beauty without fetishizing it" (Montefiore, *Feminism and Poetry*, 83).

"I have come to claim," usually referred to as the "Marilyn Monroe Poem," is a ghoulishly humorous poem from *Edward the Dyke* (*Work*, 31–32). The narrator, literally, has "come to claim / Marilyn Monroe's body / for the sake of my own. / dig it up, hand it over, cram it in this paper sack" (ll. 1–5). The narrator attracts the attention of reporters, who "are furious" but also want to know "what / am I doing for lunch?" (ll. 21, 24–25). Like Marilyn Monroe, the narrator is another woman the male reporters want to have "a crack at" (l. 41). The narrator draws them in, using their own prurient interest against them:

Now I shall take them my paper sack
and we shall act out a poem together:
"How would you like to see Marilyn Monroe,
in action, smiling, and without her clothes?"
We shall wait long enough to see them make familiar faces
and then I shall beat them with your skull.
hubba. hubba. hubba. hubba. hubba. (ll. 47–53)

Through her narrator's action, Grahn fantasizes poetic justice for the media that helped to destroy Marilyn Monroe and for all the women they objectify and influence, including "eight young women in New York City / who murdered themselves for being pretty / by the same method as you, the very / next day, after you!" (ll. 14–17). The internal rhymes "sack," "act," and "action," reinforced by the *k* and hard *c* sounds of "clothes," "make," and "skull," anticipate the crack of beating the men senseless, reported in the familiar, lascivious nonsense phrase "hubba hubba." Rich explains, "Marilyn Monroe's body, in death, becomes a weapon[,] her bone a bludgeon to beat the voyeurs, the fetishists, the poets and journalists vampirizing off the 'dumb-blonde' of the centerfolds" ("Power and Danger," 14).

The narrator is angry not only with the reporters, not only with men, but also with the women who play up to them. After the first two stanzas the poem is addressed directly to Marilyn; the narrator repeatedly adjures her to "be serious." Had Marilyn been able—or been allowed—to be serious, the poem implies, she might have been taken seriously, as the narrator wishes to be:

> Long ago you wanted to write poems;
> Be serious, Marilyn
> I am going to take you in this paper sack
> around the world, and
> write on it:—the poems of Marilyn Monroe—
> Dedicated to all princes,
> the male poets who were so sorry to see you go,
> before they had a crack at you. (ll. 34–41)

The narrator's ambivalence shows in lines 1–3 of this stanza. Read alone, line 2 is a repeat of the demand that Marilyn "be serious," but the first eight lines of the stanza make one complete sentence. As parts of the same sentence, lines 1 and 2 become related statements, with the semicolon connecting two similar ideas: "Long ago you wanted to write poems," that is, to "Be serious, Marilyn." Lines 2 and 3 follow up by indicating that the narrator, who is a poet, is "going to take" Marilyn seriously, unlike "the male poets" who were only interested in Marilyn sexually.

After the last hubba hubbas, Grahn ends the poem by reflecting its beginning. In the opening three lines the narrator had declared, "I have come to claim / Marilyn Monroe's body / for the sake of my own." In the end, fantastically having vanquished the forces of objectification, the narrator implores, "Marilyn, be serious / Today I have come to claim your body for my own" (ll. 54–55). By the last line, the narrator is not only laying claim to the idea of Marilyn Monroe's body, she is identifying with the pain and the power of it. The action is no longer taken "for the sake of" the narrator; at the end Marilyn Monroe's body is taken for—that is, understood as—the narrator's own, not in the sense of ownership, but of identification. Grahn explained in an interview in 1983 that the identification is related to class as well as gender: "When I think of [Marilyn Monroe], I get a terrible chill because I know that she came from a poor background and worked her way all the way up to being a suicide, and I don't want that to happen to any of us ever again" (Felstiner, "Judy Grahn," 100). If Marilyn Monroe's objectified female beauty helped to subjugate women, the power of her dead body, stripped to the bare bones, can empower. A woman willing to take Marilyn (and herself) seriously can use her tragedy to understand how women are pitted against one another in a misogynist culture.

Rich sees the theme of "The Marilyn Monroe Poem" recurring in Grahn's work: "Over and over Grahn calls up the living woman against the manufactured one, the man-made creation of centuries of male art and literature" ("Power and Danger," 14). In several poems Grahn specifically reclaims the stereotyped "dumb blonde," who has become the butt of her own strand of derogatory "jokes."[7] In addition to a poem about the famous blonde Marilyn Monroe, Grahn places "dumb blonde" in the list of "various names" in "The enemies of She Who call her various names": "dove - cow - pig - chick - cat - kitten - bird / dog - dish/ a dumb blonde" (ll. 6–7, *Work,* 84). "Blonde" shows up in the erotic poem "fortunately the skins" (*Work,* 53) and the parable "The most blonde woman in the world," in which Grahn rejects the equation of whiteness (blondeness) with beauty. The protagonist of the poem "threw off her skin / her hair, threw off her hair, declaring / 'Whosoever chooses to love me / chooses to love a bald woman / with bleeding pores'" (ll. 2–6, *Work,* 93). After her transformation, "her lovers" are "small hard-bodied spiders" (ll. 7–8), traditionally female weavers of destiny, fate, and time. "Hard-bodied" both connotes an insect difficult to crush and foreshadows the "grand, muscley names" for love in the language of the later poem "My name is Judith"; the spider-lovers protect, provide for, and empower the most blonde woman. "They spun her blood into long strands" (l. 11), replacing the strands of blonde hair, interacting with her, keeping her from bleeding to death. "'Now', she said, 'Now I am expertly loved, / and now I am beautiful'" (ll. 14–15).

Other parables that feature animals wittily skewer patriarchy, represented as a large and powerful but relatively stupid beast. In "The Elephant Poem" (*Work,* 33–35) and "The many minnows" (*Work,* 86) small, individually powerless beings band together to defeat large, oppressive animals. In the first, the result is "ELEPHANT TURNED UPSIDE DOWN / by a fly / a million flies" (ll. 45–47) up its phallic trunk, which Grahn compares to a weapon used in the (Vietnamese?) jungle ("56 millimeter trunk" [l. 2], "million millimeter trunk" [l. 12]). In the second, forty-seven minnows trick the "greedybeak" who has eaten up all the other "many minnows" into diving "straight into the water, in a rage. The 47 / remaining many minnows promptly ate him up / and turned him into many more many minnows" (ll. 15–17). The little people (animals) win, and the big bad guy loses, taken down with humor and ingenuity.

Grahn's variegated uses of humor all serve the purpose of upending stereotypes, the goal announced in the opening poem of *The Work of a Common Woman,* which turns on puns and unexpected, even startling oppositions.

> I'm not a girl
>   I'm a hatchet
> I'm not a hole
>   I'm a whole mountain
> I'm not a fool
>   I'm a survivor
> I'm not a pearl
>   I'm the Atlantic Ocean
> I'm not a good lay
>   I'm a straight razor
> look at me as if you had never seen a woman before
> I have red, red hands and much bitterness (*Work,* 25)

Like many of Grahn's poems, this one mainly foregoes "masculine" end rhyme for internal rhyme, sight rhyme, repetition, and assonance. The sound of soft *l*'s, *r*'s, and *o*'s accumulates—girl, hole, fool, pearl, good, look—with the seesaw rhythm of the first ten lines and is broken with the last two long lines, in which the narrator issues a command for respect.

Dykes, Queers, and Other Common Women: Repossessing the Language of Oppression

Punning double entendre is at the heart of Grahn's redefinition of the word *dyke* in "I am the wall at the lip of the water" (*Work,* 98). The eight-line poem includes three of the seven appearances of the word *dyke* in *The Work of a Common Woman*:[8]

> I am the wall at the lip of the water
> I am the rock that refused to be battered
> I am the dyke in the matter, the other
> I am the wall with the womanly swagger
> I am the dragon, the dangerous dagger
> I am the bulldyke, the bulldagger
> and I have been many a wicked grandmother
> and I shall be many a wicked daughter.

In her later works *Another Mother Tongue* (1984) and *The Queen of Swords* (1986), Grahn devotes considerable time and space to the word *dyke*. She explains in *The Highest Apple* that

> the effort of establishing and re-confirming self-definition in the voices of the contemporary Lesbian poets, has included reclaiming words with loaded, stereotypic content such as, Lesbian, dyke, whore, cunt, mother, daughter, birthing and the like—and extending as a matter of the course of our lives into the other groups to which we also variously belong: Black, feminist, working class, Jewish, fat, Indian, alcoholic, intellectual, literary, leftist, mystic, revolutionary, and immigrant American. (70–71)

In "A History of Lesbianism" (*Work,* 54–55), Grahn acknowledges both the importance of naming and the lesbian community's ambivalence toward adopting "loaded" words: "The women-loving-women / in America were called dykes / and some liked it / and some did not" (ll. 22–25).

Long before Queer Nation and (as a result) queer theory reclaimed the word *queer* from the homophobes—and certainly before lesbian feminism was willing to embrace the cosexual implications of the term—Grahn boldly tried it out in two of her poems. In "A Woman Is Talking to Death," the word *queer* for the most part retains its derogatory connotation. After the narrator has witnessed an accident in which a black man inadvertently killed a white man, she promises to testify on his behalf "—later" (l. 83). But later

> that same week I looked into the mirror
> and nobody was there to testify;
> how clear, an unemployed queer woman
> makes no witness at all,
> nobody at all was there for
> those two questions: what does
> she do, and who is she married to? (ll. 114–20)

In accepting society's homophobic equation of "an unemployed queer woman" with "nobody," the narrator backs off from the image of love as liberation and strength presented in the poem's refrain, first voiced in lines 2 and 3 of the poem: "my lovers teeth are white geese flying above me / my lovers muscles are rope ladders under my hands." After the stanza in which she names herself "queer," the narrator modifies the refrain to read, "our lovers teeth are white geese flying / above us, but we ourselves are / easily squished" (ll. 123–25), just like the young man killed in the car accident. The meaning of "lovers" as a possessive in the refrain is ambiguous; it can modify the teeth and muscles of "our" lovers, or it can modify "our" teeth and muscles, with ourselves understood as lovers. In this second sense, the narrator suggests that her strong, liberated image of herself is separate from the oppressed, "queer" reality in which sexism and homophobia compel her to leave her "lover," the driver, to suffer at the hands of racist policemen: "our lovers teeth are white geese flying / above us, but we ourselves are / easily squished." By the end of the poem, no longer using the word *queer* to describe herself, the narrator owns the refrain as matching her sense of herself, a woman who taunts death, which takes the form of repressive patriarchy.

In keeping with the poem's indictment of a destructive society, Grahn's employment of the word *queer* is not without irony. She clearly criticizes the homophobic, classist, and sexist judicial system that would fail to listen to the narrator's testimony, even as the narrator regrets her failure to use her white-skin privilege to help the black motorist. Grahn's ironic use of homophobic terms is equally apparent later in the poem when the narrator, happening upon a woman who has been beaten and raped by a taxi driver, calls herself a "pervert":

> I am a pervert, therefore I've learned
> to keep my hands to myself in public
> but I was so drunk that night,
> I actually did something loving
> I took her in my arms, this woman,
> until she could breathe right, and
> my friends who are perverts too
> they touched her too
> we all touched her. (ll. 429–37)

In "Carol and" (*Work,* 96–97), the word *queer* appears as part of a lilting, childlike rhyme, in the context of a positive portrait, lacking the immobilizing force it has in "A Woman Is Talking to Death." In *The Common Woman* (1969) Carol is the only lesbian of the seven women portrayed, and she is in the closet; in "Carol and" (1971–72), however, the character is free to behave however she chooses. The opening quatrain of "IV. Carol, in the park, chewing on straws" from *The Common Woman* (*Work,* 67) is, in Grahn's explanation, "an external mocking voice, suggesting opposition" (Grahn, "Red," 554)—but it can also be read as the internalized voice of a fearful, closeted lesbian:

> She has taken a woman lover
> whatever shall we do
> she has taken a woman lover
> how lucky it wasnt you (ll. 1–4)

Carol dreams of taking flight,

> And all the day through she smiles and lies
> and grits her teeth and pretends to be shy,
> or weak, or busy. Then she goes home
> and pounds her own nails, makes her own
> bets, and fixes her own car, with her friend. (ll. 5–9)

In the later poem, "Carol and," Grahn portrays the butch, working-class lesbian—either at home (as her *Common Woman* poem implies) or after she has come out. Outside the context of the intertextual reading, "Carol and" stands as an openly lesbian poem, presumably about a woman living an openly lesbian life:

> Carol and
> her crescent wrench
> work bench
> wooden fence
> wide stance (ll. 1–5)

> Carol is another
> queer chickadee
> like me, but Carol does
> everything
> better
> if you let her. (ll. 48–54)

Closeted in the 1969 poem, Carol does not appear to be "shy" about her sexuality in *She Who,* published once lesbian feminism and gay liberation were gathering steam in the early 1970s.

The word Grahn is most widely associated with retooling is *common*—a term whose later association with the most homogenizing aspects of white, middle-class cultural feminism robbed it of the complex, elastic use Grahn had intended for it. *The Common Woman* poems are a series of seven portraits of individual working women that confront "the emotional and social connotations" of the word *common* as applied to women (Grahn, "Red," 557). In her essay, "Red and Black with Fish in the Middle (A Discussion of Political Decisions Involved in the Common Woman Poems)," Grahn refers to "common" as one of "the magic words," like "puns, slips of the tongue, words which increase their power because they mean more than one thing."

> In status or class usage, to call a woman "common" is to insult her morality—more than meaning dull, boring, everyday, as in "common housewife," the name also means *lacking taste,* having no special class or status, nothing singular; and furtherly, more importantly, it means *belonging to just anybody,* especially sexually, of being a "common slut" or whore, of being *common* (sexual) property. (557)

Looking further than common usage, as it were, Grahn finds empowering definitions on which to draw.

> *Common* (sexual) property . . . is a reference to the former freedom of Celtic women to have many lovers, a freedom now treated derogatorily as in "any man could have her." For common refers to the old matriarchal custom of holdings belonging to an entire community, of common herds, common goods, land held in common. (This was through the female line.) Common Law is customary law, and common-law marriage is outside the instituted patriarchal legal system, and is older. The Commons are grounds belonging to the public, and the House of Commons in English Parliament refers to representatives from "the people," rather than from the aristocratic class . . . and in addition to all these meanings, the word also means ordinary and everyday. (Grahn, "Red," 557–58)

She concludes, "It is a natural poetic word" (558).

Various critics have glossed over the multiple meanings of the term; for example, one states simply that "The *Common* in the title refers to working-class writing" (Kinney, Review, 108). Rich writes that "The 'Common Woman' is far more than a class description. What is 'common' in and to women is the intersection of oppression and strength, damage and beauty. . . . The 'common woman' is in fact the embodiment of the extraordinary will-to-survive in millions of women" ("Power and Danger," 17–18). Rich echoes Inez Martinez, who writes that Grahn's "deft manipulations of sound emphasize specific questions that Grahn raises": What is it to be a woman? To be a dyke? To live in a society sterilized by male supremacy? To be a dyke in that sterile society blessed with biological life and faced with biological death? ("Poetry," 49). Both Martinez and Rich deny the poems' working-class specificity in order to expand their applicability; the poems, on the other hand, maintain Grahn's working-class sensibility even as they address a variety of subjects. Grahn reports in her introduction to *The Common Woman* that the impetus for the poems "was completely practical: I wanted, in 1969, to read something which described regular, everyday women without making us look either superhuman or pathetic" (*Work,* 60).

While *The Common Woman* poems are not *only* about class, they are, nevertheless, *always* about class. The series opens with "I. Helen, at 9 am, at noon, at 5:15" (*Work,* 61), about an ambitious woman in "trim suits and spike heels" (l. 6) who "constantly conspires" (l. 18) against both men and women in order to attain an empty "success" (l. 11) as a despised "boss" (l. 28). So that she might achieve and maintain her managerial-class status in the workplace, Helen has tried "to make it / in a male form, she's become as / stiff as possible" (ll. 3–5). Grahn plays on the meaning of "stiff" as in erect penis ("a male form") and as in corpse. Helen thinks the rigidity is worthwhile, although "somewhere underneath she / misses love and trust, but she feels / that spite and malice are the / prices of success" (ll. 8–11). Helen ultimately sacrifices her sense of self (she goes "mad," l. 27) in her attempt to succeed in a middle-class world that discriminates against women. Her class status and her gender role are inextricably linked; in a socialist-feminist sense, Helen's gender is the class status that is at the root of her oppression. Other common women in Grahn's poetic sequence are recognizably working class, like Ella (*Work,* 63)—"a copperheaded waitress" (l. 1) or Vera (*Work,* 73)—with her

> 28 dollars a week and the bastard boss
> you never let yourself hate;
> and the work, all the work you did at home
> where you never got paid (ll. 6–9)

Each of the common women takes some action that ensures her survival but always involves paying a heavy price. Helen, whose name evokes the mythical beauty of Helen of Troy, transforms herself to survive in a dog-eat-dog working world and in the end becomes a common woman who "is as common / as the common crow" (ll. 30–31). Grahn relates the crow—"something black and purple and metallic looking and thieving" (Grahn, "Red," 552)—to the first three lines of the poem: "Her ambition is to be more shiny / and metallic, black and purple as / a thief at midday"; the crow traditionally is associated with evil and death, and sometimes with the symbolically male sun.[9] Ella pays the price for defending herself from harassment and her child from abuse:

> . . . Once,
> she shot a lover who misused her child.
> Before she got out of jail, the courts had pounced
> and given the child away. Like some isolated lake,
> her flat blue eyes take care of their own stark
> bottoms. Her hands are nervous, curled, ready
> to scrape.
> The common woman is as common
> as a rattlesnake. (ll. 15–23)

Carol hides her sexual identity, and as a result,

> She walks around all day
> quietly, but underneath it
> she's electric;
> angry energy inside a passive form.
> The common woman is as common
> as a thunderstorm. (ll. 24–29)

The final, pivotal poem in the series, "VII. Vera, from my childhood," is modeled on Grahn's mother (Felstiner, "Judy Grahn," 95). With "Vera," Grahn shifts from portraying individual lives to "Solemnly swearing" to work with other women for change—so that common women will no longer have to work without recognition and end up like Vera, who has "somehow gotten to be a pale old woman" (l. 2).

> For all the world we didn't know we held in common
> all along

the common woman is as common as the best of bread
and will rise
and will become strong—I swear it to you
I swear it to you on my own head
I swear it to you on my common
woman's
head (ll. 24–32)

Like the oath that closes "Vera" and thus *The Common Woman,* the ending of "A Woman Is Talking to Death" "prophesies the emergence of a new collectivity of women" (Backus, "Grahn and the Lesbian Invocational," 835). Reading the endings of the two poems intertextually, it becomes apparent that when the common woman "will rise / and will become strong," then death "shall be poor." Both visions rest on a community of individual women who have transformed themselves personally and are rising up together to transform society.

In *The Highest Apple,* Grahn describes how "common women" developed a "community" of women in the early 1970s:

> At that time the vision of commonality was solidifying. . . . We were busy establishing a base of female controlled institutions that would begin to answer to the expressed needs of all kinds of women. Women were dramatically shifting the focus of their lives, entering the work force, changing their family structures, bonding with different kinds of lovers than they had ever imagined for themselves, launching careers and starting businesses. Commonality gave way to community, the attempt to concretize the bonding of women into a group identity. (74–75)

As Melanie Kaye/Kantrowitz observes, Grahn's reclamation of the word "common . . . continues to echo through our [lesbian] literature; Rich's dream of a common language; myself, 'are we ready to name / with a common tongue?'" (Kaye/Kantrowitz, "Culture Making," 29). Having survived robustly, the reclaimed term *common* has become a player in the essentialist/constructionist debate. Donna Haraway writes in her postmodernist "A Manifesto for Cyborgs" that "the feminist dream of a common language, like all dreams for a perfectly true language, of a perfectly faithful naming of experience, is a totalizing and imperialist one" (215). In "Cultural Feminism Versus Post-Structuralism: The Identity Crisis in Feminist Theory," Linda Alcoff begins by blasting cultural feminism, which she defines as "the ideology of a female nature or female essence reappropriated by feminists themselves in an effort to revalidate undervalued female attributes" (413). Alcoff gives as her only examples early writings by the separatist theologian/philosopher Mary Daly and by Adrienne Rich, whose title *The Dream of a Common Language* is among the most prominent lesbian-feminist uses of the word *common*. Alcoff later points out, however, that "one does not have to be influenced by French post-structuralism to disagree with essentialism" (413).

Grahn attempts to walk the dividing line in the essentialist/constructionist debate. She commented in 1987 that her book *Another Mother Tongue,* which traces the folklore and speculates about the origins of North American lesbian and gay cultures, "has become the basis for a new philosophical stance in gay men's culture, which they call essentialism, to argue against the sociological/socialist view that 'gayness' was only invented in this century and is the product of our particular industrial culture" (Constantine and Scott, "Belles Lettres," 7). Grahn calls the opposition to essentialism "the sociological/socialist view" rather than "social constructionism." This is perhaps a slip of the tongue or a mistake in the transcription of the interview. Whereas Grahn—or those gay men to whom she refers—may be making a point about homosexuality as a form of alienation under industrial capitalism, she does not elaborate; *socialist* as an oppositional term to *essentialist* is unusual enough to suggest that Grahn's use of the term is accidental, if provocative. In any case, it is a nomenclature clearly outside the academic essentialism/social constructionism debate. Further, Grahn says that essentialism is what "they call" the position for which *they* use her work. Were she to take part in the debate, Grahn would argue her position from the perspective of history and her belief in the folklore she writes about in *Another Mother Tongue:* "Actually, I don't think the two views are mutually exclusive. Certain elements of gay culture are very 20th century, but we're so much older than that it's absurd to imagine that all of this is brand new" (Constantine and Scott, "Belles Lettres," 7).[10]

Elsewhere Grahn engages directly with terms that are central to more recent literary criticism: *margin, center,* and *difference.* The relevance to both poststructuralist theory and Grahn's poetry merits quoting at length:

> If the world were shaped like a plate, "exile," "marginal" and "difference"
> would be words accurately descriptive of life at the edge of a single uni-
> verse. . . . Our social groups, countries and plant and creature groupings
> are globe shaped, and interactive; the walls can intermingle without losing
> their integrity. Reality continually folds in and out of itself, with as many

"worlds" as we have the ability and judgment to perceive, each with its own center.

In a many-centered multiverse, exiles from one place are first class citizens of another, margins of one "globe" are centers of another, "marginality" itself becomes a ribbon of road, of continual and vital interaction shaping and reshaping whatever lies within borders, and "difference" is so essentially common (and Self-centered) that it is duplication that is the oddity. It is a matter of perspective, of metaphor: to seek not what is "universal," rather to seek what has commonality, what overlaps with others without losing its own center. (Grahn, *Really*, 145)

Grahn's insistence in *The Highest Apple* that by "common" she does not mean "universal" is clearly an answer to accusations of essentialism that had been leveled against lesbian feminism by the mid eighties.

Universal, "one-world" implies everyone having to fit into one standard (and of course that one, that "uni," is going to turn out to be a white, male, heterosexual, young, educated, middle class, etc. model). . . . Common means many-centered, many overlapping islands of groups each of which maintains its own center and each of which is central to society for what it gives to society. (Grahn, *Highest Apple*, 74)

Grahn compares her sense of commonality, particularly the "international connection present in the 'She Who' series" to Audre Lorde's work, in which international, cross-cultural elements are "vividly apparent." "Commonality," as Grahn applies the term to women, "means we get to belong to a number of overlapping groups, not just one." She points to the term " 'common differences': defining and retaining racial and ethnic identities without losing either our affinity as women and or as Lesbians." While acknowledging and honoring the diversity of lesbian poets and of women in general, Grahn maintains the importance of "a common structure" to lesbian feminism and the women's movement (*Highest Apple*, 76–78).

In 1981 Grahn wrote that she "sought nothing universal to mankind in writing" *The Common Woman* poems. "In fact, in order to make certain they were really there in the flesh, I avoided all thoughts of 'universality,' 'the masses,' 'the common people' or 'mankind.'" On the other hand, she confesses to writing "deliberate pro-woman propaganda"

so as to bypass the built-in patriarchal hatred of, condescension toward, deliberate ignorance toward: 1. the details of women's lives; 2. especially of "workingclass," everyday women; 3. more especially women of color; 4. most especially of lesbians; 5. always of women who fought back, had abortions, did not love their bosses, and desired to change their lives. ("Red," 547)

Numbers 3 and 4 are problematic: although Grahn addresses racism directly in "A Woman Is Talking to Death," none of *The Common Woman* poems is clearly about a woman of color; only one is about a lesbian. Although none of the poems makes claims to universality, readers would tend to assume that the characters are white, in the absence of information pertaining to race or ethnicity—because the poems exist in the context of a white-dominated society, and because Grahn herself is white. Grahn's lesbianism could lead a reader to guess that individual "common women" are lesbians, but the specific indication of one character's lesbianism implies that the others are heterosexual, where their heterosexuality is not otherwise clearly indicated. Any of the common women *could* be a lesbian and *could* be a woman of color, but with the exclusion of specific information about race and sexuality (cf. Spelman, *Inessential Woman*), they do not "especially" appear to be so.

"What Is a Lesbian?" and what constitutes lesbian literature have been burning questions for lesbian studies and politics since the early days of lesbian feminism. Grahn wrote, performed, and published some of the first poetry within the context of the movement to attempt to provide answers. In so doing, she presented a complex picture of lesbians, opposed to the monodimensional (and pathological) portrait of "The Lesbian" that had been invented by psychiatry and sexology and that reigned supreme until the 1970s, and in contrast to the "politically correct" stereotype of the lesbian feminist purveyed by some vocal queer theorists. Grahn reached into the ancient and mythological past for images useful in constructing community and identity, even as her work intervenes in and reflects on current pressing topics. At the same time, Grahn's early work exhibits a certain prescience. Her humor resembles the wit that marks the best of queer theory and activism. Likewise, her playfulness, especially with language, shares an affinity with the "free play" of the postmodern. The wide scope and pointed criticism of her "love poetry" presages the later interrogation of the "heteronormative" romance narrative, as poems from "Edward the Dyke" to "the most blonde woman" challenge gender norms. Sometimes appearing essentialist, elsewhere clearly foundational to a constructionist project, Grahn's work resists easy categorization in either camp. And, finally, her reclamation of derogatory terms, especially *dyke,* but also *queer,* points the way for a large-scale "queer" self-naming some twenty years later.

Grahn's poetry addresses intersections of gender, sexuality, class, and race, a project that many today believe was not engaged at all until the 1980s or even nineties. Still, Grahn's primary contribution to the diversity of lesbian feminism is her persistent exploration of working-class women's lives. Although in the 1980s she wrote and spoke many times of the racial and ethnic diversity of early lesbian feminism, it fell to her colleague and friend, the African American poet Pat Parker, to illustrate how lesbian feminism in the early 1970s dealt with issues of race in the context of an analysis based most notably on gender and sexuality.

Chapter Three

"I Have a Dream Too": Pat Parker

Pat Parker was named one of the "50 Most Influential People in Gay and Lesbian Literature" in the 1980s by *Lambda Book Report,* called "a giant voice of early Lesbian feminism" by Judy Grahn, and considered by many the first African American lesbian and one of the first lesbian poets to acknowledge her sexual identity in public poetry readings. No less a black lesbian luminary than activist-publisher-writer Barbara Smith avows that "Pat Parker's poetry is the first explicitly Black lesbian feminist writing I remember reading" (*Movement* 1999:39).[1] Yet Parker and her work are far less well known than the other poets under study here, even among lesbian feminists, especially among academics. Parker's more than full-time commitment to activism and her coparenting of two children likely contributed to the fact that she published only three chapbooks in the 1970s and two bound volumes of poetry between 1978 and her death of breast cancer, at age forty-five, in 1989. *Movement in Black* (1978) collects Parker's poems, mostly from the chapbooks: *Child of Myself* (1972), *Pit Stop* (1973), and *Womanslaughter* (1978). *Jonestown and Other Madness* (1985) is a slim bound volume of eleven poems. More than infrequent publishing contributes to Parker's relative obscurity, however. Parker did not fit neatly into preexisting categories of identity, genre, or political ideology—nor did she want to. A revolutionary activist whose poetry overlaps the categories of African American, lesbian, and feminist literary traditions, Parker expressed a multifaceted, politically situated identity that calls into question the orthodoxies of every movement in which she participated. Her multi-issue agenda and complex statements about identity prefigure outspoken, organized U.S. "Third World" feminism by nearly a decade. They echo in theoretical statements by contemporary queer academics that challenge heterosexual norms and static identity politics. And they show beyond doubt that at least some lesbian feminists—and a prominent some—flew in the face of the image of a white, middle-class lesbian-feminist politics and constituency.

Evelyn C. White's observation that Parker "pushed, shoved, and fisticuffed her voice into the lesbian feminist movement" (*Movement* 1999:43) testifies to the racism that has existed there, as in the women's movement in general, the queer movement, and the larger society. But Nancy Bereano's observation about the staying power of Parker's poetry fleshes out the story; she notes that the volume "has had almost as many lives as the proverbial cat." *Movement in Black* fell out of print twice because of financial hard times for alternative presses, but it was published in various editions by three different publishers in 1978, 1983, 1989, and most recently in an expanded edition in 1999 (*Movement* 1999:frontispiece), keeping the earliest poems in print on and off for nearly thirty years.

Relatively few references to Parker were made in print before 1989, but after her untimely death both black and white lesbian feminists commented on her powerful influence on their lives, work, communities, and political movements. African American writers and activists, especially, credited Parker as a "mentor" (Folayan, "Gifts"). The Washington, D.C. group Black Women Together organized a memorial performance in honor of Parker, "to say thank-you, Pat" and publicly "acknowledge the difference your work has made in our lives." Stormy Webber read her poem "Praises to the Spirit of Pat Parker!" at the tribute, mourning "a death in the family" and acknowledging "ancestor you left us / yr strong tools / a trail clearly marked / yr precious words-." Novelist Ann Allen Shockley wrote that "as a forerunner, Pat paved the way and served as a model for younger black lesbian poets to come forth and have their voices heard in rage, joy, beauty, and song" ("Black Women Together").

Jewelle Gomez, an African American lesbian writer and activist, praised Parker for having "the courage" to be "the 'first black,' the 'first lesbian,' the first everything" (Gomez, "First"). Indeed, several tributes, biographical notes, and reviews, including one written by Parker's friend Audre Lorde, refer to her as a "visionary" (Blain, Clements, and Grundy, *Feminist Companion,* 833; Folayan, "Gifts"; Lorde, "Foreword"; Oktenberg, "Quartet"; Stato, "Pat Parker"). One memorial tribute speaks to Parker's power to help others envision themselves with pride: "She . . . convinced us (lesbians) we were the stuff of poetry" (Stato, "Pat Parker," 31). Given the nationwide outpouring of recognition and praise that followed the San Francisco Bay Area poet's death, it is not surprising that the board of the Women's Building of San Francisco considered naming a room after her in 1993.[2] New York City beat Parker's hometown to the punch: the Lesbian and Gay Community Services Center library in Manhattan is named after Parker and gay film historian Vito Russo.

Parker had a penchant for "publicly asking dangerous questions" (Folayan, "Gifts"), a willingness to speak "forcefully on behalf of those who *could* not speak for themselves" and to rage "at those who *would* not" (Brimstone, "Pat Parker," 6), and a commitment to liberation for "all sides of herself: she was a revolutionary, Black, working class, lesbian/feminist poet, and she refused to keep quiet" (Gregg 12). Parker confronted and often angered people with her relentless critique of any racist, sexist, homophobic, and/or classist status quo (M. Wolfe, "Interview" and personal communication 1997). White admiringly calls Parker a "big bold bad-to-the-bone Black lesbian" (*Movement* 1999:43). Michelle Parkerson notes Parker's multi-issue politics, which sound commonplace today because the path was forged by Parker and others in the 1970s: "Racial identity and vigilance against racism were as central to Parker's writing as her love of women and her defiance against sexism and homophobia. . . . She wrote brilliantly of the jeopardy and joy of Black lesbian life" (*Movement* 1999:35). Angela Davis states clearly that Parker's "poetry and activism foreshadowed and helped to forge the cultural and political values that continue to inspire so many of us. . . . Contemporary poets, musicians, and political activists, including those who may not be familiar with Pat Parker's work, work on a terrain that resonates with her pioneering voice" (*Movement* 1999:28). Theorists, too.

In "Pat Parker: Feminism in Postmodernity," Dympna Callaghan terms Parker's work "poetry for the nineties" (128). Callaghan discusses Parker's poem "For the white person who wants to know how to be my friend" (*Movement*, 68) in theoretical terms applicable to Parker's oeuvre as a whole: "It provokes an awareness about reading African American lesbian 'otherness' without colonising it by ignoring, dispensing with, or overemphasising the poet's gender, sexual preference and ethnicity" (129). Callaghan's project is to show the "important ways" in which Parker's work "intersects" with the "debate" over "the designation 'Third World.' . . . Parker's poetry both exemplifies and resists the concerns of contemporary postcolonial writing where the subject, the i/I of Parker's poem, is a nexus of complex power relations produced by social institutional formations" (129–30).[3] Parker opens "For the white person" by confronting readers with a contradiction that defies easy resolution: "The first thing you do is to forget that i'm Black. / Second, you must never forget that i'm Black" (ll. 1–2). Stanzas 2 through 5 challenge white people to see beyond common stereotypical associations between

African American people and soul music, soul food, violence, and sexual prowess. When "you" rely on these stereotypes, Parker writes, "It makes me wonder if you're foolish" (l. 15). In the closing stanza Parker plays on a last racist stereotype, inverting it, and questioning the integrity of "the white person": "In other words—if you really want to be my friend—*don't* / make a labor of it. I'm lazy. Remember" (ll. 18–19).

Emily Culpepper emphasizes that Parker's poems have "a genius for putting the emphasis where it belongs." She describes the effectiveness of "For the Straight Folks" (*Movement,* 111–12), which Culpepper used to end a lecture in which she "taught lesbian material to a huge lecture course for the first time, struggling with smirking alienated jocks and whispering flirting frat members" ("Genius"). The opening lines of Parker's penultimate stanza—"Fact is, blatant heterosexuals / are all over the place" (ll. 40–41)—"named the reality in the classroom and they did, yes they did, know what hit them. That is consciousness-raising" (Culpepper, "Genius"). There is nothing subtle about this poem; it exposes the "blatant" hypocrisy of heterosexism by hammering the point home at the end of stanzas 3 through 9 in capital letters:

> Have you met the woman
> who's shocked by 2 women kissing
> & in the same breath,
> tells you that she's pregnant?
> BUT GAYS SHOULDN'T BE BLATANT. (ll. 5–9)

The irony, and the injustice, is that "blatant" heterosexuality is taken for granted, not marked as "sexual" because it is the dominant norm. In the last stanza, Parker tells offended heterosexuals that she will go back into the closet, on one condition, "after you" (l.52).

"For the Straight Folks" is recorded on "Lesbian Concentrate," a 1977 album of songs and poems by lesbians responding to Anita Bryant's homophobic campaign to "Save Our Children" from "blatant" homosexuals. (Diana Press, the publisher of *Womanslaughter,* in which "For the Straight Folks" was first published, called it "the poem Anita Bryant made famous" in an advertisement for the book in 1978.) "For the Straight Folks" is one of many examples of a lesbian feminist challenging heterosexism some fifteen years before queer theory recast the issue as a theoretically complex problematizing of "heteronormativity." As Culpepper laments, Parker's "feminist theory-making in and out of academia . . . has been overlooked by too many sisters. . . . If we reduce our vision to stargazing, we fail to expand our conception of the varied forms in which ideas are developed" ("Genius").

Parker was instrumental in developing both lesbian-feminist poetry and lesbian feminism, a movement that, along with gay liberation, had grown strong enough to attract national attention from the likes of homophobic legislators and the former Miss America by the end of the 1970s. Parker and Grahn met in the San Francisco Bay Area in 1969, and from then throughout the early 1970s they "*often* read together as a pair" (Grahn, in Aal, "Judy Grahn on Women's Poetry," 69). Along with Grahn, Alta, and Susan Griffin, Parker drew together communities of women who assembled for lesbian poetry readings on the West Coast. Grahn explains that she and Parker "both knew it was impossible for us to enter the world of poetry—and consequently we invented another world of poetry, and became peers, and leaders, and friends" (Grahn, "Introduction," 15).[4] In an interview in 1985 Parker described how her early readings with Grahn functioned in much the same way as did early consciousness-raising groups, helping to create lesbian-feminist culture:

> When Judy and I started, we read mostly in small places like bookstores and coffeehouses, but there was an exhilaration because we were laying ground. There was no women's culture to speak of. The musicians we have now didn't exist. We had no validation for ourselves, for the culture, for anything. It was like pioneering—we'd go out into these places and stand up to read poems. We were talking to women about women, and, at the same time, letting women know that the experiences they were having were shared by other people. . . .
>
> If I die tomorrow, I die knowing I put my foot in a place where no one had stepped before. At that time people were not out writing poems about being lesbians. It simply wasn't done. Or, if they did, it was clothed in so many similes and metaphors that you had to take a shovel to find it. People were still writing poems and changing the pronouns. (Rushin,"Pat Parker," 28)

A Movement of Working-Class Poets

Like Grahn's poetry, Parker's work deals with class as well as gender and sexuality. In her autobiographical narrative poem "Goat Child" (*Movement*, 19–30) Parker illustrates the roots of her class politics. She describes her father, "typical / spade businessman / too much credit—too little capital" (ll.

23–25). She grew up in "what is now / suburbs of Houston only / it had weeds and space" (ll. 27–29):

> one room—tin roof playhouse
> with tarzan-making beams,
> tin #2 washtub, maggot-filled
> outhouse and super rats / (ll. 35–38)

She remembers being punished in second grade for stealing a notebook" (l. 75) from "the / doctor's son who could / afford it easy" (ll. 79–81). In the sardonic nursery rhyme "Dialogue" (*Movement*, 51–52), Parker contrasts the narrator's adult political observations with her mother's assurances that the world is safe and just. Parker writes as a poor person, "Working my whole life away, / trying to join a higher class, / & living in utter decay" (ll. 18–20).

In other poems, Parker creates working-class and poor characters to comment on economic hierarchies in the United States. Reminiscent of Grahn's *Common Woman*, "there is a woman in this town" (*Movement*, 154–57) chronicles a number of women, though Parker's characters exist on the fringes of the women's movement and the local lesbian community, including one who "was locked up" (l. 47), one who "fills her veins with dope / goes from house to house to sleep / borrows money wherever she can / . . . / none of us have trusted her" (ll. 56–63), and another, by contrast, who "owns her own business / . . . some say she is a capitalist / some say she has no consciousness / none of us trust her" (ll. 29–35). In "Movement in Black" (*Movement*, 86–93) Parker celebrates African American women's lives and achievements; in addition to named heroines past and present from Phillis Wheatley to Edmonia Lewis, many of whom were poor, Parker memorializes unnamed slaves, western pioneers, modern political activists, and a series of what Grahn would call "common" women:

> I'm the southerner
> who went north
> I'm the northerner
> who went down home
>
> I'm the teacher
> in the all Black school
> I'm the graduate
> who cannot read

I'm the social worker
in the city ghetto
I'm the car hop
in a delta town

I'm the junkie with a jones
I'm the dyke in the bar
I'm the matron at county jail
I'm the defendant with nothin' to say.

I'm the woman with 8 kids
I'm the woman who didn't have any
I'm the woman who poor as sin
I'm the woman who's got plenty.

I'm the woman who
raised white babies &
taught my kids to
raise themselves. (ll. 119–42)

Performed in five voices—Parker's, and four African American women's from the community in which she happened to be reading—this choral poem creates a dramatic community of diverse characters who chant, "I am the Black woman / I am a survivor" (ll. 191–92). It is this poem that most indelibly impressed Parker's audiences. Tribute after tribute to Parker mentions "Movement in Black." Jewelle Gomez, who participated in a mid-eighties performance, referred to it as a "ritual" that "gave others a glimmer of possibility for growth and change" (*Movement* 1999:30).

A third type of class-related poem comments directly on government policies and actions that create or reinforce economic inequality. "Where do you go to become a non-citizen?" (*Movement*, 61–62) expresses disgust with government excess and indifference to poverty, among other injustices. Each stanza concludes with a refrain unusual for such a committed activist as Parker (though one frequently heard in anti-establishment circles, to be sure): "I wanna resign; I want out." "The Law" (*Movement*, 139–40), like "Dialogue," reflects Parker's adult realization that, despite what she was taught in her youth, the powers that be discriminate, often on the basis of economic status.

the law
comes to homes

& takes the poor
for traffic tickets
the law
takes people to jail
for stealing food
the law
comes in mini-skirts
to see if your home
is bare enough
for welfare (ll. 15–26)

Parker worked at various times as a waitress, proofreader, maid, clerk, and writing instructor, and put in over sixty hours a week as medical coordinator and board member of the Oakland Feminist Women's Health Center from 1978 until 1987, when she resigned to have more time to write (Blain, Clements, and Grundy, *Feminist Companion*; Folayan and Byrd, "Pat Parker," 415; Kinsman, *Contemporary Authors*; Rushin, "Pat Parker," 29). Parker remarked in an interview following the release of *Jonestown and Other Madness* in 1985, "If I could get someone to give me $10,000 to live on for a year, I'd probably come out at the end of that year with at least three books" (Rushin, "Pat Parker," 29). In her essay "Age, Race, Class, and Sex: Women Redefining Difference," Audre Lorde explains why "poetry has been the major voice of poor, working class, and Colored women. A room of one's own may be a necessity for writing prose, but so are reams of paper, a typewriter, and plenty of time" (116).

Revolutionizing Traditions: Poetry, Critics, and the Black Aesthetic

While Grahn and Parker performed together as working class-identified lesbian feminists in the early 1970s, Parker's poetry also insistently confronted racism, an issue that Grahn addressed directly only in "A Woman Is Talking to Death." Grahn explains that Parker was unique in 1969 for more than just speaking openly as a lesbian: Parker "had come through already two or three Movements by the time lesbian-feminism was beginning to develop, and she helped develop it" (Aal, "Judy Grahn on Women's Poetry," 69). She "[got] up and [said] what had never, before, anywhere, been said . . . about women, about lesbianism, about Blacks and whites living under a racist and sexist regime which strikes out from every side as well as from above" (Grahn,

"Introduction," 11). In the same way that Grahn preceded Adrienne Rich as the preeminent white lesbian-feminist poet, Parker preceded Audre Lorde, who is placed at the center of most discussions of African American lesbian writers. Lorde was undoubtedly one of the poets who impressed Parker in the early 1970s (Grahn, "Introduction," 12), but the reverse was also true, and Parker clearly influenced Lorde's decision to publish and speak openly as a lesbian. Lorde writes that she worried about Parker after meeting her in 1969 and reading her "merciless and vulnerable and far-ranging" poems over the next few years (*Movement,* 10).[5] In her foreword to Parker's *Movement in Black,* Lorde writes, "These poems would not need any introduction except for the racism and heterosexism of a poetry establishment which has whited out Parker from the recognition" she deserves (*Movement,* 9).

Parker started writing when she was a child, and her first published poem appeared in 1963 in *Negro Digest* under the name P. A. Bullins. At the time (1962–1966, from age eighteen to twenty-two), she was married to the playwright Ed Bullins, who was the cofounder and cultural director of the Black Arts Alliance associated with the San Francisco Black Panther Party and briefly the minister of culture of the party. Parker had been a prose writer before marrying Bullins, but, she explained, she turned to poetry because Bullins "was a prose writer, and he used to *tear up* my prose! I'd write a story and he would *rip it apart!* . . . Criticism, you know? And then I decided I would begin writing poetry because he didn't know anything about that" (Cornwell, "Pat Parker," 41).

Like Bullins, Parker was active in the Black Panther Party, and she was influenced by the Black Arts poets. When Grahn asked Parker in the 1970s to name poets who had had an impact on her work, Parker "handed [Grahn] a small pile of paperbound books by poets, all of them Black, two thirds of them women" and added Grahn's name to the list. Most of the small paperbacks were published by independent black presses, "especially Dudley Randall's Broadside Press in Detroit, and the Third World Press from Chicago, extremely important sources of contemporary Black writing." Grahn sees traces of Black Arts poets Don L. Lee, Sonia Sanchez, and Nikki Giovanni in Parker's work, particularly their "vital insistence on speaking a people's art, instead of an elite or academic art" (Grahn, "Introduction," 12–13)—trademarks of the Black Aesthetic. Lee "not only celebrated blackness but wrote a number of poems exhorting those African Americans who were hesitant to act against racism to change" (Seibles, "Quilt," 182); Sanchez was among the black women poets who "constituted a formidable phalanx of the consciousness-raising activities of the 1960s" (Hernton, "Sexual Mountain," 198).

Many of the Black Arts writers of the 1960s repudiated earlier African American literature, considering it not "black" enough—that is, because the sixties militants thought that earlier writers had assimilated to white cultural and critical standards (Smith, "Black Arts," 96–8). Timothy Seibles, however, traces the notion of a Black Aesthetic back to Paul Laurence Dunbar, whom he considers the first notable African American writer to address "subjects directly relating to the experiences of black Americans," and to do so using black vernacular (or "what might be called 'Slave English'") in the 1890s ("Quilt," 158–59). But it was the gay Harlem Renaissance writer Langston Hughes, one of the poets whom Grahn notes as an influence on Parker, whom Seibles considers to have been "the primary proponent of the black literary aesthetic in America" by 1927 (Morse and Larkin, *Gay and Lesbian,* 204–6; Grahn, "Introduction," 13; Seibles, "Quilt," 167). Reviewing Parker's *Jonestown and Other Madness* in 1985, Alicia Oktenberg compares Parker to Hughes: "The body of her work rivals none except the work of Langston Hughes. He used to be called 'the poet laureate of the Negro people.' Parker can be called 'the poet laureate of the Black and Lesbian peoples'" ("Quartet," 17).

Parker clearly was part of and influenced by the movement of Black Arts poets, many of whom did not consider the writers of the Harlem Renaissance sufficiently militant. As Seibles points out, however, the Black Arts poets, with their conviction that "black was unequivocally beautiful," were "riding the momentum of the struggle for a true identity—begun, for the most part, in the twenties" ("Quilt," 181). Parker clearly acknowledged this longer lineage of politicized African American writers; according to Grahn, in addition to militant black poets of the 1960s and Langston Hughes, Parker particularly admired Gwendolyn Brooks, Lorraine Hansberry, and Zora Neale Hurston (Grahn, "Introduction," 13). In the "Roll call" section of "Movement in Black," Parker includes the writers Phillis Wheatley, Frances E. W. Harper, and Hurston.

The Black Aesthetic explicitly informs the style and content of much African American literature and art, especially after 1960. Whereas earlier black poets at times may have been "more willing to ask politely for justice and hope for the best" (Seibles, "Quilt," 181), the Black Arts poets rejected white academic and critical standards, expressed rage at white people and white society generally, incorporated the "style and rhythms and colors of the ghetto" (Hoyt Fuller, quoted in Smith, "Black Arts," 95), took rhythmic cues from black music, notably jazz and blues, turned to specific black role models as diverse as Malcolm X and James Brown (Smith, "Black Arts," 95–100), and celebrated Africa as the true "Motherland" (Seibles, "Quilt," 183). In short, Black Aesthetic theory, articulated in the 1960s by such writers as Leroi Jones/Amiri Baraka, Gayle Addison, and Larry Neal, called for "ground[ing] literature in black vernacular culture" (Smith, "Black Arts," 101), much like contemporary hip hop music.

Several of Parker's poems employ language that could be considered part (though not exclusively) urban black vernacular: the "ain'ts" of "My Lady Ain't No Lady" (*Movement*, 113); the informal, often humorous, diction of "i wonder" ("i wonder / how many matches it would take, / to lay a single-file trail / from here—/ to richard nixon's ass," ll. 1–6, *Movement*, 60) or "For the Straight Folks" ("you know some people / got a lot of nerve"); the cursing in "The *What* Liberation Front?" a poem about her dog "fuck[ing] in the streets" (l. 17, *Movement*, 71); or the culturally specific "childhood chants" recalled in "Group" ("if you're white—alright / if you're brown—stick around / if you're Black—get back," ll. 12–14, *Movement*, 136–38). Several of the poems refer to "blackness," specifically African American experiences and perspectives: black women being told they're ugly because their "lips are too big," "hair is nappy," skin is too dark, or "nose is too big" ("Group"); the alcoholism that victimizes impoverished ghetto communities ("Pit Stop," *Movement*, 104–9); pride in defiant ancestors ("Movement in Black"); or the "chains" of modern racism that remain from chattel slavery ("Questions," *Movement*, 79–82).

The characteristic of the Black Aesthetic that is most obvious in Parker's work is a reliance on black oral tradition, not just in vernacular language but in the very form of the poems. Barbara Smith explains that Parker's work is "very much in the Black oral tradition which relies on inflection, metaphor, irony, and humor to deepen our communication and make it specifically ours" ("Naming," 99). Pamela Annas notes the "oral storytelling tradition" apparent in Parker's "Pit Stop," a poem spoken by a jaded but self-aware "bar habitué," and she points out that "some of Parker's poems are jokes or anecdotes" ("Poetry," 21). Certainly, the erotic poem "For Willyce" (*Movement*, 102) with its humorous and political punch line—like Grahn's "If you lose your lover" and "parting on the left"—falls into the "joke" category:

When i make love to you
i try
with each stroke of my tongue
to say   i love you
to tease   i love you
to hammer   i love you

```
to melt    i love you
& your sounds drift down
oh god!
    oh jesus!
and i think—
here it is, some dude's
getting credit for what
a woman
has done,
    again.
```

"A Small Contradiction" (*Movement*, 123) sends up the early lesbian-feminist belief in principled nonmonogamy with a similarly well-timed punch line:

```
Me, i am
totally opposed to
monogamous relationships
    unless
      i'm
    in love. (ll. 12–17)
```

Ayofemi Stowe Folayan and Stephanie Byrd observe that "the very nature of Parker's narrative poems springs from her 'race education' in Texas and the oral traditions of African American people who supplemented this education with stories that have gone unwritten" ("Pat Parker," 417). Parker wrote and spoke many otherwise "unwritten" stories—of a variety of African American women in "Movement in Black," of bar dykes in "Pit Stop," and of victims of domestic violence in "Womanslaughter," for example (*Movement*, 141–50). The fact that "Movement in Black," though printed in a book, was conceived (and primarily successful) as a performance piece "is consistent with the Afro-American tradition of oral history" (Clarke, "Review," 223). Parker plays the role of the African griot, the "poet-philosopher-historian who kept the wisdom of the people from being lost over time," the woman who memorized and passed down complex genealogies and village histories (Seibles, "Quilt," 161).

Grahn and Wendy Cadden both liken Parker to a lawyer pleading a case; her use of repetition, revelation, and call and response is also clearly analogous to a southern black preacher (Grahn, "Introduction," 12; "Where Will You Be?"). Religious allusion figures into several of her poems, as title or epigraph—"Exodus" (*Movement,* 37), "from cavities of bones" (*Movement,* 45), "A Family Tree" (*Movement,* 55), "when i drink" (*Movement,* 110), and "when i was a child" (*Movement,* 152–53)—or as image or point of reference—baptism in "Goat Child," bigoted religious fervor in "Where Will You Be?" (*Movement,* 74–78), her mother's faith in God in "Dialogue," and her mother's repeated question in "My lover is a woman": "Lord, what kind of child is this?" (*Movement,* 98–100). Biblical allusion and the oratory style of the black church are historically significant to antiracist poetry in part because church services were the only large communal gatherings of African Americans allowed during slavery. Because it was a punishable offense to teach slaves to read and write, the black church was based entirely on oral forms rather than reading of Scripture. After abolition, preachers were among the first literate African Americans in most communities, and their ability to affect congregations with their oratory style was of paramount importance (Seibles, "Quilt," 160–61).

African American poets at least as far back as Langston Hughes constructed poems on the framework of "the call-and-response ('A-men!') rhythms of the black church" (Seibles, "Quilt," 167). As African American poets in the 1960s became more politicized about not only the content but also the form of their poems, black oral traditions such as call and response were more widely and explicitly invoked. Seibles explains that "most poems were secular sermons, direct calls to social consciousness and action, with the 'amen' response typical of the church congregation being replaced by the 'right on' of the streetwise." Seibles's comment that most Black Arts poetry "was written to be spoken, shouted, and preached" echoes in references to Parker as "a visionary, a preacher, and a pedagogue" and to her persuasive voice that could "preach/shout a poem or leisurely caress it" (Culpepper, "Genius Folayan and Byrd, "Pat Parker," 417; Seibles, "Quilt," 181).

Nearly all commentators on Parker agree that her poetry needs to be heard, not just read. Cheryl Clarke is right to point to the connection between Parker's work and "what young urban people now call *spoken word* art" (*Movement* 1999:20). Tributes refer to Parker's "stunning" oral performance, "her dynamic presence," and "the magic of [her] voice" (Callaghan, "Pat Parker," 132; Culpepper, "Genius"; Folayan, "Gifts"). That Parker at times performed with musicians (such as Gwen Avery, Avotcja, Linda Tillery, and Mary Watkins) and incorporated refrains, rhythms, and rhymes associated with music into her work augmented the auditory impact of her poetry. Barbara Smith, an obvious admirer of Parker's work, admits that she disliked Parker's poems until hearing them, but afterward testifies that Parker's reading of a particular poem "makes even more vivid the searing feelings which inspired it" (Smith, "Naming," 102). Gerald Barrax, a reviewer who belittles Parker's work, allows that it could be a "crowd pleaser" when read aloud, going so far as to call "Movement in Black" "incantatory" ("Six Poets," 260). Barrax, who dislikes Parker's work qua poetry, notices that the poems in "Liberation Fronts," the second section of *Movement in Black,* employ "incantatory rhythms, topical subject matter, and colloquial language" that make them "reminiscent of the 1960s when poetry often became public performance" ("Six Poets," 260). He misses the populist point of the Black Arts poets' emphasis on performance. They intended not "a lowering of standards of the muted word (i.e., text), [but rather] the recognition of the verbalized text" (Salaam and Ward, "Sayings," 117). Barrax, like many other academic critics, may recognize but does not value performance poetry in the black oral tradition.

Grahn, with her emphasis on the "use" of poetry, and her sense of how poetry readings can "energize" an audience and coalesce a community, clearly had learned from the same public performance movement that Parker had in the 1960s. Both undoubtedly were influenced by the Beat movement's improvised oral poetry, but the Black Arts movement seems a closer antecedent. African American Black Arts poets like Amiri Baraka/Leroi Jones and Bob Kaufman had participated in the jazz-inflected Beat scene, but they split with the Beats in the 1960s and took the performance of poetry to new political and rhetorical heights. The rage unleashed by the events of the 1960s, epitomized by the assassination of Malcolm X in 1965, led to a poetry whose energy, anger, and daring were fed by public audiences, whose emotional responses in turn pushed "revolutionist" poets such as Don L. Lee and Nikki Giovanni further (Seibles, "Quilt," 177, 182). The Black Aesthetic of the 1960s emphasized performance, with the intention of making literature "an immediate, communal form to be experienced in public" (Smith, "Black Arts," 101). Parker explained that "the point" was "to try to put the poetry in the language that we speak. . . . People forget that rhyme and meter passed down information long before we had pen and paper and books" (Rushin, "Pat Parker," 28).

As a result of their focus on public performance, poets like Parker paid more attention to sound than to formal patterns, and audiences were more likely to be impressed than were most critics. Parker remarked in 1985, "It's rare for me to get a critique of my work that's favorable." In fact, it was rare for Parker to get a critique of her work at all, especially outside of lesbian-feminist publications or by reviewers who were not African American. Cris South, one of the few white feminists to review *Movement in Black,* exemplifies Parker's sense of white reviewers' unwillingness to praise or criticize her work straightforwardly. Parker told an interviewer, "Some people say, 'I don't feel competent to critique this woman's work because she's Black, and I'm white' " (Rushin, "Pat Parker," 28). South spends the first one-third of her review elaborating on her self-absorbed opening sentences: "I am a white woman, a white woman writing a review of a black woman's poetry. And I haven't been able to forget that fact for a moment" (69). When she does turn to the poems, South barely discusses or evaluates them at all; instead, she focuses on the guilt they make her feel as a white woman who does not actively oppose racism.

As appreciated as Parker seems to have been, given the number and enthusiasm of tributes written after her death, academics and other critics were nearly as likely to ignore her work in the 1970s as they were in the 1990s. Despite her impact on lesbian activists and communities, Parker was snubbed by the professional makers of theory and literary canons, even alternative ones. Culpepper writes, "Was it racism or classism or sexism, she wryly wondered, that led folks to sometimes think that the plain speech in her poems meant they weren't hard to write?" or, one might ask, that they are intellectually unsophisticated? The Black Arts movement rejected "the dead forms taught most writers in the white man's schools" (Larry Neal, in Smith, "Black Arts," 100) and, in turn, was considered propaganda rather than art by most critics. David Lionel Smith suggests that the creation of new forms required by the rejection of white models left traditionally trained critics, including African American ones, ill-prepared to appreciate the protest poetry of the 1960s ("Black Arts," 102).[6] He explains that the reliance on African American vernacular culture "demands of its reader (or listener) a sympathy and familiarity with black culture and black idioms—and in many cases, with black nationalist cultural politics as well" (102).

In other words, Black Arts poetry—or lesbian-feminist poetry, or any other movement literature—is not as transparent or accessible to all audiences as radical movement poets would insist. When Parker says that "people write in the language of their times, or should," or that she attempts to "put the poetry in the language we speak," everything turns on her definitions of "they" and "we" (Rushin, "Pat Parker," 28). While she expresses alienation from dominant culture's "criteria for what's a good poem," there also clearly are critics who feel shut out of radical movement values, allusions, and rhetorics. Many critics' alienation and disapprobation stems from political sympathies, however, not reading comprehension. Mainstream critics with a stake in the aesthetic and political status quo would be ill-disposed to applaud any poetry with a radical message. The Black Arts movement, like the women's movement of the next decade, was easily caricatured by association with its most "egregious" extremes, examples of a "swaggering rhetoric of ethnic and gender chauvinism," of "crude, strident forms of nationalism" (Smith, "Black Arts," 93).

The charge that political poetry "confuses social theory with aesthetics" (Smith, "Black Arts," 93) was leveled at Parker's work on the rare occasion of an academic review. The reviewer of *Jonestown and Other Madness* in *Library Journal* seems to want to like Parker's poems, but labels them "at times . . . rhetorical," even though s/he concedes that "more often they are saved by Parker's sharp irony and her ability to relate political issues to events in her own life" (RR, "Review"). Gerald Barrax, reviewing *Movement in Black* in *Callaloo,* appears to appreciate Parker's poems in spite of his aesthetic and political inclinations, which lead him to undercut every positive comment he makes:

> Much of this book is charged with the electricity of Parker's commitment to the causes of Blacks, women and gays. She is a writer of admirable intentions. . . . The poet's easy wit, humor and irony often give these poems an appeal and quirky twist without which they would be either mushy or strident. . . . ["Womanslaughter"] continues into a fourth part, and the poem is too long by about that much. Not willing to trust her poetry, Parker hammers home the point too didactically. . . . The poem ends not simply in justified grief or rage but in ringing phrases that threaten to tarnish the experience it has given us. ("Six Poets," 259–62)

In 1975, Parker referred to mainstream critical standards as "all a bunch of shit, academic wanderings. . . . There's so little poetry for us because look who sets the standards" (Woodwoman, "Pat Parker Talks," 61).

Indeed, when an African American lesbian critic is setting the standards, Parker's poetry fares better in a review. Even Cheryl Clarke—who calls some of Parker's poems "self-indulgen[t] . . . apoetic, arrhythmic, and contrived," "ahistorical," "glaringly unedited, uneven, in need of revision"—spends most of her review of *Movement in Black* explicating how the book "enriches at once the tradition of black poetry and of women's poetry in America," "sharply demarcating the black lesbian poet's space in the hermetic world of Afro-American letters" (Clarke, "Review," 221, 222, 224, 217, 225). Where Cris South feels confronted and exposed as a white woman, black lesbian critics feel personally affirmed. Clarke, Barbara Smith, Becky Birtha—all three black lesbian reviewers—slip into a sort of essentialist identity politics that Parker's corpus resists because it never ossifies into one static view of The Black Lesbian Feminist. Clarke writes that "all women, *particularly black women,* who experience Parker's poems will welcome her voice" ("Review," 217; emphasis added). Smith implies a felt affiliation with Parker's viewpoint in poems such as "Brother" (*Movement,* 46), "My lover is a woman," "Womanslaughter," and "Have you ever tried to hide?" (*Movement,* 47), which Smith describes as "poems only a Black feminist dyke can write" ("Naming" 102). But at their best, these reviewers share Parker's positional politics, a stance in which identity, through experience, informs but does not circumscribe ideology. Birtha writes, "I want and need much more of Parker's work. . . . I know this is the kind of writing I need, to help me continually reaffirm my own commitment to social change."

No Place to Hide: Questioning Movements from Within

African American lesbians comprise only a portion of Parker's audience, of the movements in which she participated and upon which her poetry comments. If Parker spoke with the force of a preacher, she was not one issuing a sermon to the choir. As a woman and a lesbian she was an outsider to the Black Arts movement, and as an African American lesbian she was marginal to predominantly white segments of the women's movement. In addition to challenging oppressive hegemonic forces like the U.S. government, Parker's poetry addresses the limitations of all the movements and communities within which she fought—African American, feminist, lesbian-feminist, and gay. Parker never left the struggle; she did not allow herself to be forced out, as Grahn comments vis-à-vis Parker's feminism:

> Daring to call herself a feminist from the beginning, when even other feminists had swallowed the false line that only white middleclass women need apply—what gall, for a movement which had half its own roots in the Black Power and Civil Rights struggles—Parker remained a feminist anyway—lucky for the rest of us, giving direction, criticism, stamina, impetus, courage, and a spirit of resistance on stage and off. ("Introduction," 14)

Grahn reports having once asked Parker to describe her vision of a revolution. Parker's response, as recalled by Grahn, describes parts of all the movements of the 1960s and seventies taken together, but fits no single one of them:

"If I could take all my parts with me when I go somewhere, and not have to say to one of them, 'No, you stay home tonight, you won't be welcome,' because I'm going to an all-white party where I can be gay, but not Black. Or I'm going to a Black poetry reading, and half the poets are antihomosexual, or thousands of situations where something of what I am cannot come with me. The day all the different parts of me can come along, we would have what I would call a revolution." (Grahn, "Introduction," 11)

Parker's revolutionary goal as a lesbian-feminist leader was never the self-referential safe home of a narrowly construed (or merely stereotypically essentialist) identity politics. Different situations required the assertion of different politics—antiracist, antihomophobic, feminist—and if she understood this because of her multiply located identity, she taught it as a form of activism to others, regardless of who they were.

In 1973, Parker published her vision in the poem "i have a dream" (*Movement*, 83–84). In the first two stanzas, she appears to repudiate revolutionary dreams she has shared in the past.

> i have a dream
>   no—
>   not Martin's
> though my feet moved
>   down many paths.
> it's a simple dream—
>
> i have a dream
>   not the dream of the vanguard
>   not to turn this world—
>   all over
> not the dream of the masses—
>   not the dream of women
>   not to turn this world
>   all
>   over
> it's a simple dream— (ll. 1–16)

Parker's dream must incorporate the visions of the civil rights, black power, antiwar, and women's movements, because each of them speaks to some part of who she is. The problem with them all, however, is that they are partial.

At worst, they exclude each other's priorities, and none of them includes the dream of lesbian and gay liberation. In stanzas 3 through 7, Parker envisions holding hands with her lover in public, going "to a hamburger stand" without being "taunted by bikers on a holiday" (ll. 21–22) because of her dykish appearance, walking "ghetto streets" without being "beaten up by my brothers" (ll. 27–28), and walking "out of a bar" without being "arrested by the pigs" (ll. 30–31). The idyllic sound of the word *dream* is shattered by the violence that threatens the vision in each stanza. The dreams of Martin Luther King, Malcolm X, Huey Newton, Mao Tse Tung, George Jackson, and Angela Davis have failed Parker because they have not eradicated (and in some instances have perpetrated) the violence that threatens her as a lesbian. By the end of the poem, Parker expresses frustration ("now i'm tired—" l. 44) and anger ("now you listen!" l. 45) at the movements that have failed her. "i have a dream too" (l. 46), she declares, placing herself on par with the revolutionaries she has followed in the past, challenging them to take the step of incorporating her vision; after all, she concludes, "it's a simple dream" (l. 47).

Parker's dream of equality is indeed a simple logical leap from the dream of "justice for all," the American dream invoked by King in his "I Have a Dream" speech, but it has not been a simple task to accomplish, even by the most progressive movements with which Parker was associated. Like Audre Lorde, Parker refused to name herself either with one part of her identity (black or female or working-class or gay or feminist or poet) or with a conglomerate of her many parts (black working-class lesbian-feminist poet). Parker preferred a listing of descriptors, of identity labels as affiliations, strung together with commas—neither cut off from one another nor combined into an assimilable pigeon-(w)hole—unwilling to drop any for the sake of the other, or for a "dream" other than her own.

It is this "multiplicity" of identity, which Parker both sarcastically and earnestly terms "simple," that leads Dympna Callaghan to compare Parker's work to the postmodern sensibilities of Donna Haraway and others (Callaghan, "Pat Parker," 128, 129). Callaghan correctly points out that Parker's poems intersect with contemporary theorists' resistance to essentialist notions of "woman" (128), but Parker goes even farther. Her self-aware positioning not only opposes "racism, classism, and homophobia" (Callaghan, "Pat Parker," 128), it resists essentializing notions of "African American," "working-class," "lesbian," and all combinations of these categories. The stacking of identities, as in "working-class African American lesbian," performs the crucial task of making visible people who are erased by the false generic term *woman,* but it does not necessarily challenge essentialism. Instead, it can lead to more narrowly defined essentialisms, the pretense to knowing who or how "only a Black feminist dyke" can be. Parker's poetry questions each category with which she seems to affiliate, disallowing the easy assimilation of her positional politics to a knowable identity. Judy Grahn understood this in the 1970s, when she wrote,

> Parker was making literature out of stuff so buried under American racism and sexism, classism and antilesbianism that it wasn't even a question of breaking down or reversing a stereotype but of filling up a vacuum where the stereotype would have been if it were not *so* frightening for most people to even have such thoughts. ("Introduction," 14)

Barbara Smith hinted at a similar interpretation when she titled a 1978 review of Parker's work "Naming the Unnameable." Parker made her feelings about identity categories explicit in her biographical note to the anthology *Mark in Time* in 1971:

> I dislike "schools of writing" and pedantic labeling, i.e., academic, romantic, black mountain, beat, imagist, satirist, black, woman, black woman, etc. If a person can't figure out where I'm coming from after reading my work, then either I've failed or they've failed and definitions of me are unimportant. (183)

The work is often autobiographical and always complex, if seemingly simple because of Parker's diction. Callaghan explicates "My lover is a woman" which explores the contradictions of interracial lesbian relationship, one among many of Parker's poems that is autobiographical without being essentialist, resisting the model of "a confessional revelation of authentic identity fostered by liberal humanism" (Callaghan, "Pat Parker," 132). Parker seems to proclaim who she is, but a more accurate analysis is that she explains where she stands. Her politics of identity is situational, not essentialist.

Parker's outspoken position in 1978 is celebrated by Barbara Smith, who applauds her as "one of a handful of Black women writers who acknowledge their lesbian identity" and calling Parker, among other things, "stunningly brave" ("Naming," 99). In 1975, Parker complained that the critical standards she disdained had "been controlled by *men* for so long," not just white men (Woodwoman, "Pat Parker Talks," 61; emphasis added). A common slogan of the Black Power movement was "I am a man," and the associated Black Aesthetic was for the most part vigorously masculinist. Cheryl Clarke terms Parker's poetry "a departure from the racialist, nationalist radical Afro-American poetry" of the 1970s, "because it dares to present a black lesbian's experience of oppression in the world as well as her vision" ("Review," 224). Parker directly confronted the sexism of radical black poetry and politics from her position as a black lesbian. "For Michael on his third birthday" (*Movement,* 54) begins with the epigraph, "What are you, Michael? / Black and Beautiful." With this four-stanza poem Parker both affirms that "Black is beautiful" and challenges the equation of black and beautiful with male. Three stanzas recall the killing existence of slavery, "Death the only fact" (l. 10), but, in the last stanza, "The gun has turned around," and the poet proclaims "MEN—Beautiful and Black" (ll. 15–16). On the surface, this is a legacy of self-love willed to a black male toddler. But in the context of Parker's critique of sexism in black communities, the "gun . . . turned around" and the capitalization of "MEN" can also be read as the poet turning her critical eye on the disappearance of African American women in the loudly proclaimed black-nationalist focus on "MEN—Beautiful and Black." In this reading, the poem is both an affirmation and an object lesson for the young Michael.

In "Brother" and "Womanslaughter," Parker commits the ultimate movement heresy of naming black men's violence against women. (The topic provoked an outpouring of invective from critics of Alice Walker's *The Color Purple* in 1982, for one prominent example.) "Brother" illustrates Parker's ability to succinctly diagnose a social ill; the poem literally has a punch line, but it is not of the humorous sort:

Brother
   I don't want to hear
   about
   how *my* real enemy
   is the system.
i'm no genius,
   but i do know
   that system
you hit me with
   is called
     a fist.

The epigraph to "Brother" comes from Harriet Tubman, one of the women Parker would memorialize by name as a "survivor" in "Movement in Black" six years later. The implication of the quotation is that the poet, like Tubman, has the tenacity and moral authority to fight to the finish for the "two things I've got a / right to, and these are death / or liberty. One or the other / i mean to have." Barbara Smith states that "Brother" is the sort of poem "that only a Black feminist dyke can write," not because white women are unable to see the problem but because only a Black woman (and, one might add, a Black woman with radical movement experience) could "legitimately criticize supposedly revolutionary Black men who batter women" without being susceptible to accusations of racism ("Naming," 102). Perhaps Smith feels that this poem could only have been written by a "Black feminist *dyke*" because so many radical movement women had come out of the closet by the late 1970s, or perhaps her assessment stems from a lesbian-feminist belief that a lesbian would be more likely to criticize men than a straight woman with a misguided stake in a heterosexist system. Smith does not clarify this point in her review.

Some of Parker's early poems, first collected in *Child of Myself* and reprinted in the section of *Movement in Black* titled "Married," address psychological abuse of women in heterosexual relationships. In "Goat Child" Parker describes the lessons she learned from a husband who offered to teach her "'the ways of woman'" (l. 356):

> i learned hate
> i learned jealousy
> i learned my skills—
> to cook—to fuck
> to wash—to fuck
> to iron—to fuck
> to clean—to fuck
> to care—to fuck
> to wait—to fuck (ll. 358–66)

In "You can't be sure of anything these days" (*Movement,* 36), Parker describes betrayal by "a really far out man" (l. 1) who "Says he wants an intelligent, creative / woman to be his *partner* in life" (ll. 7–8) but then ends up expecting his wife to perform traditional "women's work" (l. 18).

In "Exodus," Parker issues a warning: "Trust me no more— / Our bed is unsafe" (ll. 1–2). By the last stanza, with its ominously unfinished quatrain, the marriage bed is no longer "our bed" but "your bed." When it was "our bed," the self-definition that completed the quatrain was, first, "a cancerous rage" and, second, "a desperate slave." In the last stanza, the narrator has left the conjugal bed but dares not yet name her new independent self. The quatrain is unfinished, leaving off the last line:

> Trust me no more
> Your bed is unsafe
> Rising from folds of cloth— (ll. 17–19)

By the end of *Child of Myself*, Parker is writing love poems to women, having escaped the "folds of cloth" that represent a repressive role as wife to a sexist man.

Parker's long narrative poem "Womanslaughter" tells the story of an abused wife who did not escape—her sister, who was repeatedly assaulted and finally murdered by her husband.

> There was a quiet man
> He married a quiet wife
> Together, they lived
> a quiet life.
>
> Not so, not so
> her sisters said,
> the truth comes out
> as she lies dead.
> He beat her.
> He accused her
> of awful things
> & he beat her.
> One day she left. (ll. 83–95)
>
> One day a quiet man
> shot his quiet wife
> three times in the back.
> He shot her friend as well.
> His wife died. (ll. 141–45)

The husband was convicted of manslaughter for "a crime of passion" (l. 186) rather than murder, because "Men cannot kill their wives. / They passion them to death" (ll. 231–32). Parker, as feminist griot, remembers and retells an otherwise untold story, one that many black nationalists considered counterrevolutionary because they saw it as maligning black men, already emasculated by white society.

In the final, triumphal stanzas of this otherwise grief-stricken and furiously groping poem, Parker vows to take up and transform the role that would have belonged to her recently deceased father, whose presence is felt in the thrice-repeated quatrain, "'It is good, they said, / that Buster is dead. / He would surely kill / the quiet man'" (ll. 79–82, 150–53, 203–6). Three years after her sister's funeral, Parker writes that she is "again strong" (l. 239), able to act collectively where her father would have lashed out individually and ineffectually:

> I have gained many sisters.
> And if one is beaten,
> or raped, or killed,
> I will not come in mourning black.
> I will not pick the right flowers.
>
> I will not celebrate her death
> . . . .
> I will come with my many sisters
> and decorate the streets
> with the innards of those
> brothers in womenslaughter.
> . . . .
> I will come to my sisters,
> not dutiful,
> I will come strong. (ll. 240–45, 249–52, 256–58)

This final stanza has been criticized for "hammer[ing] home the point too didactically" and, by contrast, lauded as "a declaration of the kind of commitment that will bring about the life-saving revolution," "sum[ming] up the anger of many of us" (Barrax, "Six Poets," 262; Smith, "Naming," 102; South, "Review," 73). It was undoubtedly in the latter spirit that "Womanslaughter" was received at the International Tribunal on Crimes Against Women in Brussels in 1976, where Parker read the poem as testimony about violence against women in the United States. "Womanslaughter" also appears in a book published to coincide with the tribunal, *Poetry from Vio-*

lence, in which several women of color, including Dorinda Moreno, Marcela Trujillo, Nellie Wong, and Mitsuye Yamada, write about violence in their communities.

Parker's collective vision in the final stanza of "Womanslaughter" resonates with the themes of many of her poems; specific images and words in the stanza are directly and significantly intertextual with at least six other poems. For example, the lines "No more, can I dull my rage / in alcohol & deference" (ll. 253–54) recall the witty and tragic litany of reasons to drink elaborated in "Pit Stop" (*Movement,* 104–9)—including the desire to drown anger, shame, and sorrow. "Pit Stop" concludes with the narrator excusing herself from the bar because "i cannot afford to lose / this race. / i cannot afford to die, / in this place" (ll. 103–6). "Womanslaughter" gives specific purpose to the renunciation of "alcohol & deference": there are lives to be saved and deaths to be avenged in collective feminist activism, which cannot be executed effectively from a bar stool.

The "innards" with which Parker vows to "decorate the streets" recall the word *innards* in three other poems, "My hands are big" (*Movement,* 43–44), "Don't let the fascist speak" (*Movement,* 63–66), and "i wish that i could hate you" (*Movement,* 124). In each case, Parker uses the word *innards* to symbolize a core sense of self involving childhood memory, oppression, and injustice. By vowing to figuratively disembowel not only the rapist and the murderer but the whole society that supports them ("those brothers in womenslaughter"), Parker pledges to turn the woman-hating status quo inside out, exposing and transforming racist patriarchal culture. By inverting the misogyny of patriarchy's "innards," perhaps the ever present threat of "womanslaughter" would be replaced by "woman's/laughter."[7]

In "My hands are big," Parker explains that she is a product of her upbringing, informed by oppression, unable to fit easily into the pleasant scenario of harmonious feminist sisterhood imagined by women unfamiliar with racism and poverty:

> some of
> > my sisters see me
> > as big & twisted
> > > rough & torn
> > > callused & sectioned
> > > definitely not pleasant,
> > to be around— (ll. 7–13)

My hands are big & rough
  like my mother's
my innards are twisted & torn
  like my father's
my self is
  my big hands—
    like my father's
  & torn innards
    like my mother's
  & they both felt
    & were—
& i am a product of that—
& not a political consciousness (ll. 43–55)

These "innards" are at the core of Parker's self-concept. They are her inheritance from her parents, poor black people who were oppressed, but who in turn persecuted the lesbian daughter who would not listen to them and stay "married & miserable" (l. 29). Contradictory—"twisted / and torn" (l. 45)—as this self-image is, it is part of the baggage Parker carries to the women's movement.

Parker's "Don't let the fascist speak" addresses the sacrosanct liberal principle of unfettered free speech, questioning for whom that right is actually guaranteed. In this poem, Parker figures her "innards" as the site of her visceral memory of racist injustice. When Parker hears "the voices of students / screaming / insults   threats / *'Let the Nazis speak'*" (ll. 8–11), her "innards churn / they remember" (ll. 26–27) the separate and unequal education she received in all-black public schools, police brutality against Black Panthers who were exercising their alleged right to free speech, and "images / of jews in camps— / of homosexuals in camps— / of socialists in camps" (ll. 74–77). Her "innards" as site of memory and of conscience are also the base for moral decision as they make her aware that

there is
no contradiction
what the Nazis say
will cause
  people
  to hurt
    ME. (ll. 114–20)

Finally, in "i wish that i could hate you," a poem about jealousy, her "innards" are the basis for decisions. "i wish that i could hate you / when you brush against me in sleep / your breath slapping life in my innards / & i feel my body go soft in wanting you" (ll. 1–4). Despite any decision she makes with her head, she will follow her gut feeling.

Renaming Love: Poetry in a Women's Tradition

The last three lines of "Womanslaughter"—"I will come to my sisters, / not dutiful, / I will come strong"—echo the intimate lyric "Let me come to you naked" (*Movement,* 120), in which Parker envisions a politicized erotic relationship in which she can freely express various aspects of herself: "naked," "dark," "old," "weak," "angry," "callused," and finally,

> even more

> Let me come to you strong
> come sure and free
> come powerful

> and lay with you (ll. 13–17)

Both "Let me come to you naked" and "Womanslaughter" appear in the "Love Poems" section of *Movement in Black,* and both reenvision the tradition of women's love lyric. Like Grahn's "grand, muscley" names for love, Parker's love poems are "powerful"; love has the capacity to "give birth / to revolution" ("Metamorphosis," ll. 22–23, *Movement,* 132). Several of Parker's love poems center on romantic and/or erotic relationships, but others are platonic, and some are collective, anonymous, and purely political.

"Gente" (*Movement,* 135) is the first of Parker's love poems to depart entirely from the template of a romantic or erotic relationship. The poem is about a political group of women of color with whom Parker played softball (sudi mae, "We Have," 6–7, 25). Gente formed in 1974 as an alternative to white-dominated sports teams sponsored by lesbian bars, and as a means of socializing primarily with other lesbians of color. According to Grahn, Parker and others organized Gente because of racism within the lesbian-feminist movement. It was among the first groups of its kind, Grahn explains, a precursor to *This Bridge Called My Back.*[8] Parker writes in the poem "gente" that "it feels good / to be able to say / my sisters / and not have / *any* reservations" (ll. 21–25). Ironically, "feels good" echoes one of the refrains in "My lover is a woman," in which "feel good" refers to being intimate with her white lover, despite the disapprobation of both women's families and circles of friends. Perhaps the irony is not so great, however, since "My lover is a woman" is specifically about the difficulties of interracial relationships, while "gente" is about the ease of socializing among women of color. Other "love poems" are about learning to overcome racist beauty standards and love oneself ("Group," *Movement,* 136–38), the "contradictions" of "The Law" (*Movement,* 139–40), making peace with her sister's violent death ("Autumn Morning," *Movement,* 151), acquiescing to her dying mother's definition of respect as deference ("when i was a child"), and questioning the limits of feminist "sisterhood" ("there is a woman in this town").

Parker's attention to renaming herself and her world place her squarely in a tradition of women's poetry, as exemplified and explained by Grahn, and as schematized by Pamela Annas in her essay "A Poetry of Survival: Unnaming and Renaming in the Poetry of Audre Lorde, Pat Parker, Sylvia Plath, and Adrienne Rich." Annas explores the implications for poets of the fact that all language carries cultural assumptions. If the poet is outside the dominant norm—not white, male, and heterosexual—she attempts to "reclaim words and images, to revise the way words are put together as well as the words themselves, to review the whole tradition of poetry, to repossess and reinhabit language" ("Poetry," 10). Annas posits five stages of "unnaming and renaming" to describe how women poets achieve this revision, whose "necessity . . . seems clear by now" (10). The stages range from acceptance of dominant norms through dual consciousness, refuting "the other-defined self," redefining and renaming the self, and renaming the world from the perspective of the redefined self ("Poetry," 11–12).

Annas describes Parker's work as "distinguished by a tension between unnaming and renaming" ("Poetry," 19). In this schema, "My Lady Ain't No Lady" is a poem of unnaming, since it defines the poet and her lover against traditional types, the class- and race-laden images of "lady" and "gentleman" (19–20). "Womanslaughter" and "Don't let the fascist speak" both exist "in the contrary and powerful space between unnaming and renaming," a charged form that explores contradictions (21–22). "Movement in Black" is a long exercise in renaming the self (22), while "i have a dream" renames the world, that is, "brings the world, through language, into an alignment with the self" (12). Annas details an observation that most other commentators have made about Parker's poetry: Barbara Smith discusses Parker's "process of self-creation" ("Naming," 100), Callaghan examines the ways in which "identity" in Parker's work "is at once constituted by affirmation and negation" ("Pat Parker," 134), Lyndie Brimstone remarks on Parker's "relentless search for a definition of self" ("Pat Parker," 4), Joan Nestle states that "for Pat Parker, knowledge of what must be jettisoned is the most powerful starting place" ("Place," 9); I have written elsewhere of Parker's concern with "defining *herself,* in opposition to the ways in which the 'they' of white, straight, male-dominated society would describe us all" ("Giving Voice"). Jay Wright describes a similar tradition in black poetry, in which a figure "suffers the pains of transition from one state of existence to another and strives by some act to gain identity" ("Desire's Design," 17), confirming Cheryl Clarke's observation that Parker writes from and into both black and women's literary traditions ("Review," 217, 224).

"Womanslaughter" is one example of how Parker's work fits into a tradition of feminist and lesbian poetry as well as African American poetry. The poem was modeled after Grahn's "A Woman Is Talking to Death," which is "made the way it is because [Grahn] was already so familiar with" Parker's "Goat Child,"

> the first deliberately autobiographical poem by a woman that I had ever heard, although there was no reason (try sexism) why a woman's entire life couldn't be the storyline of a poem, a modern epic. For people hearing it at the time, the idea that women even *had* life stories was amazing and nearly unheard of. (Grahn, "Introduction," 13)

A vital aspect of the lesbian-feminist movement that Parker and Grahn helped to create, according to Verta Taylor and Leila J. Rupp, is the vigorous critique of the movement and of lesbian-feminist communities from within ("Women's Culture," 34). Parker's statement at the end of "Womanslaughter" that "it will matter not / if she's Black or white— / if she loves women or men" (ll. 246–48) hints at a broad critique of lesbian feminism and the larger women's movement. Just as Parker names the sexism and homophobia of African American movements and communities, she names the exclusions of women's communities and organizations. "Parker's way of working," according to Grahn, "has always been to keep her ears open among a community of people,"

> and take on the personal responsibility for saying what was on people's minds and important to them. What was not being said other places, or

what was being muddied and needed clarification. And what white women could not hear at a meeting, we just might hear on a stage, boomed through a microphone. What men would not hold still for on the street, they might listen to in a more formal situation. Parker selects the work she reads for its effect on her audience, will it teach us anything—not, will it please us, will we like her, can she entertain us. This does not keep her from using sharply pointed sarcasm, irony, and a variety of hysterically funny senses to make her ideas come across. ("Introduction," 12)

"Have you ever tried to hide?" and "Brother" are printed on facing pages in *Movement in Black,* and the two perform parallel critiques of feminism and the black power movement. While the "punch line" of "Brother" confronts a black man's fist, "Have you ever tried to hide?" ends by shouting "SISTER! your foot's smaller, / but it's still on my neck" (ll. 20–21). While this poem directly confronts the racism of white feminists in the early 1970s, it also acknowledges the participation of other African American women in the movement. Most of the poem, in fact, addresses an African American "you":

> Have you ever tried to hide?
>   In a group
>   of women
>   hide
>   yourself
> slide between the floor boards
> slide yourself away child
>   away from this room
>   & your sister
> before she notices
>   your Black self &
> her white mind (ll. 1–12)

Parker is describing her reaction to hearing a white woman at a meeting ask, "How do we know that the panthers / will accept a gift from / white—middle—class—women?" a question that rendered Parker and other working-class/women of color in the group invisible.

In "there is a woman in this town," Parker interrogates the willingness of feminists, including herself, to claim all women as their sisters, recalling her stated indifference at the end of "Womanslaughter" to a woman's race or sexual orientation in the name of political solidarity against domestic violence.

In a repeated pattern of four stanzas, Parker sketches a woman, describes the community's response to her, and asks "Is she our sister?":

> some say she is lonely
> some say she is an agent
> none of us speak to her
>
> Is she our sister?
>
> some say she is mis-guided
> some say she is an enemy
> none of us know her
>
> Is she our sister? (ll. 5–8, 14–17)

The evidence mounts with each cycle: "none of us have loved her / . . . none of us trust her / . . . none of us go out with her / . . . none of us invite her home / . . . none of us have trusted her / Is she our sister?" The poem does not come to a clear resolution, except to indicate that being oppressed does not make a person pure. "Once upon a time, there was a dream" (l. 71), Parker concludes, but this one is not "simple." It is a complicated dream, one that has not worked out in the utopic way its architects had planned, but one that nevertheless "lives for those who would be sisters / it lives for those who need a sister / it lives for those who once upon a time had a dream" (ll. 78–80). The intensity of this poem, like so many of Parker's poems, comes from the brilliantly insightful question, not the answer.

As Jewelle Gomez observes, asking pointed, needling questions is "a power more subtle than the bombast of those who think they have all the answers" (Gomez, "First"). Parker's poem titled, simply, "Questions" (*Movement,* 79–82) asks how to enact the axiom "'Until all oppressed people / are free— / none of us are free.'"

> the chains are different now—
> lay on this body strange
> no metal clanging in my ears
>
> chains laying strange
> chains laying light-weight

laying credit cards
laying welfare forms
laying buying on time
laying white packets of dope
laying afro's & straighten hair
laying pimp & revolutionary
laying mother & daughter
laying father & son

   chains laying strange—
   strange laying chains
      chains

how do i break these chains (ll. 1–17)

The question mark is implied in the last line of the section—or is it? Without the punctuation, the line becomes descriptive rather than interrogatory. A presidential proclamation, a civil war, and a constitutional amendment broke the chains of slavery, but the way to end these "different" chains "laying light-weight" seems less straightforward. Without the question mark, they become how-do-i-break-these chains, perplexing social ills without an antidote.

In section 2, the chains are made of sexism, in section 3, they are made of homophobia, and Parker asks/states twice, "how do i break these chains." In section 4, "the chains are here," and Parker characterizes them abstractly rather than concretely; they are "chains of ignorance & fear." In this final section, the lines are clearly questions:

how do i break these chains
to whom or what
   do i direct pain (ll. 62–64)

sisters—how do i break your chains
brothers—how do i break your chains

mothers—how do i break your chains
fathers—how do i break your chains

  i don't want to kill—
  i don't want to cause pain—

how—
how else do i break—your chains (ll. 73–80)

Parker returns to the idea of everyone being oppressed by the existence of oppression, as "these chains" have become "your chains." Renouncing a violent solution, Parker calls for all people to take responsibility for addressing the question "how do i"—now *we*—"break—your chains."

Parker's most frequently anthologized poem asks another question, "Where Will You Be?" (*Movement*, 74–78), calling all "perverts" to account for themselves in a repressive society. As in the "Mock Interrogation" section of Grahn's "A Woman Is Talking to Death," perversion here is a sin of omission, of failing to act in the face of danger from without (a fanatically religious, repressive, bureaucratic state) and from within (our complicity with the silencing norms of heterosexism).

> They will come in robes
> to rehabilitate
> and white coats
> to subjugate
> and where will you be
> when they come?
> . . . .
>
> Every time we watched
> a queer hassled in the
> streets and said nothing—
> It was an act of perversion.
>
> Everytime we lied about
> the boyfriend or girlfriend
> at coffee break—
> It was an act of perversion. (ll. 43–48, 57–64)

In the second half of the poem Parker exhibits her disdain for the identity labels behind which people attempt to hide, sounding something like a nineties queer activist/theorist arguing against both the ethics and efficacy of assimilation.

> & it won't matter
> if you're

homosexual, not a faggot
lesbian, not a dyke
gay, not queer (ll. 97–101)

It won't matter
if you're
    Butch, or Fem
    Not into roles
    Monogamous
    Non Monogamous (ll. 120–25)

They will come for
the perverts
and where will
you be
When they come? (ll. 139–43

    By focusing incessantly on necessary questions, Parker resisted facile, partial answers, leaving social remedies and personal identities in a state of healthy interrogative flux. She insisted on naming herself black, woman, lesbian, working class, poet, but refused to boil her perspective down to any easily appropriable definition. In her insistence on multiple, shifting identities, Parker was a poet whose grassroots vernacular theorizing prefigured some of the most important insights of queer theory. Like Grahn, she challenged what would later be termed "heteronormativity" by redefining "love poems." Parker also directly called the bluff of normative categories of identity in poems such as "For the Straight Folks" and "For the white person . . ." Parker's class and race politics, directed at both the lesbian community and the larger world, expose as false the stereotype of lesbian feminism as an essentialist, white, middle-class movement. Her own multiply situated, positional politics have much in common with the sort of stance more often associated with the 1990s than the 1970s by most contemporary commentators, demanding a reexamination of an era and a politics that have been written off prematurely as naive and finally irrelevant.

Chapter Four

"High Over Halfway Between Your World and Mine":
Audre Lorde

Like the poetry of Judy Grahn, Audre Lorde's is a poetics of location, of constructed lesbian heritage. And like her friend Pat Parker before her, Audre Lorde took a firmly rooted, multiply located stand based on an identity forged through multiple differences—expressing an identity poetics. In this sense, Audre Lorde both draws on the poetics of lesbian feminism and prefigures the politics of postmodernism. Lorde is a pivotal character connecting lesbian feminism and queer theory; in her multiple self-positioning as "Black lesbian feminist warrior poet mother,"[1] she stands historically and rhetorically at the crux of the so-called generation gap between lesbian-feminist and queer theoretical notions of identity.

Much was made by critics in the 1990s of Lorde's "postmodern" stance on identity. In Lorde's autobiographical novel *Zami*, Kathryn Provost sees "a speaker fully aware of linguistic contradictions and slippage, of difference/*différance* [*sic*], and of how these characteristics come into play in the making of meaning and subjectivity" ("Becoming," 48). Similarly, in "*Zami* and the Politics of Plural Identity," Erin Carlston offers an astute reading of the novel as a proto-theory of "positionality." Nancy Fraser and Linda J. Nicholson describe Lorde's and other black feminists' antiracist declamations in theoretical terms, as exposing "the earlier quasi-metanarratives, with their assumptions of universal female dependence and confinement to the domestic sphere, as false extrapolations" ("Social Criticism," 33).[2] Christine di Stefano points out that Lorde's multiple "differences" make gender essentialism an impossible stance, thus challenging feminism with a postmodern sensibility ("Dilemmas," 65). Thomas Foster places Lorde's poem "School Note" in the textual company of such postmodern luminaries as Jacques Derrida, Antonio Gramsci, Sandra Harding, Julia Kristeva, and François Lyotard. Sagri Dhairyam looks at Lorde's work from a decidedly poststructuralist, postcolonialist perspective in " 'Artifacts for Survival': Remapping the Contours of Poetry with Audre Lorde," and Gloria T. Hull suggests "viewing Lorde's poetry in the light of Kristeva's theory" to illuminate both the poetry and the poststructuralist theory ("Living," 172).

And in fact, Lorde's insistence on her "multiple selves"[3]—her many public declarations and poetic expressions—speak to a postmodern sensibility. She eschews the temptation "of easy blackness as salvation" in her poem "Between Ourselves" (*Between*, 14–17; *Black*, 112–14). She positions herself as perpetually shifting location, simultaneously occupying seemingly contradictory spaces in "School Note" (*Between*, 4–5; *Black*, 55):

> for the embattled
> there is no place
> that cannot be
> home
> nor is (ll. 21–25)

Over and over she insisted on the string of identifiers that proclaimed her "Sister Outsider," a figure Donna Haraway would term emblematic of a postmodern, cyborgian sense of self.

But Audre Lorde was a lesbian feminist; she said so again and again. She said so in her 1979 interview with Adrienne Rich, calling herself "a Black lesbian feminist with cancer" (*Sister*, 108). She says so in her 1980 essay "Age, Race, Class, and Sex: Women Redefining Difference," where she refers to herself again as "a Black lesbian feminist" (*Sister*, 120). And she says so in the title of "Man Child: A Black Lesbian Feminist's Response" (*Sister*, 72–80). In her "Open Letter to Mary Daly," she warns that white lesbian feminists exclude black women at their peril (*Sister*, 69). She offered a diffuse definition of lesbianism to interviewer Karla Hammond in 1981, citing Barbara Smith's "Toward a Black Feminist Criticism" and echoing Lillian Faderman's and Adrienne Rich's famously lesbian-feminist definitions (Hammond, "An Interview," 20, 21). Lorde is frequently included in literary critics' discussions of lesbian-feminist poetry, often in the company of Judy Grahn, almost always with Adrienne Rich. Several of the tributes to Parker connect the two.[4]

Does Lorde's avowed and recognized lesbian feminism mean that her work does not share an affinity with queer theory? Definitely not. Does that affinity negate her lesbian feminism? Not at all. These are questions possible only from an either/or perspective. I hesitate before terming Lorde "both/and," however. She so incisively criticized the limits of hegemonic categories, so forcefully exposed the racism of white women's studies and activism, that I am tempted to call her "both/and/neither." Lorde never termed herself "queer" in the postmodern sense, and though she called herself "lesbian-feminist," she never stopped there. The long version of her self-naming included a great deal more, including a reading of those who would truncate her list:

> As a forty-nine-year-old Black lesbian feminist socialist mother of two, including one boy, and a member of an interracial couple, I usually find myself a part of some group defined as other, deviant, inferior, or just plain wrong. . . .
>
> I find I am constantly being encouraged to pluck out some one aspect of myself and present this as the meaningful whole, eclipsing or denying the other parts of self. But this is a destructive and fragmenting way to live. ("Age, Race," 114, 120)
>
> Perhaps for some of you here today, I am the face of one of your fears. Because I am a woman, because I am Black, because I am lesbian, because I am myself—a Black woman warrior poet doing my work—come to ask you, are you doing yours? ("Transformation," 41–42)

Queer critics who turn to Audre Lorde's work use her multiple positioning, the moral/political force invoked by the particular locations she inhabits, and her widespread influence on lesbian and feminist politics and theory to shore up their constructivist position and to oppose what they see as lesbian feminism's naive essentialism. Lorde is, in Marilyn Farwell's terms, "one of the few lesbian-feminists appropriated by postmodernists" (Farwell, *Heterosexual Plots*, 94). Lorde herself made clear that she abhorred the appropriation of her experience and voice in her 1981 speech "The Uses of Anger: Women Responding to Racism." She reads from a letter sent to her by a white feminist, " 'Because you are Black and Lesbian, you seem to speak with the moral authority of suffering.' Yes, I am Black and Lesbian," Lorde responds, "and what you hear in my voice is fury, not suffering. Anger, not moral authority. There is a difference" ("Anger," 132).

The queer move of laying claim to Lorde is used against lesbian feminism, at least to the extent that Lorde's lesbian feminism is downplayed. Her proclamation of her "multiple selves" is rooted in the original meaning of "identity politics" formulated by the Black feminist Combahee River Collective. The group's manifesto explains that its politics stemmed from the fact that "no other ostensibly progressive movement has ever considered our specific oppression as a priority or worked seriously for the ending of that oppression"

(275). The lack of an essentialist notion of identity is conspicuous. The distinction between perceived identity as a pretext for oppression and one's sense of self is clearly articulated by their statement that "as Black women"—the identity/pretext—"we find any type of biological determinism a particularly dangerous and reactionary basis upon which to build a politic" (277). Like the women of the Combahee River Collective, Lorde understood the importance of defining one's own identity in this hostile context. "If we don't name ourselves, we are nothing," she told an interviewer in 1980. "As a Black woman I have to deal with identity or I don't exist at all. I can't depend on the world to name me kindly, because it never will. . . . So either I'm going to be defined by myself or not at all. In that sense it becomes a survival situation" (Hammond, "An Interview," 19). For many individuals and groups whose socially constructed subjectivities are radically situated by material oppression, identity is not taken lightly, even if it is understood as contingent.

Identity, one's name, is a sign, but not merely, casually one; it is a sign with vital power, according to Lorde, without which "there is no contact with personal power; without that contact of power there is no movement; and without movement, there's surely death" (Hammond, "An Interview," 19). This rendering of "identity politics," a term and stance that has become anathema to queer theory, shares a great deal with the use of "strategic essentialism" endorsed by Spivak, Fuss, and others. A decade or more before it was queerly theorized, it was understood and employed by Audre Lorde and her "sister outsiders."[5]

But queer theory does not acknowledge that, at least in part, the validation of multivocal, shifting identity was *learned* from Audre Lorde and others like her, who found their voices and forged their "postmodern" identity politics in the crucibles of lesbian feminism, the civil rights movement, and other identity-based movements for social justice. There is a historical genealogy between Lorde's work and postmodern queer understandings of socially constructed identities, not merely a coincidental similarity. Without question, Lorde's work irrevocably changed and indelibly marks contemporary theory, yet her work is not cited as foundational within queer theory, which is indebted to it. As Barbara Christian explains, Lorde "enlarged the race-feminist theory of that period [the 1980s], so much so that the concept of difference as a creative force is today as 'natural' a part of our analyses of the world as the notion that oppressions exist" ("Remembering," 5). White feminist/queer academics did not discern on their own the importance of differences among women (or as Teresa de Lauretis put it famously, "within women"); they began to accept the idea, and then to translate it into the professional discourse of theory, thereby co-opting it, only after an enormous amount of pressure from working-class/lesbian/women of color.[6]

The multiplicity of identity that Lorde describes was meant to trouble the easy, too broad identification of "sisterhood"—but it is sometimes problematically essentialist itself, even in its refusal to overgeneralize "woman" or "lesbian," or to assign indelible somatic significance to "black." Lorde tends, for example, to rely upon a standpoint epistemology encapsulated in her frequent introductory phrase, "As a Black lesbian feminist, I . . ." ("Uses," 59; "Age," 120). This may be shorthand for the constructivism Lorde evinces elsewhere, but in key essays and speeches it is not clearly stated as such. Harriet Malinowitz succinctly encapsulates postmodernists' attraction to Lorde, Lorde's contribution to postmodernist feminism—and also the way in which "Lorde's entire conceptualization of speech, silence, and truth . . . are at complete odds with postmodern conceptions of the same" ("Lesbian Studies," 256–67). Despite the apparent contradictions, Lorde's credibility "as a Black lesbian feminist" nevertheless is grabbed up by postmodernism. Farwell sees this as an example of the fluid boundaries between lesbian feminism and queer theory, and of the variation within both theoretical camps:

> While lesbian-feminists point the lesbian subject in a utopian direction, they imply and at times articulate a more problematic lesbian subject, one whose definition is not enclosed or finalized but in process, a figure whose sameness with other women does not preclude differences . . .
>
> If lesbian-feminists like Rich and Lorde have deconstructive moments, then postmodernist theorists of the lesbian subject have essentialist moments. In the first place, postmodernists, like lesbian-feminists, represent a broad spectrum of thinking. While all postmodernists are united in their opposition to stable identity categories, the degree to which they refuse efforts of categorization differentiates them. (Farwell, *Heterosexual Plots*, 95)

"All the Parts of Who I Am": Self-Naming in Lorde's Essays

Lorde first invoked her litany of identity in late 1977, the year she was diagnosed with breast cancer. At that time, according to her son, Jonathan Rollins, "her life took on a kind of immediacy that most people's lives never develop. The setting of priorities and the carrying out of the highest prioritized tasks assumed a much greater importance. And there's . . . a real change in the tone of her writing."[7] Lorde describes her epiphany in "The Transformation of Silence Into Language and Action," delivered in December 1977 at the "Lesbian and Literature Panel" at the Modern Language Association Convention: "In becoming forcibly and essentially aware of my mortality, and of what I wished and wanted for my life, however short it might be, priorities and omissions became strongly etched in a merciless light, and what I most regretted were my silences" (41).[8] She explains that she had feared that speaking her mind might have caused "pain, or death," but, faced with death, she understood it as "the final silence" and realized that she must begin to speak out as if any day could be her last. "I was going to die, if not sooner then later, whether or not I had ever spoken myself. My silences had not protected me," she said, and then she uttered a single sentence that became a sort of motto, and, like lines from Grahn's "Common Woman" poems, has been reprinted on cards, buttons, and the like: "Your silence will not protect you" ("Transformation," 41).[9]

"The Transformation of Silence Into Language and Action" marks Lorde's first self-naming in a major speech or essay as "Black lesbian poet." As early as 1962 she insisted on naming herself equally "Black, Woman, and Poet," but "lesbian" would not enter the litany until she faced breast cancer. It remained there until the disease killed her in 1992. Although she published openly lesbian poems as early as 1972 ("Martha") and 1974 (the better-known, and sexually explicit, "Love Poem"), and spoke openly of her relationship with Frances Clayton, as late as fall 1977 Lorde's public string of identifiers did not include the word *lesbian*.[10] "Transformation" also marks the introduction of the word *warrior* to Lorde's publicly spoken self-naming, at about the same time that warrior imagery became a prominent motif in her poetry: "Within those weeks of acute fear came the knowledge—within the war we are all waging with the forces of death, subtle and otherwise, conscious or not—I am not only a casualty, I am also a warrior" (41).

In fact, several of the themes of "Transformation"—silence and speech, death and survival, anger and struggle—are evident in *The Black Unicorn,* the poetry collection published in the period following Lorde's diagnosis and her simultaneous "transformation." In addition, Lorde delivered three other influential speeches in this period: "Uses of the Erotic: The Erotic as Power" (August 1978), "The Master's Tools Will Never Dismantle the Master's House" (September 1979), and "Age, Race, Class, and Sex: Women Redefining Difference" (April 1980).[11] It is in these texts, taken as a group, that Lorde's new strategy of self-identification becomes clear. *The Black Unicorn* was her first book of poems to be so centrally informed by her lesbianism. In

"Uses of the Erotic," "The Master's Tools," and "Age, Race, Class, and Sex" Lorde names herself "Black lesbian feminist," as she first did in "Transformation." Lorde employed various permutations of the string of identifiers, "Black lesbian feminist woman warrior mother poet" in interviews and speeches from 1978 until her death.

In "Age, Race, Class, and Sex," Lorde describes the importance of insisting upon all the parts that make up her complex identity stance:

> My fullest concentration of energy is available to me only when I integrate all the parts of who I am, openly, allowing power from particular sources of my living to flow back and forth freely through all my different selves, without the restrictions of externally imposed definition. Only then can I bring myself and my energies as a whole to the service of those struggles which I embrace as part of my living. ("Age," 120–21)

Lorde's essays make clear that "the parts of who I am" and the "power from particular sources" include multiple modes of being, understanding and expressing oneself: the erotic, the poetic, the emotional, and the intellectual. Part of her rejection of "the master's tools" is the rejection of the hierarchies of prose over poetry, theory over action, intellect over emotion. "What does it mean when the tools of a racist patriarchy are used to examine the fruits of that same patriarchy?" she asks ("Master's Tools," 110–11). In "The Master's Tools" she writes about the need to recognize and make positive use of the differences among women. But she also intends to validate a panoply of visions, genres, and methods of inquiry—when she writes that "divide and conquer must become define and empower" ("Master's Tools," 112), when she accuses heterosexual white academic feminists of "the grossest reformism" ("Master's Tools," 111), and when she utters her most resounding statement:

> *For the master's tools will never dismantle the master's house.* They may allow us temporarily to beat him at his own game, but they will never enable us to bring about genuine change. And this fact is only threatening to those women who still define the master's house as their only source of support. ("Master's Tools," 112)

Lorde's attention to form is evident elsewhere as well. In "Transformation" she focuses on language: "For those of us who write, it is necessary to scrutinize not only the truth of what we speak, but the truth of that language by which we speak it" (43). In "Age, Race, Class, and Sex" she exposes the explicit link that often ties genre to class: "Of all the art forms, poetry is the most economical. It is the one which is the most secret, which requires the least physical labor, the least material, and the one which can be done between shifts, in the hospital pantry, on the subway, and on scraps of surplus paper" (116). In "Poetry Is Not a Luxury" she takes aim at the notion that theory, in the form of nonfiction prose, is somehow more important than other forms of expression. (And, for that matter, at the notion that theory can only take the form of nonfiction prose.) Nancy Bereano, in her introduction to Lorde's *Sister Outsider: Essays and Speeches,* asserts that "Audre Lorde's voice is central to the development of contemporary feminist theory," contradicting Lorde's statement, reported by Bereano, "that she doesn't write theory. 'I am a poet,' she said" ("Introduction," 7). Clearly, Lorde wrote both, poetry and theory; in her own lexicon, there can be no true separation of the two. For, as Lorde writes in "Poetry Is Not a Luxury" (published just before her cancer diagnosis), poetry is theory inchoate:

> That distillation of experience from which true poetry springs births thought as dream births concept, as feeling births idea, as knowledge births (precedes) understanding. . . . [Poetry] forms the quality of the light within which we predicate our hopes and dreams toward survival and change, first made into language, then into idea, then into more tangible action. Poetry is the way we help give name to the nameless so it can be thought. (36, 37)

In the many instances in which "Poetry Is Not a Luxury" is reprinted, quoted, or alluded to, it is rarely noted that the essay was originally a response to a specific devaluation of the importance of poetry in a political context. Lorde wrote it in 1977 as a letter to *Chrysalis: A Magazine of Female Culture,* after the editors announced that they had decided to stop printing poetry in order to save money. Lorde argues that poetry is not inconsequential to political struggle; poetry is meta-theory, the first articulation of idea as feeling and image.

A Lesbian-Feminist Poetics of Deconstruction: The Black Unicorn

If poetry comes first for Lorde, that makes it primary, not a stepping-stone on some teleological path toward "theory." Over and over, she named herself *poet* and emphasized her contribution to the movement, to women's "survival," as forged through poetry: "The white fathers told us: I think, therefore I am.

The Black mother within each of us—the poet—whispers in our dreams: I feel, therefore I can be free. Poetry coins the language to express and charter this revolutionary demand, the implementation of that freedom" ("Poetry," 38).[12] Lorde refuses to "see feel/think as a dichotomy," asserting that poetry is not effete and certainly not second to theory, "the worship of rationality and that circular, academic, analytic thinking" ("An Interview," 100–1).

Critics of all stripes exhibit a strange resistance to Lorde as poet, however, preferring to discuss (and presumably to read) her prose work. Sagri Dhairyam notes that only one critic has ever placed Lorde's poetry in a traditional literary context, but the critical aversion to Lorde's poems goes further.[13] The lion's share of published criticism and references to Lorde's work centers on her essays and novel. References to her prose work outnumber references to her poetry by more than two to one in the *MLA Bibliography*, which does not even consider the multitude of other brief citations of her prose, although she published ten books of poems compared to only three collections of essays and one novel. Dhairyam attributes this to Lorde's "slippery status between activist and writer of literary merit" and notes that in bookstores "Lorde's work is not usually found in poetry sections, but is probably available in Black studies or women's studies sections." She sees this as testimony to poetry's standing as "the most 'literary' of genres" and thus the most resistant to institutional recognition of outsiders—black, female, lesbian, etc. (Dhairyam, "Artifacts," 240, 243).

For that ready audience of politicized lesbian poetry readers primed by Parker, Grahn, and others, Lorde poses a different problem. In a glowing review of *The Black Unicorn* published in *Conditions: five, The Black Women's Issue,* Fahamisha Shariat explains that Lorde's poetic diction, unlike Parker's, can be difficult to decode:

> Although Audre Lorde may not be totally clear on a first, or even a second reading—sometimes her language approaches the surreal—her poems are rich enough to send us back for new discoveries with each reading. There are over sixty poems here. I think every blakwoman [*sic*] can find some that speak to her. ("Review," 176)

Add to this her unflinching antipatriarchal, antiracist message, and one can explain other critics' dismissals:

> In her seventh book, Audre Lorde attempts a symbolic picture of black womanhood; an effort which fails completely. . . . The book fails because

the vision is backed by a lackluster imagination, and an inability to transform external detail into emotional experience. (*Kirkus Reviews*)

  Most of the poems are simply bad. (Siconolfi)

  The rhetoric is familiar, and since Lord [*sic*] is by and large uncon-
cerned with the mechanics of poetry, her voice is undistinguished. . . . It
has an enormous appeal for those who share the author's views and would
like to see their own feelings and experiences confirmed in print. (*Publisher's Weekly*)

That one of these unflattering reviews was written by a priest is almost
humorous, given Lorde's accounts in *Zami* and in several interviews of her
travails as a girl in Catholic schools. That the reviewer who clearly does not
"share the author's views" cannot manage to spell her name correctly is also
telling. Does one need to share Lorde's (or any other poet's) views to appreciate her art? Or are some reviewers more implicated in her political critique
than others? This raises the question, then, for whom is Lorde's poetry difficult, in what ways and for what reasons? Lorde's essays and speeches tend to
simpler, declarative sentences that are at once easier to comprehend, excerpt,
purloin, and—taken out of context—misconstrue. More easily recognizable
as "theory," they are perforce less nuanced than the poems.[14]

  Lorde's investment in the role of poetry, similar to Grahn's, makes *The
Black Unicorn* an excellent place to look for abundant examples of her identity poetics. Some come in rather direct form, as when she writes of herself
in the plural: "I look in my own faces" ("Between Ourselves," l. 75, *Black,*
112–14) or "I am blessed within my selves" ("Outside," l. 55, *Black,* 61–62).
Thematically and structurally, the poems in *The Black Unicorn* present a
poetics of deconstruction that resists the either/or mandate of patriarchal,
white Western culture. The poems, parallel to Lorde's multiple positioning,
are often made up of layer upon layer of undone, transcended, and incorporated dualisms. In the end Lorde does not seek to leave identity behind, but
to put it in its place—or rather places, plural.

  Her unicorn is black, after all—alluding to the African *Chi-Wara* pictured
on the cover of the book and echoing the unicorn of Black Arts poet and
publisher Dudley Randall's "Black Poet, White Critic"—but this is no simple reversal of images, no "easy Blackness as salvation" ("Between Ourselves,"
l. 36, *Black,* 112–14).[15] The unicorn's blackness, with whose "fury" the speaker
of the title poem identifies, is ornery (*Black,* 3). It has attitude, and it has history. Marked in the last lines by the most salient fact, that it "is not / free"

(ll. 15–16), the black unicorn is also described, in a progression of adjectives at the end of lines at the beginning and end of the short poem, as "greedy," "impatient," "restless," and "unrelenting" (ll. 1, 2, 13, 14). In other words, blackness is the marker of identity in large part because of oppression—a social construction of identity politics (an identity poetics) straight out of the Combahee River Collective statement. Lines 1 and 2 end-stop with periods: "The black unicorn is greedy. / The black unicorn is impatient." (ll. 1–2). The parallel construction of line 3 makes it seem about to do the same—"The black unicorn was mistaken"—but in classic Lordean style the sentence runs over into the next line and on, for seven lines total, acknowledging and then quickly undermining a racist expectation.[16] The black unicorn was not wrong, but wronged.

> The black unicorn was mistaken
> for a shadow
> or symbol
> and taken
> through a cold country
> where mist painted mockeries
> of my fury. (ll. 3–9)

Sharon Holland perceptively argues that the wrong perpetrated was slavery, with this middle passage of the poem (ll. 3–9, of sixteen lines total) referring to the literal Middle Passage.[17] Equally, the poem expresses the passage from repressed black girlhood to politicized black womanhood that Lorde so eloquently describes in *Zami*. The theme reverberates through *The Black Unicorn,* in poems like "From the House of Yemanjá" (the Yoruba orisha [deity] who is the mother of all the others, *Black,* 6). The first stanza reads,

> My mother had two faces and a frying pot
> where she cooked up her daughters
> into girls
> before she fixed our dinner.
> My mother had two faces
> and a broken pot
> where she hid out a perfect daughter
> who was not me
> I am the sun and moon and forever hungry
> for her eyes. (ll. 1–10)

The relentless hunger of line 9, repeated in the last stanza, relates to the "greedy" and "unrelenting" unicorn of the title poem. Though raised to behave "genteelly" and "with respect" ("'Never Take Fire from a Woman,'" ll. 3, 8, *Black,* 111), Lorde's narrative voice throughout the volume speaks as a less than "perfect daughter" ("From the House of Yemanjá," l. 7). She is the paradoxical black unicorn, straining against every form of containment—hence the use of first person ("my fury," l. 9) in the middle of "The Black Unicorn."

The traditional Western association of the white unicorn with youth and virginity alone suggests the reading of "The Black Unicorn" as a coming-of-age metaphor, but Lorde again undermines the expected dichotomies. Maturity is not achieved through phallic violation but rests in a mystical female image.[18] The autonomous possession of sexual power "deep in her moonpit / growing" (ll. 11–12) suggests woman identification, that is, lesbianism. Reviewing *The Black Unicorn* for *Gay Community News* in 1979, Loraine Bethel pointed out that in the title poem's confluence of racial and sexual images Lorde also "puts the white lesbian/feminists on notice" that their rehabilitation of the mythological (white) unicorn rests in "European colonialists' distortion of African folklore" (1). Fourteen years later, Brenda Carr phrased a similar sentiment for an academic audience in a journal article subtitled "Politics of Voice, Tactical Essentialism, and Cultural Intervention in Audre Lorde's Activist Poetics and Practice":

> Provisionalising a universal subject position may be seen as one of the projects of the entire volume, as the title poem "Black Unicorn" indicates. . . . Such a representational shift asks us to question our assumption that Western culture is universal by foregrounding the connection between cultural formations and positioning in such identity factors as race and gender. (142)

The poem takes on ubiquitous dichotomies—good/bad, slave/free, black/white, male/female, gay/straight—but offers an unfamiliar, unsettled resolution. The last line consists of the single word that describes the black unicorn's desired, but not actual, state: "free." The last stanza is a run-on sentence whose lines at first seem to parallel the opening stanza. But without the end-stopping punctuation of the first stanza, the tension of the last four lines of the poem bespeak the urgency of the personal and political struggle that shape the entire book:

The black unicorn is restless
the black unicorn is unrelenting
the black unicorn is not
free. (ll. 13–16)

The poem ends by explaining what the speaker/dominant symbol "is not" and implies what she is as a result: besieged, tenacious, in struggle.

Battle Position(ality): Lorde's Warrior Imagery

Like *lesbian,* the word *warrior* began to appear on equal semantic and grammatical footing with *Black, feminist, woman,* and other markers of Lorde's identity in various permutations of her oft-quoted litany in the late 1970s. *Warrior* thus appears to be, equally with those other terms, a marker of identity and ground for identity politics. Lorde not only intends to name herself but to call forth like and like-minded others to do battle with the oppressive status quo. Obviously, warrior is not a traditionally recognized category of identity or oppression. The term functions as a stance, a battle position(ality). Its prominence in Lorde's identity poetics litany makes it clear that the other more conventional identity markers function as stances as well. Lorde draws on both, identity and positionality, in her postmodern identity politics. Gloria (Akasha) T. Hull describes Lorde's strategic self-naming in *Our Dead Behind Us,* a volume of poems published in 1986:

> Lorde's seemingly essentialist definitions of herself as black/lesbian/mother/woman are not simple, fixed terms. Rather, they represent her ceaseless negotiations of a positionality from which she can speak. Almost as soon as she achieves a place of connection, she becomes uneasy at the comfortableness . . . and proceeds to rub athwart the smooth grain to find the roughness and the slant she needs to maintain her difference-defined, complexly constructed self. ("Living," 155–56)

In *The Black Unicorn*'s warrior poems, Lorde draws on historical and legendary African woman warriors (a move toward culture and identity), but selectively, to suit her creative and political vision (a social constructionist move akin to Grahn and Anzaldúa).[19] Thus in the poem "125th Street and Abomey" (*Black,* 12) Lorde forges links to her "warrior sisters / who rode in defense" of the "queendom" of Seboulisa, mother of all the Yoruba orisha (ll. 18–19), and she echoes the phrase with a line in "For Assata" (*Black,* 28), her poem about 1970s black radical dissident Assata Shakur: "Assata my sister warrior / Joan of Arc and Yaa Asantewa / embrace / at the back of your cell" (ll. 28–31). Lorde explains in her "Glossary of African Names Used in the Poems" that Seboulisa is known as "The Mother of us all" in Abomey ("capital and heart of the ancient kingdom of Dahomey" in present-day Benin [*Black,* 119]); Yaa Asantewa was an "Ashanti Queen Mother . . . who led her people in several successful wars against the British" (*Black,* 121). Both figures are mothers, but not in any stereotypical Western sense: Seboulisa, a local manifestation of the West African Yoruba deity Mawulisa, embodies both male and female principles; Yaa Asantewa led her people against an imperialist army.

"125th Street and Abomey" belongs to part 1 of *The Black Unicorn,* a cycle of nine poems that begins with "The Black Unicorn" and makes central use of West African imagery. (In the other three parts of the book, West African imagery appears but is not the dominant trope.) As a geographical location, "125th Street and Abomey" is the crossroads of Harlem and Dahomey, which was known for its fierce warrior women (Bascom, *Yoruba,* 12; Herskovits, *Dahomey* 2:86).[20] Lorde positions herself both as inheriting the Dahomean amazons' legacy and as embattled in racist North America. The parallel image of "warrior sisters"/"sister warrior" in "125th Street and Abomey" and "For Assata" (in part 2) illustrates Lorde's vision of the intersection of the ancient strength of the Dahomean amazons and the contemporary strength of the oppressed African American woman activist, both figured as warriors. This is not an uncritical search for her history but a self-conscious use of it to create a political stance and a striking literary metaphor.

At the end of "125th Street and Abomey," Lorde compares herself to "Seboulisa mother goddess with one breast / eaten away by worms of sorrow and loss" (ll. 32–33). She asks for Seboulisa's recognition as "your severed daughter / laughing our name into echo / all the world shall remember" (ll. 35–37). Severed from Seboulisa by "Half earth and time" (l. 23), Lorde is connected to her as well because they are both "severed," one-breasted women. To Seboulisa, Lorde surrenders what is "most precious and least needed / my well-guarded past / the energy-eating secrets" (ll. 8–10). Through Seboulisa, then, Lorde expresses the sentiment familiar from "The Transformation of Silence Into Language and Action": "Your silence will not protect you" (*Sister,* 41). She trades her fear and silence for "woman strength / of tongue" (ll. 21–22), the ability she boasts of at the end of the poem, of "laughing our name into echo / all the world shall remember" (ll. 36–37). This insistence on her existence through poetry is Lorde's weapon of choice, since, as she writes in both "Transformation" (42) and the poem "A Litany for Survival" (*Black,* 31–32), "We were never meant to survive." "But women have survived. As poets," she reminds readers of "Poetry Is Not a Luxury" (39).

In "For Assata," Lorde turns her warrior's weapon, her voice, to the case of Assata Shakur, imprisoned in 1973 for shooting a police officer on what many feminists and black activists considered trumped up charges.[21] The poem describes Shakur, incarcerated and unsmiling like all the mute "sisters" in prison with her (l. 4); her "face is in shadow / obscured by the half-dark / by the thick bars" (ll. 6–8). Lorde compares Shakur to herself and to famous women warriors fighting for freedom and self-determination: Joan of Arc in fifteenth-century France and Yaa Asantewa in nineteenth century Ashanti (present-day Ghana), both fighting against British imperialism.[22]

In "125th Street and Abomey" Lorde offers to Seboulisa "as libation" an "offering / of old victories / over men over women over my selves" (ll. 12–14); in "For Assata" Lorde dreams of new victories:

> I dream of your freedom
> as my victory
> and the victory of all dark women
> who forego the vanities of silence
> who war and weep
> sometimes against our selves
> in each other
> rather than our enemies
> falsehoods (ll. 19–27)

Having drawn a contemporary political struggle in realistic terms (the imprisonment and silencing of black women) in the first stanza, in the second stanza Lorde sounds themes and images established in part 1 through poems like "125th Street and Abomey" as tropes for *The Black Unicorn:* community, silence, warriors in battle, multiple identity. Lorde identifies with Assata, "I dream of your freedom / as my victory" (ll. 19–20), and she identifies them both with "all dark women" (l. 21) who refuse to be silenced and who choose political struggle. Here, as elsewhere, Lorde presents no easy conception of whom she struggles against: herself, the multiplicity of her selves, her more obvious enemies (racism, sexism, etc.), and "falsehoods" (l. 27). Lines 26–27 allow for two readings of "our enemies / falsehoods." One implies the possessive, so that it is the lies of the enemy that she struggles against. The second implies a colon after "enemies," so that "falsehoods" themselves are "our enemies," regardless of their source.

On another level, "For Assata" is a poem about internalized oppression as a block to sisterhood, community, and revolution, similar to Pat Parker's vision in "Have You Ever Tried to Hide?" Lorde would explore this theme further in her 1983 essay "Eye to Eye: Black Women, Hatred, and Anger": "The language by which we have been taught to dismiss ourselves and our feelings as suspect is the same language we use to dismiss and suspect each other. . . . The road to anger is paved with our unexpressed fear of each other's judgment" (*Sister*, 169). In "For Assata," Lorde succinctly expresses the destruction of internalized racism, of women "who war and weep / sometimes against our selves / in each other / rather than our enemies" (ll. 23–26).

"For Assata" meets "125th Street and Abomey" where their common images and concerns cross: both connect present-day activists with a powerful West African female legacy; both figure antiracist activism as a warrior's stance; both make reference to Lorde's sense of her multiple "selves" and the importance of overcoming the ravages of silence. Both, in short, play on a dual sense of identity and positionality, enacting Lorde's postmodern lesbian-feminist identity poetics. The two poems meet just as Joan of Arc and Yaa Asantewa and Assata Shakur meet, just as Harlem and Dahomey meet, just as the speaker and Seboulisa meet, just as Lorde meets them all.

"Eshu's Daughter": Translating Among Tongues

Lorde stands at the crossroads of communities, histories, geographical locations—of her multiple selves and various elements of a world marked by difference—positioning herself in *The Black Unicorn* as akin to the Yoruba deity who is worshipped at the crossroads. Eshu (also called Elegba, Legba, and Elegbara) the linguist and trickster, is mentioned by name in only three of the poems, "Dahomey," "Timepiece," and "Between Ourselves," but his image and significance resonate throughout the book and Lorde's prose work of the time period. Eshu is the "mischievous messenger between all the other *Orisha-Vodu* and humans," according to Lorde's glossary, "an accomplished linguist who both transmits and interprets" (*Black*, 119). Lorde's friend and comrade Parker plays the trickster, too, as Cheryl Clarke notes, through her "indeterminacy, her performance of multiple roles, and her interpretive power" (*Movement* 1999: 15).[23] The trickster figure's importance to Lorde is evidenced, at least in part, by the fact that her explanation of Eshu is by far the longest of any in her glossary; clearly, Lorde wants her readers to understand his role. Lorde's position, as visionary poet straddling various intersecting identities and communities, mirrors her definition of Eshu; like the trickster-god, she overcomes dichotomies, embodies multiple differences, and moves among diverse communities and identities.

Lorde androgynizes Eshu, who is unmistakably male in the traditional tales, known for his sexual aggressiveness and almost always depicted with an erect penis (Herskovitz, *Dahomey* 2:201–30). Lorde feminizes the trickster in order to play his role, explaining that "in many Dahomean religious rituals, his part is danced by a woman with an attached phallus," a sort of Yoruba cross-dresser (*Black,* 120). In *Another Mother Tongue*, Judy Grahn cites Lorde as telling her that Eshu "originally . . . was a female, Afrikete, in the old thunder god religion that preceded Yoruba." In Grahn's version of Lorde's interpretation, Eshu "is *always* danced by a woman who straps on a straw phallus and chases the other women" (Grahn, *Another* 124–25; emphasis added). Lorde constructs the culture and history by which she is constructed, bending it to her own purposes, in recognition of its limits and of the role of the teller in the tale. She makes clear in the glossary of *The Black Unicorn* that Eshu is male, if his role is often performed by a female, but she consciously searches out and chooses to explore the implications of the female version of the trickster. Herskovitz reports one legend in which Legba takes the name "Aflakete," tonally quite close to Afrekete/Afrikete, meaning, "I have tricked you" (*Dahomey* 2:229). Lorde "tricks" the tradition by claiming what Grahn terms, generically, the "Gay" aspect of Eshu. In *Zami*, Afrekete is the sexual and spiritual partner whose presence transforms and invigorates the protagonist, helping her reconnect the pieces of herself split apart after a major breakup, but, more important, showing her how to celebrate herself, as a black lesbian, passionately.[24]

Afrekete does not appear by name in *The Black Unicorn,* but Eshu does, and Lorde's identification with him is clear. Her poetic voice assumes his legendary powers, and in one poem she figures her multifaceted self as his inheritor: "I look in my own faces / as Eshu's daughter" ("Between Ourselves," ll. 75–76, *Black,* 112–14). In Eshu's first appearance in the volume, in the poem "Dahomey" (*Black,* 10–11), "four women joined together dying cloth / mock [Eshu's] iron quiver / standing erect and flamingly familiar" (ll. 10–12). While he is powerful, and prominently male, he is not feared by women, nor does he dominate them. Similarly, in the following stanza Lorde balances the male Shango, orisha of "lightning and thunder, war, and politics" (*Black,* 121), by invoking a strong female presence: "Thunder is a woman with braided hair / spelling the fas of Shango" (ll. 19–20). Without the female diviner, the *fa,* or destiny, prescribed by Shango cannot be known; as Lorde explains in the glossary, at least in one area, "In Nigeria, the head of the Shango cult is frequently a woman, called the Alagba" (*Black,* 121). While Shango is powerful, "one of Yemanjá's best-known and strongest sons," his fame and might derive from "mother / Seboulisa" (ll. 3–4), who is a manifestation of Yemanjá, "mother of the other *Orisha*" (*Black,* 121). Eshu appears in the second stanza, Shango in the third, but "mother / Seboulisa" is "found" by the speaker in Abomey in the first stanza, placing her at the head of the poem's structure, just as she exists at the top of the Yoruba pantheon.

"Dahomey" illustrates in microcosm how, throughout the volume, Lorde frames her personal history and contemporary struggle in the larger context of an ancient past with a continuing vibrant culture. A poet and novelist who often writes of her struggle to understand her parents (especially her mother) and her relationship to them, Lorde begins "Dahomey" describing their presence as central to her search for understanding when she visits Abomey: "It was in Abomey that I felt / the full blood of my fathers' wars / and where I found my mother / Seboulisa" (ll. 1–4).[25] Aurally, line 2 reads "father's wars," suggesting the daily battles against racism that her dark-skinned father fought.[26] In Abomey, the speaker states that she also "found my mother" (l. 3). As is common in Lorde's poems, the stanza is one long sentence, with meanings spilling over the ends of lines and suggesting multiple interpretations. Her "fathers' wars" in print suggests many fathers, that is, ancestors; her "mother" is "found" on the next line to be the orisha Seboulisa (ll. 3–4). The connection between the speaker, her biological parents, her figurative parents (i.e., ancestors), and the Yoruba orishas is set up in the first four lines of the poem. Stanzas 2 and 3 concentrate on aspects of Yoruba life and culture, introducing the interplay between individuals and the orishas Eshu and Shango, as interpreted by Lorde.

Lorde's identification with Eshu's power as a lover and a translator come together in the "tongue" imagery she employs in more than a dozen poems in *The Black Unicorn,* including the fourth and final stanza of "Dahomey":

> Bearing two drums on my head I speak
> whatever language is needed
> to sharpen the knives of my tongue
> the snake is aware although sleeping
> under my blood

since I am a woman whether or not
you are against me
I will braid my hair
even
in the seasons of rain. (ll. 27–36)

In this stanza Lorde presents herself as a mix of warrior, lover, and translator among her selves and her communities. The "two drums" (l. 27) are means of communication, capable of rumbling like thunder. The connection to Shango, and thus to war and politics, is made through the repetition in lines 32–34 of the image of a woman with braided hair, from the third stanza.

At the same time, Lorde connects the allusion to Shango to her identification with Eshu as lover, when she writes, "I am a woman whether or not / you are against me" (ll. 32–33)—implying not merely an adversarial definition of "against" but a bodily one as well. The image of lovers' bodies moving "against" one another is a trademark erotic trope in Lorde's work. In "Uses of the Erotic" she explains that the erotic includes "moving into sunlight against the body of a woman I love" (58). The second stanza of the erotic poem "Meet" begins, "Coming to rest / in the open mirrors of your demanded body / I will be black light as you lie against me" (ll. 17–19, *Black,* 33). In "Recreation" she writes, "you create me against your thighs" (l. 12, *Black,* 81). Again, in "Fog Report" (*Black,* 70), the image works to encompass the lovers' simultaneous difference and togetherness, a deconstruction of the typical binarics of self and other, lover and loved—binaries gendered, raced, and otherwise:

When I speak
the smell of love on my breath
distracts you
and it is easier for me
to move
against myself in you
than to solve my own equations. (ll. 4–10)

These paradoxical erotic bodies lying "against" one another echo in "Dahomey," where the warrior/politician Shango melds with the lover/poet Eshu in the voice of Lorde's first-person narrator, a traveler to her people's historic and legendary past who discovers there her contemporary role—a synthesis of all of these, expressed through poetry.

In the poem "The Women of Dan Dance with Swords in Their Hands to Mark the Time When They Were Warriors" (*Black,* 14–15), Lorde similarly presents herself as a powerful and sensuous woman who rejects the self-destructive choice of silence and the negative stereotypes of Western patriarchy. "I come as a woman / dark and open," she writes in the first stanza (ll. 7–8), not as an archetypal demon—"I did not fall from the sky" (l. 1) like Lucifer (Isaiah 12:14)—nor as a vengeful, Biblical punishment (Exodus 10:4–19), "descend[ing] like a plague of locusts" (l. 3). The poem's title alludes to the ritual dance of the amazons of Dahomey, as described by a nineteenth-century anthropologist: "In their dances—and it is the duty of the soldier and the amazon to be a proficient dancer—with eyes dilated, the right hand is working in a sawlike manner for some time, as if in the act of cutting round the neck, when both hands are used, and a twist is supposed to finish the bloody deed" (Herskovitz, *Dahomey* 2:85). Lorde identifies in the poem with the amazon's open ritual display of strength, rejecting the stereotypical role of women as silent and, like the Biblical Eve, manipulative.

> I do not come like a secret warrior
> with an unsheathed sword in my mouth
> hidden behind my tongue
> slicing my throat to ribbons
> of service with a smile (ll. 14–18)

For Lorde, "Silence will not protect you"; it will kill you. She refuses to bite her tongue, to swallow the words that are her weapon. And because of her refusal, she has the use of her tongue for pleasure as well as battle. After rejecting self-denial in stanza 2, Lorde embraces erotic passion in the third and final stanza:

> I come like a woman
> who I am
> spreading out through nights
> laughter and promise
> and dark heat (ll. 23–27)

In this, the third use of the word "come" in the poem, its sexual meaning is most evident. (The verb appears and takes on a sexual connotation in most of *The Black Unicorn's* erotic poems: "Meet," "Journeystones VI," "Touring," "Scar," "Timepiece," "Recreation," "Woman," "Letter for Jan.") As she comes, she becomes "who I am," at the same time appropriating the name of the Hebrew God (Exodus 3:14); but she rejects the Western God's vengeance, allying herself instead with Yoruba deities, Eshu in particular.

Lorde's tongue is her translator's tool, giving her the ability to speak truth to her multiple communities, her warrior/orator's weapon, as she "sharpen[s] the knives of [her] tongue" ("Dahomey," l. 29), and her lover's instrument, for "licking" and "tasting" ("Meet," ll. 15, 5). For Lorde, the erotic includes but is not limited to the sexual, a stance most forcefully articulated in her essay "Uses of the Erotic: The Erotic as Power" (*Sister,* 53–59). Against the backdrop of the feminist antipornography movement, Lorde opposed the erotic to the pornographic, which she describes in the essay as "a direct denial of the power of the erotic, for it represents the suppression of true feeling. Pornography emphasizes sensation without feeling" (54). Lorde links the erotic to poetry, describing both as vital expressions of emotion, knowledge, and strength. While poetry serves "as a revelatory distillation of experience" ("Poetry," 37), "The erotic is the nurturer or nursemaid of all our deepest knowledge" ("Erotic," 56). She describes "the erotic as a considered source of power and information within [women's] lives" (53), a font so forceful that it threatens patriarchy, "So we are taught to separate the erotic demand from most vital areas of our lives other than sex" (55). Lorde resists the separation, asserting that the erotic provides "the power which comes from sharing deeply any pursuit with another person" (56).

In "Uses of the Erotic" Lorde sets forth ideas that she had and would continue to illustrate in her poems: "Yes, there is a hierarchy. There is a difference between painting a back fence and writing a poem, but only one of quantity. And there is, for me, no difference between writing a good poem and moving into sunlight against the body of a woman I love" (58). In "Recreation," for example, Lorde explores the creativity of the erotic, describing lovemaking not just for fun (the "Recreation" of the title), but also as a form of renewal (a continually available source of mutual re-creation):

> Coming together
> it is easier to work
> after our bodies
> meet
> paper and pen
> neither care nor profit
> whether we write or not
> but as your body moves

under my hands
charged and waiting
we cut the leash
you create me against your thighs
hilly with images
moving through our word countries
my body
writes into your flesh
the poem you make of me. (ll. 1–18, *Black,* 81)

In the essay "Uses of the Erotic" and in her poetic uses of the erotic, Lorde once again seems, as it were, queerly lesbian feminist. Her refusal of the pornographic, of sex for sex's sake, would be at odds with the explosion of pro-s/m, "politically incorrect" sexual discourse that marked the sex-radical 1980s and queer 1990s, but her explicit, undeniably sexual poetry contradicts the queer dismissal of lesbian feminism as prudish or antisex.[27] Lorde's seemingly "essentialist" insistence in the essay that "as a Black lesbian feminist, I have a particular feeling, knowledge and understanding" contradicts the essay's closing statement, her very "queer" understanding that women insisting on the power of their erotic desires challenge "a racist, patriarchal, and anti-erotic society" (59).

Blood: Vitality and the Threat of Violence

It makes sense, given Lorde's conception of the erotic as anything pursued with passion and commitment, that her erotic poems are rarely limited to sexual themes. Five of the "tongue" poems also employ "blood" imagery, reminding readers that what Lorde is passionate about is not merely pleasure but life itself, which is everywhere threatened by oppression. Explaining to white feminists the daily threat of violence to "Black women and our children," Lorde wrote, "Some problems we share as women, some we do not. You fear your children will grow up to join the patriarchy and testify against you, we fear our children will be dragged from a car and shot down in the street, and you will turn your backs upon the reasons they are dying" ("Age," 119).

Lorde returns again and again to the story of "the white cop who shot down 10-year-old Clifford Glover" in 1973 ("The Same Death Over and Over, or Lullabies Are for Children," l. 17, *Black,* 64). The third stanza of "Power" (*Black,* 108–9), one of Lorde's best-known poems, reads:

> The policeman who shot down a 10-year-old in Queens
> stood over the boy with his cop shoes in childish blood
> and a voice said "Die you little motherfucker" and
> there are tapes to prove that. At his trial
> this policeman said in his own defense
> "I didn't notice the size or nothing else
> only the color." and
> there are tapes to prove that, too. (ll. 22–28)

Lorde's committed, passionate feminism extends to concern for all black children, for, as the speaker of "The Same Death Over and Over . . ." explains to a white feminist poet, "the white cop . . . / did not fire because he saw a girl" (ll. 17–18). In "Power," where she meditates on Glover's murder and the policeman's acquittal, Lorde expresses an urgent need to turn her desperation and fury into creative power ("poetry"), rather than destructive and self-destructive violence ("rhetoric"):

> . . . I am lost
> without imagery or magic
> trying to make power out of hatred and destruction
> trying to heal my dying son with kisses
> only the sun will bleach his bones quicker. (ll. 16–20)
> I have not been able to touch the destruction within me.
> But unless I learn to use
> the difference between poetry and rhetoric
> my power too will run corrupt as poisonous mold
> or lie limp and useless as an unconnected wire (ll. 40–44)

Lorde wants to transform the violence of racist power into the empowerment provided by poetry, but fears other possible outcomes. In the second stanza, she describes a nightmare scenario in which she opts for self-preservation over collective empowerment, unable or unwilling to save children like Clifford:

> I am trapped on a desert of raw gunshot wounds
> and a dead child dragging his shattered black
> face off the edge of my sleep
> blood from his punctured cheeks and shoulders
> is the only liquid for miles and my stomach

churns at the imagined taste while
my mouth splits into dry lips
without loyalty or reason
thirsting for the wetness of his blood (ll. 6–14)

In the fifth and final stanza Lorde imagines giving in to "the destruction within me," succumbing to the desire for revenge, however misdirected and ultimately self-defeating, sardonically parroting stereotypes of violent, black male teenagers:

and one day I will take my teenaged plug
and connect it to the nearest socket
raping an 85-year-old white woman
who is somebody's mother
and as I beat her senseless and set a torch to her bed
a greek chorus will be singing in 3/4 time
"Poor thing. She never hurt a soul. What beasts they are." (ll. 40–51)

"Power" is a poem awash in blood whose importance is memorialized by Lorde's careful vocalizing of the dangers of succumbing to the violent racist system that murders children, acquits policemen, and sucks people into cycles of violence that may seem like reasonable responses to oppression. Lorde's "tongue" is visible both in terms of voice (used appropriately, in the service of poetry, to avoid taking the violent route) and in stanza 2 as part of the "mouth" that is "thirsting for the wetness of his blood" (i.e., the potentially self-destructive path that is mere "rhetoric," which forecloses the future by letting down future generations).

Lorde makes clear that Glover's murder is not what officials like to call "an isolated incident" in the dedication to "A Woman/Dirge for Wasted Children" (*Black,* 66–67), "for Clifford." In this three-stanza poem the first and third stanzas refer directly to Clifford Glover; in the short middle stanza Lorde makes the connection to all "wasted children": "Centuries of wasted children / warred and whored and slaughtered / anoint me guardian / for life" (ll. 20–23). Ultimately, though, she expresses an inability to stop the killing, as the poem ends, "I am bent / forever / wiping up blood / that should be / you" (ll. 36–40). As in "Power," Lorde responds to violent bloodshed with a passionate commitment to voice: "I burn / like the hungry tongue of an ochre fire / like a benediction of fury" (ll. 7–9). Remembering that the tongue is related to Eshu/Elegba, "the rhyme god" (Grahn, *Another* 125), and that poetry for Lorde "lays the foundations for a future of change" ("Poetry" 38), the invocation of "tongue" here calls up Eshu as both "the guardian of human beings" and "the personification of Accident in a world where Destiny is inexorable" (Herskovitz, *Dahomey* 2:229, 222), that is, the Dahomean belief that the trickster/linguist god, if correctly entreated, will intervene to change one's fate. Lorde, as poet-trickster-linguist, attempts to intervene in the violence that decimates black America, pouring her ardent, activist commitment to life into the poetic process.

Edges and Crossroads

Blood and tongue, death and life, silence and speech, violence and the erotic—all meet at the crossroads, a traditional Yoruba location for shrines to Eshu and a figurative space evoked in several of Lorde's poems. Lorde herself, as postmodern lesbian feminist, as poet-theorist, as "Black lesbian feminist warrior poet mother," embodies and enacts the meetings of many paths. Eshu's shrines also stand outside every Yoruba home, a place that figures prominently in much black feminist writing. *Home Girls,* for one example, is the landmark collection of black feminist writing, published in 1983, in which Lorde's "Tar Beach" and Hull's "Poem (for Audre)" both appear.[28] Carole Boyce Davies's work on black women writers' use of imagery related to "home"—cultural, mythical, geographical—demonstrates the connection between a sense of home, usually imagined as a stable place, and the crossroads, or the site of motion and travel:

> The politics of location brings forward a whole host of identifications and associations around concepts of place, placement, displacement. . . . It is about positionality in society based on class, gender, sexuality, age, income. It is also about relationality and the ways in which one is able to access, mediate or reposition oneself, or pass into other spaces given certain other circumstances. (*Black Women,* 153)

As Chinosole demonstrates, home in African American women's writing is a complex image related to identity, displacement, survival, and, in Lorde's case, a complex mélange that exists in "the house of self" (387). Or, to return to Lorde's own formulation, "there is no place / that cannot be / home / nor is" ("School Note," ll. 22–25, *Black,* 55).

No wonder, then, that Lorde perches on edges, boundaries, and other liminal spaces. In many of her poems the speaker and/or the situation rest on the knife's edge where two or more aspects of herself meet—clashing, meshing, overlapping in turn—or where she encounters difference in another, often a lover. In "Meet" (*Black*, 33–34), the speaker recounts a sexual rendezvous between a black woman and a white woman on the cusp of the celestial seasons: "Woman when we met on the solstice / high over halfway between your world and mine / rimmed with full moon" (ll. 1–3). Their life-giving, regenerative lovemaking takes place against the backdrop of the larger world, depicted both as ancient/life giving (represented by West African references) and contemporary/violent (referenced by allusions to "the ditches of Chile and Ouagadougou," l. 38). The metaphorical and actual differences that meet in the poem take many overlapping forms: physical ("your red hair burned my fingers as I spread you / tasting your ruff down to sweetness," ll. 4–5), geological ("deep in your caverns of decomposed granite / even over my own laterite hills," ll. 12–13), visual ("you will be white fury in my navel / I will be sweeping night," ll. 33–34), relational ("now you are my child and my mother / we have always been sisters in pain," ll. 42–43), vital ("we must taste of each other's fruit / at least once / before we shall both be slain," ll. 50–52). Their lovemaking incorporates the paradoxes of the outside world as well, as their "hands touch and learn / from each others hurt" (ll. 36–37).

This meeting across differences is generative, as is made clear by the poem's mating imagery. The speaker foretells that her lover "shall get young as I lick your stomach" (l. 31), as in "get *with* young," since the speaker will invite her lover in the next stanza to "Come in the curve of the lion's bulging stomach / lie for a season out of the judging rain / we have mated we have cubbed" (ll. 44–46). "Taste my milk in the ditches of Chile and Ouagadougou" (l. 38), the speaker offers, as if she is nursing her lover back to health in a dangerous world. The lovers will return to that world, however; their meeting is momentous, but also momentary, even if there is promise of another encounter. Lorde writes in the last stanza, "we have high time for work and another meeting / women exchanging blood / in the innermost rooms of moment" (ll. 47–49), but there is no guarantee. She ends the poem, "we must taste of each other's fruit / at least once / before we shall both be slain" (ll. 50–52); their work and their love, in an unjust world, are perilous.

Foreshadowing their parting in the second stanza, where the speaker makes sensuous predictions of the passion the lovers will share, the speaker pledges, "and I promise to leave you again / full of amazement and illuminations" (ll. 22–23). The couplet illustrates Lorde's utilization of edges in poetic form, not just as images. The edge first seems distinct, as line 22 includes a grammatically complete thought, even though in it the desirous lover paradoxically vows to leave. As with most lines of Lorde's poetry, this one ends without punctuation, allowing the stanza to transgress the line's (and sentence's) edge. Thus, the speaker is promising both to fulfill her lover's expectations (since now the "again" of line 22 makes clear that the lover has been amazed and illuminated before) and to leave her as must happen at the end of the encounter, made clear at the end of the poem. The form of the poetry—the fluidity of grammatical meaning across line breaks creating multivalent and sometimes paradoxical images—enacts Lorde's multi-layered dynamic sense of identity in a way less available in forms whose structure demands a more static linear logic. (Hence, perhaps, her stated preference for poetry over theory.)

For Lorde, to dwell on the edges and at the crossroads is neither to inhabit private space nor to claim individual identity. When she names herself "sister outsider" she makes clear her sense that she is not alone but one of many who are linked by their multiple differences and resistance to dominant culture.[29] Lorde's use of first-person plural in "A Litany for Survival," another important "edge" poem, demonstrates her sense of solidarity and community as well as illustrating her role as a leader in the community of sister outsiders (*Black,* 31–32). Lorde begins the first two stanzas of the four-stanza poem with the invocation, "For those of us." In the first stanza she describes "those of us" who inhabit society's liminal spaces; in the second stanza she elaborates that "those of us" therefore live in fear of "the heavy-footed" who "hoped to silence us" (l. 21). The controlling sound of the first stanza is the *s* that occurs twenty-three times in fourteen lines, echoing the initial *s* of "survival" in the title. The stanza ends with Lorde's hope for "us," to endure and to create "a now that can breed / futures" for our children "so their dreams will not reflect / the death of ours" (ll. 10–11, 13–14). The dominant consonant of the second stanza is the *f* of "fear." Repetition emphasizes Lorde's theme through phrases as well as sounds. In stanza 3, alternating lines end "we are afraid"; the cumulative effect is to impart the double bind of oppression. "We are afraid" whether it is day or night, whether we are satiated or hungry, loved or alone, outspoken or silent. The last, very brief stanza moves beyond portraying the oppression of sister outsiders to leading the way in a didactic prescription for change: "So it is better to speak / remembering / we were never meant to survive" (ll. 42–44). Lorde echoes the end of stanza two: "For all of us / this instant and this triumph / We were never meant to survive" (ll. 22–24). In "A Litany for Survival," then, Lorde advocates a group solidarity based upon sharing the experience of differentness, not a specific difference, she emphasizes the importance of "remembering," accentuating its importance by isolating the word on its own line in the last stanza, and she admonishes her sister outsiders to follow the lead she establishes by speaking out, since they have everything to gain and nothing to lose: "We were never meant to survive."

In the Footsteps of Parker and Grahn: Creating Lesbian Community

Lorde's role as a focal point of the lesbian community, particularly for women of color, led to the making of a documentary titled, after the poem, *A Litany for Survival.* In 1990 a literal if temporary community of some one thousand participants from more than twenty countries gathered in Boston for "I Am Your Sister: Forging Global Connections Across Differences—A Conference Celebrating Audre Lorde and Her Work." Conference "work-sessions" explicitly took ideas and excerpts from Lorde's prose and poetry as starting points for discussions, performances, and consciousness-raising, with the unifying theme of meeting "Eye to Eye" (the title of one of Lorde's essays) across multiple differences.[30] Since the early seventies, but increasingly in the late seventies and through the eighties, Lorde's readings, like Parker's and Grahn's, created community as they gathered lesbians at bookstores, rallies, and assorted meeting places. In the words of Gloria I. Joseph, "She educates, teaches, organizes and politicizes with her extra-ordinary poetry readings" ("Personal," 23).

Several poems in *The Black Unicorn* function to create literary lesbian "community," as do Grahn's *The Common Woman.* In addition to many unnamed, on some level universal or symbolic women (e.g., "Woman," *Black,* 82; or the "Woman" of "Meet") and many first-person references to herself and/or her lover ("we," "our"), Lorde peoples the volume with a variety of individual, named women. Friends, sister poets, activists, and possibly former lovers appear in poems such as "Harriet" (*Black,* 21), "To Martha: A New Year" (*Black,* 46), "In Margaret's Garden" (*Black,* 47), and "Letter for Jan" (*Black,* 88–89). In these poems Lorde writes, if briefly, in more intimate terms of individual relationships than she does in many of the West African-inflected poems of part 1 or the poems that follow "A Litany for Survival" in their incantatory motif. "Solstice," the last poem in the book (*Black,* 117–18),

is written in the first person but clearly presents a model for readers to follow, echoing earlier poems and similarly themed essays:

> May I never remember reasons
> for my spirit's safety
> may I never forget
> the warning of my woman's flesh
> weeping at the new moon
> may I never lose
> that terror
> that keeps me brave
> May I owe nothing
> that I cannot repay. (ll. 33–42)

By contrast, "Letter for Jan" apparently responds to an actual letter from a
poet who thought she was "chicken not to speak" (l. 1) to Lorde when she
had the chance (*Black*, 88–89). The poem's reference to Lorde's blackness and
Jan's fear that Lorde "was mama as laser" (l. 3), who might "reject you back
into your doubt / smothering you into acceptance / with my own black
song" (ll. 36–38), raise the possibility that Jan is white and that her fear is due
to the racism that keeps women apart. Lorde interprets Jan's fear as related
to the power of the erotic and the poetic that she channels:

> When all the time
> I would have loved you
> speaking
> being a woman full of loving
> turned on
> and a little bit raunchy
> and heavy
> with my own black song. (ll. 45–53)

"Journeystones I–XI," like *The Common Woman,* is a cycle of poems that
evokes a number of individual women, creating a sense of the diversity of
women the speaker has encountered in her life. Each woman is named in the
first line of a brief stanza (from five to ten lines) that recalls her importance
to the speaker. Lorde's diverse collection of friends, lovers, and sister outsiders provides another sense in which she is a poet of "multiple selves"; this

time, literally, there are multiple (textual) individuals who make up the conglomerate referred to as "the lesbian community."

Just what and who constitutes this community has been contended since the term came into widespread use among (some) lesbians in the early 1970s, of course. As Phelan reminds us,

> The historical development of lesbian communities alerts us to the fact that there is no one such thing as "lesbian culture" for all of us to belong to; rather, there are many lesbian cultures or subcultures. "Lesbian culture" cannot be a monolith or a totality that encompasses all of our lives, and this is actually a strength. (*Getting Specific*, 68)

Some of the noisiest problems of competing needs and historical mistrust among various groups were evident at "I Am Your Sister," whose goal was to explore differences and begin to move through them to coalition and alliance. (Reports and commentary on the conference focused almost as much on complaints from participants as on the proceedings [Folayan, "I Am Your Sister"; Felman, "I Am Your Sister"].) In the tug-of-war between lesbian feminism and queer theory, Audre Lorde's work becomes, in a sense, the rope on which both teams pull. Seen from another perspective—the one I have advanced here—Lorde as rope entwines the two related camps. Lorde's identity poetics, her postmodern lesbian feminism, points up the extent to which the contest depends upon the absence of the sort of multiply positioned, category-resistant voice that the work of radical women of color represent. To claim what is queer about Lorde without acknowledging what is lesbian-feminist erases a good portion of lesbian, and queer, history.

Chapter Five

An Uncommonly Queer Reading: Adrienne Rich

So what's a chapter about a (*the?*) white middle-class lesbian feminist doing in a book about reinserting working-class/lesbians of color into the history of lesbian theory? Although I argue that lesbian feminism is neither as white, middle class, nor antiqueer as it has been portrayed, neither do I assert that lesbian feminism is *not* white, middle class, nor, well, lesbian feminist. To discuss lesbian feminism, especially through its poetry, requires a look at the work of Adrienne Rich, the woman who, with her friend and colleague Audre Lorde, stands at the definitional core of lesbian feminism for so many commentators. Published the same year as Lorde's *The Black Unicorn* and contemporaneous pivotal essays, Rich's *The Dream of a Common Language* had a similarly far-reaching impact on lesbian feminism and lesbian theory more generally. While there are obvious differences between the two writers and the two volumes of poetry, there are numerous connections as well— links that usually go unexamined when Lorde is selectively cited as evidence of queer theory's political rectitude while Rich is vilified for the wrongdoings of a stereotyped (white, middle-class, separatist, radical-feminist) lesbian feminism. My point here, and throughout *Identity Poetics,* is that we falter when we discuss the segmented parts of "the lesbian community," of "lesbian feminism," and of the contemporary lesbian political/theoretical project as entirely distinct and opposing camps instead of acknowledging the fluidity, the overlap, and (to use a term especially significant to any analysis of Rich) the continuum of relevant ideas.

Most of the errors of lesbian feminism, imagined and actual, have been syncretized at various points to the figure of Adrienne Rich, as represented by a few key passages, even phrases, plucked like distinct feathers from a complex organic whole (by which I mean whole essays as well as a develop-ing oeuvre): *lesbian continuum, compulsory heterosexuality, common language, radical feminism.* In the words of the deconstructionist critic Elizabeth

Meese, Rich's work has been "enlist[ed] in the service of critical disputes," in the work of at least one critic, "based only on a few convenient examples" and "uncomfortably independent of evidence and persuasive argument" (*(Ex)tensions,* 171).[1] Arlene Stein, in her postmortem on lesbian feminism, *Sex and Sensibility: Stories of a Lesbian Generation,* refers directly to Rich only three times, and each time it is to repeat her own take on Rich's "lesbian continuum": a "blur[ring] [of] the boundaries between lesbians and heterosexual feminists," which "exemplified" cultural feminism (112).[2]

Sometimes, Rich herself is not even mentioned by name when her ideas take a hit, as, for example, in the first subheading of Donna Haraway's influential "A Manifesto for Cyborgs," where Rich's "Dream of a Common Language" becomes "An Ironic Dream of a Common Language for Women in the Integrated Circuit" (190). Later in the essay Haraway blasts Rich's phrase, devoid of attribution and context, again: "The feminist dream of a common language, like all dreams for a perfectly true language, of a perfectly faithful naming of experience, is a totalizing and imperialist one" (215). Once more, when she restates two of her main points, Haraway knocks Rich, a nameless stand-in for all the faults of prepostmodern feminism. "Cyborg imagery . . . is a dream not of a common language, but of a powerful infidel heteroglossia. . . . Although both are bound in the spiral dance, I would rather be a cyborg than a goddess," she writes, ridiculing, among other things, the women's spirituality movement *of which Rich is not a part* (223).

Haraway's readers are supposed to understand the references and, for those who do, they are reinforced by Haraway's repudiation of Rich as a "radical feminist" who "like Susan Griffin [and] Audre Lorde" has "profoundly affected our political imaginations—and perhaps restricted too much what we allow as a friendly body and political language" ("Manifesto," 216). Lorde alone is resurrected in the next paragraph, in which Haraway extols the virtues of the concepts "women of color," "*Zami,*" and "sister outsider"— keeping what she finds useful and throwing out the identity politics context, including radical and lesbian feminisms, in which it grew. Haraway qualifies her dismissal in a notational coda, allowing that while Rich's radical feminism is too rigid, Rich, Lorde, and Griffin as "poets are very complex, not least in treatment of themes of lying and erotic, decentered collective and personal identities" ("Manifesto," 232*n*32).

Haraway quite persuasively argues for her postmodern position, but she meanwhile reduces Rich to a sort of synecdoche for radical feminism. Haraway herself calls her reading of radical feminism a "schematic caricature" ("Manifesto," 199, 202, 228*n*13) and a "reductive critique" ("Manifesto,"

228*n*15) in the service of her larger goal of pointing out th
and radical feminisms and positing a postmodern cyborg
never allows the full complexity of Rich's vision, especially ...
its development by the mid eighties, when the cyborg manifesto was pu-
lished. By that time, Rich had published her essay "Notes Toward a Politics
of Location" (delivered as a speech in 1984), which she dubbed "a struggle for
accountability" (*Blood, Bread,* 211), that is, a struggle to account for her relative privilege and to problematize her earlier proclamations on "the common
oppression of women" (*Blood, Bread,* 210). Although in this essay Rich takes
herself to task for "the limits of my understanding a year ago, five years ago—
how did I look without seeing, hear without listening?" (*Blood, Bread,* 223),
in fact Rich had written on race and class, not just gender and sexual oppression, in essays as early as the 1970s: "Teaching Language in Open Admissions" (1972), "Toward a Woman-Centered University" (1973–74), "Motherhood: The Contemporary Emergency and the Quantum Leap" (1978), and,
centrally, in "Disloyal to Civilization: Feminism, Racism, Gynephobia"
(1978).[3] As early as 1975, in "Women and Honor: Some Notes on Lying,"
Rich was proposing a necessary "complexity" for feminism (*On Lies,* 193).
She developed the idea further in "The Meaning of Our Love for Women Is
What We Have Constantly to Expand," in which she repudiates the siren call
of "dyke separatism" in favor of "radical complexity," even in the all-female
context of a precursor Dyke March during Gay Pride in 1977 (*On Lies,* 227):

> Racism is not a "straight" issue, motherhood and childcare are not
> "straight" issues, while there is one black or Third World lesbian, or one
> lesbian mother, in the world. Violence against women takes no note of
> class, color, age, or sexual preference. Lesbians and straight-identified
> women alike are victims of enforced sterilization, indiscriminate mastec-
> tomy and hysterectomy, the use of drugs and electroshock therapy to tame
> and punish our anger. There is no way we can withdraw from these issues
> by calling them "man-connected problems." There is no way we can afford
> to narrow the range of our vision. (*On Lies,* 228)

While in the 1970s Rich sometimes tended to emphasize rather generally
the need to include "all women" ("Toward a Woman-Centered University,"
145; "Conditions," 213; "Meaning," 229), by the time of "Cyborg" Haraway
is faulting Rich for a politics she has publicly moved beyond—and one that,
nevertheless, played a part in creating the stance Haraway is advocating.
At least in one sense, Haraway's postmodern cyborg depends upon Rich's

(and others') earlier identity politics; Haraway argues that Rich, Lorde, and Griffin's

> insist[ence] on the organic, opposing it to the technological . . . can only be understood in Sandoval's terms as oppositional ideologies fitting the late twentieth century. They would simply bewilder anyone not preoccupied with the machines and consciousness of late capitalism. In that sense they are part of the cyborg world. ("Manifesto," 216)

Just so, Haraway responds to identity politics and is involved in its discursive world. To paraphrase the work of Diana Fuss, identity and postmodernist politics are coimplicated systems. At the same time, in the 1985 essay Rich explores her own positionality and shelves "the whole primacy question" of radical feminism that is closely associated with the work of Mary Daly (Hedley, "Surviving," 41–42). While Haraway—and Linda Alcoff, in another watershed essay of the late 1980s, "Cultural Feminism Versus Poststructuralism"—reductively read Rich's earlier work,[4] Rich herself moved in directions that some critics a few years later would compare to the work of Spivak and Derrida (Herzog,"Adrienne Rich," 269; Meese, *(Ex)tensions*, 176–77). (By 1992, at least one critic, James McCorkle, views Rich as a "Postmodern American Poet," according to his inclusion of her work in his critical study *The Still Performance: Writing, Self, and Inteconnection in Five Postmodern American Poets*.) Even Phelan, critical as she is of the flaws of identity politics throughout her work, sees in Rich's mid-eighties essay a kindred spirit to her own politics of specificity, "an almost revolutionary statement of responsibility" in her "politics of location" (*Getting Specific*, 8–9)— that is, her identity poetics, forged through activist engagement with the civil rights movement, the anti-Vietnam War movement, lesbian feminism, and the writings of, among others, the several poet-theorists who make up this book.

Rich is targeted in Haraway's "caricature" of radical feminism and Alcoff's opposition to cultural feminism, but she is never named by them as lesbian feminist nor, indeed, as lesbian at all. The elision is significant because of lesbian feminism's positional, oppositional stance—correctly construed as gender essentialist in many cases, but clearly constructionist with respect to lesbianism. Following the Combahee River Collective, Alcoff succinctly explains identity politics in this vein—"to recognize one's identity as always a construction yet also a necessary point of departure" ("Cultural Feminism," 432)—but does not see it applying to Rich. And perhaps understandably not: Rich's work is clearly not poststructuralist, but neither is it simply essentialist nor static over time.

Haraway picks on the phrase *common language,* which, while both powerful and a fitting metaphor for Haraway's analysis of radical feminism, is nevertheless a term Rich used in print only three times: as the title of her 1978 collection of poems and in two of the poems it includes, "Origins and History of Consciousness" (*Dream,* 7–9) and "Cartographies of Silence" (*Dream,* 16–20). Despite critical readings to the contrary, both poems clearly seem to illustrate Rich's ambivalence about assuming the sameness of women as a basis for feminist politics. Both question "the true nature of poetry," defined in "Origins" as "The drive / to connect. The dream of a common language" (ll. 11–12). "Drive" and "dream" indicate a striving for community and communication, not an achievement of it. In "The Fact of a Doorframe," an earlier poem, Rich similarly called poetry "common":

> Now, again, poetry,
> violent, arcane, common,
> hewn of the commonest living substance
> into archway, portal, frame
> I grasp for you . . . (ll. 16–20)

In this 1974 poem, the edifice constructed by poetry, the doorframe in which the poet stands,

> means there is something to hold
> onto with both hands
> while slowly thrusting my forehead against the wood
> one of the oldest motions of suffering (ll. 1–4)

Hardly simple or crystal clear, poetry as described here can be an opaque language ("arcane," l. 7; "stubborn," l. 21) and is not an obvious tool of easy communication among women.

Rich opens "Origins and History of Consciousness" in a dismal writer's lodgings, where poems are "crucified on the wall, / dissected" (ll. 2–3); "No one lives in this room / without living through some kind of crisis" (ll. 5–6). This last sentence of stanza 1 is echoed syntactically in the beginning of stanza 2 and grammatically carried through the entire stanza:

> No one lives in this room
> without confronting the whiteness of the wall

behind the poems, planks of books,
photographs of dead heroines.
Without contemplating last and late
the true nature of poetry. The drive
to connect. The dream of a common language. (ll. 6–12)

To the extent that "common language" should be taken to mean all women becoming or sounding alike—a typical but not necessarily accurate interpretation of Rich's poetic phrase—the *dream* of a common language is not the same thing as a waking reality.

"Origins" is primarily a somnambulant poem. In stanza 3 the narrator dreams "of going to bed / as walking into clear water ringed by a snowy wood" (ll. 16–17), washed clean by the dream experience, where "like a warm amphibious animal" (l. 21) she is *"clear now / of the hunter, the trapper / the wardens of the mind—"*(ll. 25–27). The sentence that ended stanza 1 is shifted slightly, so that at the end of the first section (of three) it reads, "No one sleeps in this room without / the dream of a common language" (ll. 32–33). Section 2 also turns on the difference between dreaming and waking. "It was simple" (l. 34), the section begins, to meet and fall in love with her woman lover. "What is not simple," on the other hand, is "to wake from drowning" (l. 40) in their lives' realities before they became lovers, into an awareness of the violence of the city around them. Section 3 presents two types of waking: the simple type, "to wake from sleep with a stranger, / dress, go out, drink coffee, / enter life again" (ll. 55–57), and the more complex type, to consciously choose a lesbian relationship that will be public and accounted for. The poem declares in the last stanza that "life" only begins when the lovers "start to move / beyond this secret circle of fire" (ll. 67–68); the dream, the unreality, belongs to the night, and the narrator refuses to "call it life" (l. 67).

Thus, in "Origins," there are at least two ways to read "the dream of a common language." Either it is a phrase that describes poetry and its relationship to the private, unreal dream world of the night, or, if by "common language" Rich is supposed to imply an unproblematic connection between or sameness of all women, then it is an elusive dream, not a waking fact. In "Cartographies of Silence," Rich's other use of the phrase in a poem, "each / speaker of the so-called common language feels / the ice-floe split, the drift apart / as if powerless, as if up against a force of nature" (ll. 2–6). This poem is not about easy, naturally transparent communication but about the contours of "lies, secrets, and silence," to quote the title of Rich's first prose collection. Language here is not actually common, but allegedly ("so-called") common. So, while some critics disparage "the dream of a common language" as Rich's essentialist vision for a radical-feminist future, viewed in context the poet's intent might well be understood as quite the opposite.

If the phrase was parodied by critics in the eighties and nineties, it was as easily misconstrued as it was incorporated by lesbian feminists in the seventies and early eighties. Like Judy Grahn (and sometimes with her), Rich often appeared under the banner of the term *common*.[5] Writing in the "Lesbian Writing and Publishing" special issue of the lesbian-feminist journal *Sinister Wisdom,* Melanie Kaye(/Kantrowitz) marked the motif as crucial to the idea of "classics" in twentieth-century lesbian literature: "judy grahn . . . reclaimed the word 'common' (a reclamation that continues to echo through our literature; rich's dream of a common language; myself, 'are we ready to name / with a common tongue?')" ("Culture," 29). Some critics oversimplified, or simply misread. Reviewing *The Dream of a Common Language* in *Gay Community News,* Lorraine Bethel praised Rich for naming "universal female truth[s]," missing the nuances with which Rich's poetry grapples with patriarchal language and the complexities of different women's lives. It is in the reviewer's terms, not Rich's, that "the dream of a common language of love between women is one all of us have had all our lives" ("Poetry," 9). Thus Rich's prophecy in the poem "North American Time" (written in 1983) that she is destined to be misunderstood is equally applicable to lesbian-feminist supporters and queer detractors:

> Everything we write
> will be used against us
> or against those we love.
> These are the terms,
> take them or leave them.
> Poetry never stood a chance
> of standing outside history. (ll. 11–17)

Other critics of the late seventies and early eighties did see the nuance in Rich's postulation of the form and promise of communication among diverse women through poetry. Mary Gentile's explication of Rich's antiseparatist politics of language illustrates the tension between radical-feminist reductivism (at once the postmodern accusation against Rich and the reason she was valorized by radical feminists) and Rich's antiessentialist appreciation of differences among women. Gentile begins with Rich's "drive / to connect. The dream of a common language," as have so many others who fault Rich's formulation as essentialist. Gentile explains, instead,

> Rich sees the richest, the strongest, the most intelligent in lesbian/femi-nism as arising from attempts to understand and draw connections among all women's common experience while trying to learn from their differ-ences. . . . She rejects always the reductive, the simplistic, the inflexible. ("Adrienne Rich," 142)

The tension is encapsulated in the contradictory readings of "the dream of a common language" and in the coexistence of Rich's attempts to craft a lan-guage that speaks to (and for?) "all women" (*On Lies,* 17, 145, 213, 229) with her clear attempts to listen to and account for diverse women, all of whose voices make up the "radical complexity" she calls for (*On Lies,* 193, 227). Ulti-mately, and increasingly over the course of her published work, Rich figures the "common language" as a multilayered conversation or chorus, not a homogenous white woman's voice. This is perhaps most obvious in her 1983 volume, *Sources,* and in the 1982 essay, "Split at the Root: An Essay on Jewish Identity," in which Rich explores anti-Semitism and her own Jewish heritage.

Haraway's critique of the cultural hegemony of the commonality theme in radical feminism is not wrong, but it is too facilely applied to Rich by many critics. At the same time, Rich is everywhere and nowhere in later fem-inist and lesbian theory, appropriated by the technique Margaret Homans has called the "disappearance into" a later theory of an earlier one. Such is the case with the many invocations of Rich's term *compulsory heterosexuality* devoid of citation and lesbian-feminist context. Among many others, the prominent queer theorist Judith Butler performs this sleight of hand—and in an essay devoted, no less, to the importance of what she calls "citational-ity" (*Bodies,* 18). The term *compulsory heterosexuality* has its uses to queer the-ory, no doubt, but its radical- and lesbian-feminist roots apparently do not. Joan Retallack notes that Butler's "mirror image" of subversive performativ-ity is "after Freud-Lacan/Foucault/Rich, of culture as inescapably masculin-ist and 'compulsorily heterosexual,'" but Butler is similar to other queer the-orists in being more likely to cite the first three than Rich (Retallack,": Rethinking:" 354).

Perhaps Butler's reluctance to claim Rich's contribution is understand-able, if still inexcusable, in light of the controversy surrounding Rich's essay "Compulsory Heterosexuality and Lesbian Existence." Objections centered not on Rich's formulation of the coerced nature of women's heterosexuality but on her proposition of "the term *lesbian continuum*"

> to include a range—through each woman's life and throughout history— of woman-identified experience, not simply the fact that a woman has had or consciously desired genital sexual experience with another woman. If we expand it to embrace many more forms of primary intensity between and among women . . . we begin to grasp breadths of female history and psychology which have lain out of reach as a consequence of limited, mostly clinical, definitions of *lesbianism*. (*Blood, Bread,* 51–52)

Embraced by many, the concept of the lesbian continuum (similar to and contemporaneous with Lillian Faderman's expansive definition of lesbianism in *Surpassing the Love of Men*) also was attacked by feminist and lesbian critics of various persuasions for its lack of historical specificity, erasure of sexuality, prioritizing of gender over race, failure to recognize the costs of publicly claiming lesbian identity, and/or requirement that all women be (or be seen as) lesbians. In the early 1980s Bonnie Zimmerman was one of many critics opposed to what she called the " 'expanded meaning' school" of lesbian identity articulated by Rich's lesbian continuum, calling it

> reductive and of mixed value to those who are developing lesbian criticism and theory and who may need limited and precise definitions. . . . Too often, we identify lesbian and woman, or feminist; we equate lesbianism with any close bonds between women or with political commitment to women. These identifications can be fuzzy and historically questionable. . . . By so reducing the meaning of lesbian, we have in effect eliminated lesbianism as a meaningful category. (Zimmerman, "What," 205–6)[6]

Diana Collecott questions whether, "in the face of such facts as the history of African-American women, we are justified in affirming what Adrienne Rich called 'the lesbian continuum', or should we focus on discontinuity, the absence of a universal lesbian identity?" ("What Is Not Said," 240). Gloria Bowles elaborates most of the common complaints in her 1981 essay, "Adrienne Rich as Feminist Theorist," including the charge that Rich appropriates the distinct experiences of African American women by looking to their lives and literature for evidence of the lesbian continuum (322–25).

But Rich's contention is an echo of African American feminist Barbara Smith's reading of Toni Morrison's novel *Sula* in "Toward a Black Feminist Criticism" (1977). Smith highlights the strong emotional connection between the novel's two main female characters and calls it "lesbian," reading *Sula* as a lesbian novel "not because [the] women are lovers, but because they are the central figures, are positively portrayed, and have pivotal relationships with one another" (164).

> *Sula* . . . works as a lesbian novel . . . because of Morrison's consistently critical stance toward the heterosexual institutions of male/female relationships, marriage, and the family. Consciously or not, Morrison's work poses both lesbian and feminist questions about Black women's autonomy and their impact upon each other's lives. (Smith, "Toward," 165)

Furthermore, criticisms of Smith sound a lot like the criticisms of Rich. Deborah E. McDowell's charge, reiterated by Hazel V. Carby in *Reconstructing Womanhood,* is that Smith's definition of lesbianism is "vacuous" ("New Directions," 190) and that she "undercuts her own credibility" ("New Directions," 189) by presenting a "definition of lesbianism [that] is vague and imprecise; it subsumes far more Black women writers, particularly contemporary ones, than not into the canon of Lesbian writers. . . . Smith has simultaneously oversimplified and obscured the issue of lesbianism" ("New Directions," 190).

Like "Compulsory Heterosexuality," Rich's 1976 MLA address, "It Is the Lesbian in Us" (*On Lies,* 199–202), faced accusations of overgeneralization and oversimplification. The controversial essays are the only two to which Rich appends afterwords in her volumes of collected essays, in order to respond to the intense debate and criticism they provoked. In the case of "Compulsory Heterosexuality," Rich asks readers to view the essay "as one contribution to a long exploration in progress, not as my 'last word' on sexual politics" (*Blood, Bread,* 68). Rich acknowledges the various "resonances" of the word *lesbian* for the audience of "It Is the Lesbian in Us," conceding that in the interest of time (MLA presentations typically last twenty minutes) she may have "oversimplified the issue" of the connection between lesbianism and creativity. Nevertheless, she maintains in her afterword that she meant "to say something more complex" than to either a) issue a "lesbian imperative" (Alkaly-Gut, "Lesbian Imperative"; Ostriker, *Writing,* 121; Peters, "'Whatever Happens,'") or b) erase the specificity of lesbian oppression, with her thundering statement, "It is the lesbian in us who is creative, for the dutiful daughter of the fathers in us is only a hack" (*On Lies,* 201).

Both famous formulations seek to place lesbians in a gendered female context rather than an ostracized sexual location. As Rich writes in "Compulsory Heterosexuality," "I perceive the lesbian experience as being, like motherhood, a profoundly female experience, with particular oppressions, meanings, and potentialities we cannot comprehend as long as we simply bracket it with other sexually stigmatized existences" (*Blood, Bread,* 53). Or, in another way of looking at it, Rich pulls all women into a lesbian universe—defined in terms of woman identification, not only sexual intimacy—centering lesbians and woman-to-woman energy, as some might have described it in the seventies. Both the lesbian continuum and the lesbian in us are consciously expansive but do not exclude *lesbian existence,* Rich's specific term in "Compulsory Heterosexuality and Lesbian Existence" for what is commonly called lesbianism. (It is Rich, after all, who insists on the lesbian specificity of her *Twenty-One Love Poems* when two heterosexual friends praise their universality [Bulkin, "An Interview," 58].) Somehow, the second term in the title gets lost in the controversy, and so the queer emphasis on sexuality over gender leads in a more or less straight line to the repudiation of Rich's landmark early essays, either by ignoring them or through reductive criticisms. Such responses (or nonresponses) are by now so automatic that an undergraduate told me in 1998 that my lesbian-feminist poetry class was the first time she was reading "Compulsory Heterosexuality" with the permission to think about it on her own without a queer critique already a part of the text. (One almost wonders why the professors at her previous institution were assigning the essay. Was it to demonstrate the implied stupidity of lesbian feminism, emblematized by a particular reading of Rich?)

Rich as Rhetorical Proto-Queer

Ironically, the lesbian continuum and the lesbian in us were faulted on nearly the same grounds as the term *queer* would be criticized by detractors two decades later. Although the bases for inclusion in queer nation or the lesbian continuum differ, the rhetorical move and motivations are similar: to gain political allies, to draw attention to sexual identities that are suppressed by heterosexism, and crucially to construct disruptive, insurgent categories of identity that fly in the face of the terms' typical usages. From this perspective, Smith's lesbian-feminist reading of *Sula* is perfectly queer, naming "lesbian" a text that disrupts the narrative of woman as heterosexual. At the same time, it is queerly lesbian feminist, in that it does not require "genital sexual experience" as a criterion for the construction of lesbianism.

Queer at once reclaims a derogatory term for same-sex love and challenges lesbians and gay men to loosen the boundaries that have defined communities and their politics. *LGSN,* the newsletter of the Gay and Lesbian Caucus for the Modern Languages, became one of many sites of contention over the term *queer* in 1993, when editors proposed changing the name of the publication to *QSN* and asked for caucus members' input.[7] The next few issues included letters from both sides of the debate, including one from Colleen Ramos, whose praise for the possibilities inherent in the word *queer* is representative of a variety of pro-queer arguments:

> "Queer" has the advantage of signifying a broad, indeterminate range of so-called perversions, thus permitting those who identify as lesbian or gay to form alliances with bisexuals, transvestites, transsexuals, and others on the margins of straight society. . . . Moreover, "queer" makes me rethink who "we" are. It forces us to face the fact that "we," as a historical construction, are in the process of changing from a protective insular community, based upon essentialist convictions of lesbian or gay identity, to a larger movement based upon the riskier but powerful concept of queer as the disavowed alterity within our normatively heterosexual society. "Queer" thus marks a radical shift from identity politics to deconstructive politics. ("Letter," 3)

Other letter writers responded negatively to the proposed name change on various grounds: that *queer* remains a painfully derogatory term, that its false gender neutrality silences women, that its use is faddish and will pass. Responding generally to the widespread replacement of *lesbian and gay* with *queer,* Zimmerman asks rhetorically, "What comes after queer? Human?"[8]

If "It Is the Lesbian in Us . . ." and the lesbian continuum bear parallels to queer in its take on sexuality as a construction in opposition to patriarchy/heteronormativity, this raises the heretical question (in both directions), was Rich in the 1970s and eighties in some respects a queer theorist before her time? I have asserted that the work of Judy Grahn and Pat Parker, largely out of circulation in the nineties, needs to be read. I have maintained that Audre Lorde must be read in her proper context. I am veering close to arguing that Adrienne Rich must be taken *out* of context to be appreciated for her contribution to queer theory. This is true in that it was the debates of the eighties that led to some of Rich's key theoretical contributions being taken out of context, considered suspect, and then flogged like a dead horse. Read now, the nascent queerness in some of those ideas as well as the antiracist themes are evident. Critiques of Rich's "cultural feminism," which tend to focus on an interpretation of part of a sentence from "Compulsory Heterosexuality," make sense, for example, in the early eighties context of the "sex-radical" perspective, perhaps—and yet Rich never said that women in the past weren't having sex; far from it. (See, for example, Bulkin, "An Interview," 62). From the post-sex wars queer perspective, we can read Rich's lesbian resistance to "heteronormativity" (read "patriarchy") differently than it was read by its detractors in the early eighties—and perhaps more in the sense that it was intended. That is to say, from a queer perspective, or from the "queer" era, we should be able to read Rich from a standpoint less embroiled in the arguments of their day—but only if we refuse to accept the ossification of old answers to still pertinent questions. In this vein, Elizabeth Meese sees in Rich a deconstructive resistance to "the oppositions the phallogocentric analytical method uses to produce heterosexism, racial dominance, and class oppression masquerading as knowledge" (*(Ex)tensions*, 173), even traces of a characteristically postmodern "intellectual drift" (*(Ex)tensions*, 172). Marilyn Farwell makes specific claims for the "lesbian" on the continuum as "determined . . . by her positioning toward other women. . . . The lesbian image focuses attention on a revised female positionality" (*Heterosexual Plots*, 93). Farwell argues that the notion is "more complex than is usually acknowledged" (*Heterosexual Plots*, 90) and likens it in certain ways to the work of the poststructuralist film theorist Teresa de Lauretis (*Heterosexual Plots*, 121).

Missed Connections: Silence and Naming

Part and parcel of renouncing lesbian feminism in the person of Adrienne Rich is ignoring the connections between the political visions and identifications of middle-class/white lesbian feminists and working-class/lesbian feminists of color. Working-class/lesbian feminists of color tend to be rendered invisible unless it is time for enfranchised white academics to prove we are not racist, and middle-class/white lesbian feminists typically are ignored except to recite their sins. Thus, while Rich is castigated for her lesbian feminism, Lorde is—I am tempted to say—exonerated.

Both Lorde and Rich gained prominence as poets and as activists before coming out as lesbians, and before publishing openly lesbian volumes of poetry—*The Black Unicorn* and *The Dream of a Common Language*, respectively—in 1978. Rich describes meeting Lorde in the early 1970s in New

York, and their ensuing friendship, in an essay about the women's poetry movement of the era tellingly titled "A Communal Poetry":

> I knew that I had found a remarkable new poet and that she was also a colleague, someone I might actually talk with. Meeting one day on the South campus of CCNY [City College of New York], we began a conversation that was to go on for over twenty years, a conversation between two people of vastly different temperaments and cultural premises, a conversation often balked and jolted by those differences yet sustained by our common love for poetry and respect for each others' work. For most of those twenty-odd years . . . we exchanged drafts of poems, criticizing and encouraging back and forth, not always taking each others' advice but listening to it closely. (*What Is Found,* 169)

Lorde echoes Rich's narrative of their friendship, revealing in a lengthy 1979 interview with Rich that "in my journals I have a lot of pieces of conversations that I'm having with you in my head" (*Sister,* 103).

The two poets centrally pursue several of the same themes in their works—violence, power (which both use as the title of a poem), motherhood, community, heroic (and ordinary heroic) women, anger—and employ some of the same key images, such as New York City, nature, the solstice. The dialogue between their poetry is sometimes explicit. Rich literally dedicates the poem "Hunger" in *The Dream of a Common Language* to Lorde (12–14). The poem takes up the problem of world hunger, expanding the reach of Rich's feminist politics to problems "in Chad, in Niger, in the Upper Volta" (l. 29), that is, to the continent that is central to Lorde's poetic cosmology in *The Black Unicorn.* The poem meditates upon the centrality of women, particularly mothers, to feeding the world and upon the responsibility and privilege of North American feminists. In the third stanza Rich touches on many themes she and Lorde both explored in the late seventies:

I stand convicted by all my convictions—
you, too. We shrink from touching
our power, we shrink away, we starve ourselves
and each other, we're scared shitless
of what it could be to take and use our love,
hose it on a city, on a world,
to wield and guide its spray, destroying
poisons, parasites, rats, viruses—
like the terrible mothers we long and dread to be. (ll. 44–52)

Rich ends the poem with a call to activist coalition that exemplifies their activist poetics and their relationship, "Until we find each other, we are alone" (l. 76).

Lorde seems at times to have Rich in mind when responding generally to white feminists' reactions to learning about the realities of racism in the lives of women of color. Lorde explained to Rich in their 1979 interview, "I'll be having a conversation with you and I'll put it in my journal because stereotypically or symbolically these conversations occur in a space of Black woman/white woman where it's beyond Adrienne and Audre, almost as if we're two voices" (*Sister,* 103). Lorde's explanation is echoed in poems such as "The Same Death Over and Over," in which the speaker explains that the real problem is not just "the small deaths in the supermarket" that white middle-class women since Betty Friedan had been describing, but rather "the smoking ruins in a black neighborhood of Los Angeles / and the bloody morning streets of child-killing New York" (ll. 1, 7–8). Lorde's speaker is not denying her interlocutor's statement; she writes, " 'I'm trying to hear you' I said" (10), " 'I'm not fighting you' I said" (14). To the extent that this poetic exchange may be viewed as taking place in Lorde's symbolic "space of Black woman/white woman," it echoes Rich's description of their relationship: "We also debated, sometimes painfully, the politics we shared and the experiences we didn't share. The women's liberation movement was a different movement for each of us, but our common passion for its possibilities also held us in dialogue" (*What Is Found,* 169).

Lorde's and Rich's poems were published in many of the same feminist journals in the 1970s, including *Aphra, Ms., Chrysalis,* and *Amazon Quarterly,* for which Lorde served as the poetry editor. By 1973, they had performed at poetry readings together, and they began to know each other better when both were nominated for the National Book Award for that year (Wood, "Interview," 14). (Rich won the award but accepted in the name of co-nominees Lorde and Alice Walker; together, the three coauthored an acceptance speech refusing the notion of competition among other women writers.) As both their friendship and their importance to feminism developed, their names and works were increasingly associated with each other. Rich's *Poems: Selected and New* was advertised on the jacket of Lorde's 1976 collection *Coal,* and Rich's words of praise appear on the jackets of Lorde's *The Black Unicorn* and *Chosen Poems.* By 1976, Lorde was being published by the large New York publishing house W. W. Norton, Rich's publisher since 1966.[9] In the 1980s and 1990s, scholars and other commentators often discussed Lorde's and Rich's work together as vital to the lesbian and gay movement (e.g., Col-

lecott,"What Is Not Said," 244–45; Kushner, "Last Word") or when analyz-
ing similar themes in their poetry and prose (e.g., Annas, "Poetry"; Bowen,
"Completing," 227; Braxton, "Introduction"; Carruthers, "Re-Vision";
Yorke, "Constructing").

Just as both appeared on the now famous 1978 MLA panel, "The Transformation of Silence Into Language and Action," Rich like Lorde explores
the significance of silences in her poems and essays. Speaking to an interviewer in 1980 about the importance of breaking insidious silences, Lorde
refers to Rich, "As Adrienne has said, what remains nameless eventually
becomes unspeakable, what remains unspoken becomes unspeakable"
(Hammond, "An Interview," 18). Rich's first prose collection, significantly
titled *On Lies, Secrets, and Silence,* includes three essays that take silence as a
central theme: "Disloyal to Civilization," from the 1978 panel, "It Is the Lesbian in Us . . . ," the essay to which Lorde was referring, and "Women and
Honor: Some Notes on Lying" (1975), in which she equates silence with dis-
honesty and dishonor, observing that "Lying is done with words, and also
with silence" (186). Rich describes the lie of silence that is the closet in the
afterword to "It Is the Lesbian in Us . . .": "The word *lesbian* must be
affirmed because to discard it is to collaborate with silence and lying about
our very existence; with the closet-game, the creation of the *unspeakable*"
(*On Lies,* 202). In "Women and Honor" Rich combines the themes of
silence, the closet, and compulsory heterosexuality: "Heterosexuality as an
institution has also drowned in silence the erotic feelings between women. I
myself lived half a lifetime in the lie of that denial. That silence makes us all,
to some degree, into liars" (190).[10]

The Dream of a Common Language takes silence and its antidote, voice, as
a central theme, from the focus on denial in the first poem, "Power" (3), to
the lamentation of the things "No one ever told us" (l. 43) in "Transcendental Etude," the last one (72–77). Like Lorde, Rich aims to transform silence
into language and action through poetry, recognizing that the journey can be
arduous. "No one who survives to speak / new language" avoids this, she
writes in "Transcendental Etude" (ll. 105–6), but the rewards are great: self-
knowledge, mutuality in love and desire—in short, "a whole new poetry" (l.
148). Though this phrase has been criticized as a naive statement of language
reflecting something called reality, it can be understood as part of a positional
identity poetics, as I have been arguing throughout. (See, for example, sections 7 and 8 of Rich's poem "Cartographies of Silence" [*Dream,* 16–20] for
one of many places where Rich acknowledges the limitations of language.)
Other poems explore multiple forms that silence takes ("Cartographies of

Silence"), unspoken elements of actual women's relationships ("Paula Becker to Clara Westhoff," *Dream*, 42–44, "A Woman Dead in Her Forties," (*Dream*, 53–58), secrets ("Sibling Mysteries," *Dream*, 47–52), censorship (*Twenty-One Love Poems*,5, *Dream*, 27), and lies ("Cartographies of Silence").

Rich is equally occupied in *The Dream of a Common Language* with giving name to the unspoken, the taboo, "the unnameable," and it is in this sense that the book as a whole dreams of a common language, giving voice to variously silenced and unnamed experiences of and among women. Of course, this is also problematic. Rich cannot do it alone—nor does she mean to, but as the emblematic lesbian-feminist (or often, in the mainstream, token lesbian) poet, she is assumed to be trying to. As Catherine Stimpson points out, Rich

> resists being laid down as the star track in what ought to be a multiple-trek [*sic*] tape of the language of such women as Judy Grahn, Susan Griffin, Marilyn Hacker, Audre Lorde, Susan Sherman. "To isolate what I write," she has warned, "from a context of other women writing and speaking feels like an old, painfully familiar critical strategy." (141)

The Dream of a Common Language literally puts words in the mouths of some women, such as the mountaineer Elvira Shateyev in "Phantasia for Elvira Shateyev" (*Dream*, 4–6) and the painter Paula Becker, close friend to the wife of the poet Rainer Maria Rilke, in "Paula Becker to Clara Westhoff." Other poems, such as "Sibling Mysteries," "To a Woman Dead in Her Forties," and a number of the *Twenty-One Love Poems*, speak the poet-narrator's perspective on what has gone unsaid in relationships of her own. Several speak to women's lives and relationships more generally (and, some might argue, in a problematically essentialist way): "the raging stoic grandmothers" in section 13 of "Natural Resources" (*Dream*, 60–67), the mother who is "the woman . . . / . . . making for the open" of "Mother-Right" (ll. 15–16, *Dream*, 59), the "woman" and the "we" running throughout "Transcendental Etude," "the daughters and the mothers / in the kingdom of the sons" in section 3 of "Sibling Mysteries."

Rich's preoccupation with "lies, secrets, and silence" makes her, with Lorde, a forerunner of the queer theorist Eve Sedgwick, whose *Epistemology of the Closet* is an extended meditation on the construction of Western culture through the silences of dominant discourses, especially with respect to the canon of Great Literature. Both Rich and Sedgwick concentrate on silences as presences, weapons, secrets, and lies, not neutral absences. Both discuss the politics of silence, or, in Sedgwick's term, "ignorance," which intimately relates to specific knowledges. Sedgwick argues that the knowledge/ignorance dyad in Western culture is always about sexuality, traceable to Eve's eating the fruit from the tree of knowledge in Eden. By the late nineteenth century homosexuality, "the Love that dare not speak its name," became the "one particular sexuality that was distinctively constituted *as* secrecy" (*Epistemology*, 74, 73). The enforced silence of the closet is, in Sedgwick's terms, "itself a performance," like coming out, a series of "speech acts" (*Epistemology*, 3). In "Transcendental Etude," a poem about shedding the lies and breaking the silences of conventionality, Rich writes, "The longer I live the more I mistrust / theatricality, the false glamour cast by performance" (ll. 82–84). Ignorance, for Sedgwick as for Rich, is presence, not absence: "unknowing *as* unknowing, not as a vacuum or as the blank it can pretend to be but as a weighty and occupied and consequential epistemological space" (Sedgwick, *Epistemology*, 77), "silence and lying about our very existence; with the closet-game, the creation of the *unspeakable*" (Rich, *On Lies*, 202).

Sedgwick's and Rich's remedies for this state of affairs differ significantly, however. In her activist passion for justice, Rich makes clear that at times she is seeking to name truths, a goal antithetical to the insights of poststructuralist, Sedgwickian queer theory. Rich's "Transcendental Etude," certainly, seeks to strip away the silences enshrouding the primacy of women to each other ("nothing that was said / is true for us" [ll. 68–69]), to uncover "the truths we are salvaging from / the splitting-open of our lives" (ll. 85–86). The words *true* or *truth* appear in five of the major poems in *The Dream of a Common Language:* "Origins and History of Consciousness," "Cartographies of Silence," "Sibling Mysteries," "A Woman Dead in Her Forties," and "Transcendental Etude." Many others seek to reveal "the truth" of a situation, such as "Power," "Hunger," "The Lioness," several of the *Twenty-One Love Poems,* and "Natural Resources."[11] Rich succeeds, if not at finding absolute truth, in naming women's oppression and lesbian existence so that they may not be erased by silence.

Sedgwick states an equally activist, if more narrowly academic, goal of pursuing "anti-homophobic inquiry" (*Epistemology*, 14), though her method is more deconstructive than expositional. She refuses deconstruction as an end in itself, however, observing that "a deconstructive understanding of these binarisms makes it possible to identify them as sites that are *peculiarly* densely charged with lasting potentials for powerful manipulation—through precisely the mechanisms of self-contradictory definition or, more succinctly, the double bind" (*Epistemology*, 10). A deconstruction does not of itself disable a binarism, it merely exposes the interdependence of the two terms. Sedgwick states her fervent desire that all types of antihomophobic activism and inquiry proceed. She, if not the majority of her readers, acknowledges that, despite her own queer position, "the space of permission for this work and the depth of the intellectual landscape in which it might have a contribution to make owe everything to the wealth of essentialist, minoritizing, and separatist gay thought and struggle also in progress" (*Epistemology*, 13). These are hardly glowing terms for other types of "antihomophobic" inquiry and activism in the current queer-theoretical-friendly climate, but it is a nod in the direction of attribution (and coalition?) nonetheless. Nothing, alas, is said directly of the activism of the recent past in the passage, but the homage seems clearly implied. Indeed it should be, in light, for example, of Meese's deconstructive reading of "the lesbian continuum" as a

> move "beyond" the conventional binary oppositions, rather than simply negating them. Rich (re)figures lesbianism and heterosexuality along the continuum's subversive relational structure which connects women in their difference, asks each woman to identify the differences within herself, and relates one to another. (*(Ex)tensions*, 171)

Not unlike Meese, Sedgwick reads the lesbian continuum as "tend[ing] toward *universalizing* (i.e., more or less constructivist [*Epistemology*, 40]) understandings of homo/heterosexual potential," though based on a gender separatism that forecloses "an alliance or identity between lesbians and gay men" based on "gay-*separatism*, minoritizing models of specifically gay identity and politics" (*Epistemology*, 89).

The difference between Sedgwick's and Rich's approaches is fraught with one of the central issues of the putative lesbian feminism/queer theory divide, the centering of study and theory on gender *or* on sexuality. Sedgwick calls *Epistemology of the Closet* feminist "in the sense that its analyses were produced by someone whose thought has been macro- and microscopically infused with feminism over a long period," but she chooses to place "the book's first focus . . . on sexuality rather than (sometimes, even, as opposed to) gender" (*Epistemology*, 15). Sedgwick's impulse to preserve "understandings of sexuality that will respect a certain irreducibility in it to the terms and relations of gender" (*Epistemology*, 16) is a vital goal for LGBT studies (and certainly for queer theory), clearly. But Sedgwick would seem to commit the error elucidated by Elizabeth Spelman in *Inessential Woman* when she insists that an antihomophobic study is somehow more so by being untainted by the complications, as it were, introduced by questions of lesbians and sexism and/or people of color and racism. (The authors under study in *Epistemology of the Closet*—Melville, Wilde, Nietzsche, James, Proust—bear out this reading, a problem also of Sedgwick's earlier book *Between Men* and her edited volume *Novel Gazing*.) How, then, to make sense of Sedgwick's introductory "*Axiom* 3: There can't be an a priori decision about how far it will make sense to conceptualize lesbian and gay male identities together. Or separately" (36)? Sedgwick's choice of texts indicates the "decision" she *has* made, as a passage from "Compulsory Heterosexuality" makes clear Rich's: "The term gay may serve the purpose of blurring the very outlines we need to discern, which are of crucial value for feminism and for the freedom of women as a group" (*Blood, Bread*, 53). It is not that Sedgwick studies sexuality qua sexuality while Rich focuses on gender; they part ways along gendered lines. Sedgwick trains her lens, specifically, on gay men.

Oddly, under the rubric of "*Axiom* 2: The study of sexuality is not coextensive with the study of gender . . ." (27), Sedgwick makes a practically lesbian-feminist argument when she asserts that sexuality, fluid over one's lifetime, is an "apter deconstructive object" than gender (34). In the sense that lesbian feminism is a self-consciously constructivist politics, its proponents make the same argument in different terms. Sedgwick's statement, too, is worse the wear of the years that have passed since it was published, during which the growth of the transgender movement—ironically, part of the queer movement itself—has called into question Sedgwick's supporting idea that "virtually all people are publicly and unalterably assigned to one or the other gender, and from birth" (34).

Dissimilarities between Sedgwick and lesbian feminists such as Rich and Lorde are clear, but points of connection are obvious enough to suggest the productiveness of an ongoing conversation. Sedgwick expresses a desire that *all* types of antihomophobic activism proceed "without any high premium placed on ideological rationalization between them" (*Epistemology*, 13), implying, at least, that the contradictions are insurmountable on an intellectual basis. What would come of an actual coalitional movement, if we can imagine it, in which Lorde and Rich and Sedgwick shared the podium as keynote speakers at a convention? A platform at a rally on the Washington Mall? A holding cell as detainees after a massive civil disobedience action? What if, in the sort of provocative, brilliant essays and speeches they are wont to produce, Sedgwick quoted Judy Grahn and Audre Lorde, Rich quoted Pat Parker and Judith Butler, and both Sedgwick and Rich cited each other?

Chapter Six

"Caught in the Crossfire Between Camps": Gloria Anzaldúa

As the lesbian writer whose name is most likely to turn up in texts by both Rich and Butler, Gloria Anzaldúa with her concept of "*mestiza* consciousness" is one answer to these rhetorical riddles. Of all the poets under study in *Identity Poetics,* Anzaldúa is the one most frequently and approvingly invoked by queer and other poststructuralist theorists. Yet, Anzaldúa traverses the boundary between queer theory and lesbian feminism (poststructuralist theory and identity politics) as surely as she straddles boundaries of race, nation, language, genre, and gender—a process of *mestizaje* whose articulation is the objective of her germinal 1987 book, *Borderlands/La Frontera: The New Mestiza.*

In one of the many poems liberally interspersed throughout the otherwise prose-dominated first half of the book, Anzaldúa figures the crossroads she inhabits as a place of struggle:

Una lucha de fronteras / A Struggle of Borders[1]

Because I, a *mestiza,*
continually walk out of one culture
and into another,
because I am in all cultures at the same time,
alma entre dos mundos, tres, cuatro,
me zumba la cabeza con lo contradictorio.
Estoy norteada por todas las voces que me hablan
simultáneamente.
[soul in between two worlds, three, four,
my head rings with the contradictory.
I am disoriented by all the voices that speak to me
simultaneously.] (99)[2]

Given the argumentative rhetoric of the lesbian-feminist/queer theory "debate" and Anzaldúa's position straddling the divide, the connotation of *lucha* as "battle" and the cognate *frontera* as the "front" may seem apt, if exaggerated. But Anzaldúa rejects the battle for supremacy of one over the other; instead, she expresses the state of being both/and/neither, the border existence of the new mestiza, a culturally specific, complex, and self-conscious articulation of identity poetics. In an oft-quoted passage from *Borderlands/La Frontera,* Anzaldúa reworks Virginia Woolf's famous proclamation, declaring the mestiza a transgressor of boundaries and a creator of a new culture based on elements of the old ones, on components of her identity, and on interpersonal relationships both actual and potential:

> As a *mestiza* I have no country, my homeland cast me out; yet all countries are mine because I am every woman's sister or potential lover. (As a lesbian I have no race, my own people disclaim me; but I am all races because there is the queer of me in all races.) I am cultureless because, as a feminist, I challenge the collective cultural/religious male-derived beliefs of Indo-Hispanics and Anglos; yet I am cultured because I am participating in the creation of yet another culture, a new story to explain the world and our participation in it, a new value system with images and symbols that connect us to each other and to the planet. (102–3)

Anzaldúa seeks not to transcend differences but to inhabit them in all their messy multiplicity. "*Soy un amasamiento,*" she writes, "I am an act of kneading, of uniting and joining" (103). She "kneads" her personal experiences, reclaimed cultural symbols, history of oppression, and political resistance into a text at once analytic and mystical, literary and visionary. Throughout, in the mixed-genre style of the book's first half and the poetry of its second half, she presses the point that hers is a multifaceted existence and politics that cannot be separated into component parts with claims to priority or unique allegiance.

To the extent that a distinct body of Latina lesbian literature can be periodized,[3] its critical mass emerged later than the initial lesbian-feminist literary explosion of the 1970s, the black lesbian-feminist outpouring of the late 1970s and early 1980s (represented in the anthology *Home Girls*), and the multiracial "women of color" boom of the early 1980s (highlighted by the publication of *This Bridge Called My Back* in 1981). Notably marked by the publication of texts such as Anzaldúa's *Borderlands/La Frontera,* the anthology *Compañeras: Latina Lesbians* in 1987, and the anthology *Chicana Lesbians* in

1991, it came—is still coming—at a theoretically post–identity politics moment. The paradox is obvious, and it is apparent in much Latina lesbian writing, which incorporates both a positional identity politics and the multiplicity more commonly associated with postmodernism. As articulated by Chicana feminist critic Norma Alarcón, who herself employs the tools of poststructuralist theory, this complex standpoint is "too readily viewed as representing 'postmodern fragmented identities'":

> The so-called postmodern decentered subject—a decentralization which implies diverse, multiply constructed subjects and historical conjunctures—insofar as she desires liberation must move towards provisional solidarities, especially through social movements. In this fashion, one may recognize the endless production of differences to destabilize group or collective identities, on the one hand, and the need for group solidarities to overcome oppression through an understanding of the mechanisms at work, on the other. ("Chicana Feminism," 376)

In other words, a sense of identity and group solidarity are necessary in the face of racism, sexism, and homophobia, despite the widely accepted poststructuralist analysis of unitary identity as illusory. Phelan explains the "revolutionary force" of Anzaldúa's mestiza; hers is

> the ability to refuse the reifications of cultural nationalism without abandoning the nation entirely, and to provide links to class-based movements without becoming subsumed within them. Because she never simply "is" any one element of her blended being, the mestiza cannot be captured in the oppositions that are presented as inevitable; class *or* nation, sex *or* race, or any other reified opposition. (*Getting Specific*, 74–75)

While "race," for example, may be understood as a bankrupt historical and social construction, racism is all too materially prevalent. Hence, Latina lesbian feminism, including Anzaldúa's new mestiza politics, embraces at least a "strategic essentialism" in culturally specific manifestations. Chela Sandoval explains that "assimilationist, integrationist, revolutionary, supremacist, [and] separatist" tactics may be used in the service of "U.S. Third World Feminism," which should be understood as "a theory and method of oppositional consciousness." Anzaldúa's mestiza consciousness is a leading *teoría,*[4] as Sandoval makes obvious in an encyclopedia entry defining "U.S. Third World Feminism" that she titles "Mestizaje as Method" (361).[5]

Borderlands/La Frontera epitomizes Chicana lesbian identity poetics. Anzaldúa's invocation of indigenous symbols, precolonial history, and evolutionary biologisms (especially in chapter 7, "*La conciencia de la mestiza:* Towards a New Consciousness") would mark her work as irretrievably essentialist if these and other textual elements were not constantly subverted to a constructionist purpose. As Judith Raiskin explains, "Anzaldúa envisions a collapse of the systems of categorization through the 'mestiza' and 'queer' consciousness created by them" ("Inverts," 159). She can get away with a passage like this one—"The mestizo and the queer exist at this time and point on the evolutionary continuum for a purpose. We are a blending that proves that all blood is intricately woven together, and that we are spawned out of similar souls" (107)—because of its juxtaposition with this one, and others like it:

> [The mestiza] puts history through a sieve. . . . This step is a conscious rupture with all oppressive traditions of all cultures and religions. She communicates that rupture, documents the struggle. She reinterprets history and, using new symbols, she shapes new myths. . . . Deconstruct, construct. (104)

Anzaldúa uses the categories and the crossroads created by their intersections to create mestiza consciousness. She may use the language of essentialism, but she uses it differently, metaphorically, in a manner that serves radically subversive ends (Raiskin, "Inverts," 159, 161). The development of a mestiza consciousness, which Anzaldúa describes as an ongoing dynamic process, uses cultural and other identitarian tools but does not reify group identity status.

Borderlands/La Frontera *in the Context of* El Movimiento

In the service of their creative political project, Chicana lesbian feminists like Anzaldúa build upon and react to other identity politics movements, each with their own mix of "tactical essentialism" and overt constructionism. *El Movimiento,* the Chicano power movement that began in the 1960s, serves prominently both as model and foil. Just as women of color were active in lesbian feminism from the beginning, Chicanas (including Chicana lesbians) always participated in El Movimiento though much of their early contribution remains unrecognized. The surge of Chicana feminism in the 1980s, responding to both the sexism of El Movimiento and the racism of the women's and lesbian-feminist movements, "has given new life to a stalled Chicano movement" (Alarcón, "Chicana," 372). Like the cultural-nationalist Chicano movement, Chicana feminist writing often relies on precolonial (and to some extent postcolonial) Mexican and indigenous imagery. For El Movimiento the *Virgen de Guadalupe* proved a powerful symbol. *La Virgen,* a manifestation of the Catholic Virgin Mary, is said to have appeared in 1531 and, speaking the Aztec language Nahua, told a poor *indio* that she would be the protector of his people. Anzaldúa explains that *"la Virgen de Guadalupe* is the single most potent religious, political and cultural image of the Chicano/*mexicano.* She, like my race, is a synthesis of the old world and the new, of the religion and culture of the two races in our psyche, the conquerors and the conquered" (52). Anzaldúa identifies more closely with a predecessor of la Virgen, the azteca-mexica Coatlicue, symbolic of a more vigorous precolonial female agency. According to Anzaldúa, Coatlicue is the earliest "Mesoamerican fertility and Earth goddesses," from whom is descended Coatlalopeuh (the name la Virgen called herself when she appeared in the sixteenth century, homophonous to the Spanish Guadalupe). The "creator goddess," Coatlicue "had a human skull or serpent for a head, a necklace of human hearts, a skirt of twisted serpents and taloned feet" (49), images that show up repeatedly in Anzaldúa's writings.

Like Lorde's invocation of Seboulisa, Anzaldúa employs the image of Coatlicue to express creative power in a female figure specific to her culture of origin. Invoked by Anzaldúa as Sappho is invoked by Grahn, Coatlicue is vital to Anzaldúa's writing process and to her continual creation of mestiza consciousness. In chapter 4 of *Borderlands/La Frontera,* titled "The Coatlicue State," Anzaldúa describes at length the wrenching process of literary and self-creation.[6] The poems "Letting Go" (186–88), "Poets have strange eating habits" (162–63), and "Creature of Darkness" (208–9) similarly convey Anzaldúa's difficult and spiritual creative journeys. "Letting Go" most closely parallels her description of "The Coatlicue State" as it describes the nearly grotesque compulsion to undergo painful transformations.

> You must plunge your fingers
> into your navel, with your two hands
> split open,
> spill out the lizards and horned toads
> the orchids and the sunflowers,
> turn the maze inside out.
> Shake it. (ll. 3–9)
>
> It's not enough
> letting go twice, three times,

a hundred. Soon everything is
dull, unsatisfactory.
Night's open face
interests you no longer.
And soon, again, you return
to your element and
like a fish to the air
you come to the open
only between breathings.
But already gills
grow on your breasts. (ll. 62–74)

Like "Letting Go," the other two poems employ animal imagery associated with the Coatlicue state. In "Poets have strange eating habits," the narrator rides a "balking mare" (l. 3) into the earth's "*abismo*" (l. 24), or "abyss," repeatedly, like "an addiction" (l. 57), taking on attributes of birds and snakes. "Creature of Darkness" depicts the immobilization of the Coatlicue state that precedes the transformed emergence into creative action. While hiding in the darkness wanting "not to think" (l. 10), the narrator relates to the salamander, the mole, the bat, and, once again, the snake that is so closely identified with Coatlicue, Lady of the Serpent Skirt.

Other poems employ precolonial as well as traditional Chicano/mexicano images. Snakes appear again in "*La curandera*" ("The Healer," 198–201), for example. Chicanas' ancient lineage is lauded in "*No se raje, Chicanita*/Don't Give In, *Chicanita*" (222–25).

. . . they will never take that pride
of being *mexicana*-Chicana-*tejana*
nor our Indian woman's spirit.
And when the Gringos are gone—
see how they kill one another—
here we'll still be like the horned toad and the lizard
relics of an earlier age
survivors of the First Fire Age—*el Quinto Sol.* (ll. 23–30)

La Llorona, one of the three dominant female archetypes of Chicano/a culture, the ghostly mother who wails in the night for her lost children, is the subject of "My Black *Angelos*" (206–7). Anzaldúa explains that "*la Guadalupe,* the virgin mother who has not abandoned us, *la Chingada* (*Malinche*), the raped mother whom we have abandoned, and *la Llorona*" have all been used against Chicanas—*la Llorona* "to make us long-suffering people" (52–53). But in "My Black *Angelos*," while the narrator initially fears *la Llorona,* the wailing woman is depicted as powerful and ultimately is incorporated into the narrator herself. Her "Taloned hand" reminiscent of Coatlicue,

> She crawls into my spine
> her eyes opening and closing,
> shining under my skin in the dark
> whirling my bones twirling
> till they're hollow reeds.
>
> *aiiiiii aiiiiiaaaaaaaa*
> *Una mujer vaga en la noche*
> [A woman wanders in the night]
> *anda errante con las almas de los muertos.*
> [travels errantly with the souls of the dead.]
> We sweep through the streets
> *con el viento corremos*
> [with the wind we run]
> we roam with the souls of the dead. (ll. 27–37)

La Llorona here is depicted as a dark angel, not a demon or witch, by an author for whom darkness is one aspect of her self-concept. Anzaldúa describes Coatlicue, her totem deity, as one of the "darkened" aspects of the goddess Tonantsi-Coatlalopeuh and ultimately Guadalupe. She also identifies *La Llorona* in the poem as somewhat disrespectable, a wandering or errant woman who is thus free.

The poems of the first two sections of the second half of the book reside primarily in El Valle, Anzaldúa's South Texas border homeland. Like the first half of the book, the poetry half begins with stories and histories of la Raza. The first poetry section, "*Más antes en los ranchos*" ("Before, on the ranches"), consists of five narrative poems, vignettes centered on a presumably auto-biographical narrator, her grandmother, a woman washing and hanging out sheets, unnamed mexicanos, the animals they live among (birds, a fawn, a horse, chickens)—and frequently the white men who endanger them all. The second poetry section, "*La Pérdida*" ("The Loss"), contains seven poems focused more specifically on oppression and the desire to escape it. Subjects include the conditions of Chicanas working in the fields, sexually harassed and raped by white bosses ("*sus plumas el viento*" ["the wind her feathers"], 138–41), the sterility of the literally trashed land left to the poor Chicanos/as ("Cultures," 142), the perils and desires of "illegal" Mexican border crosses, known as *mojados*, or "wetbacks" ("*sobre piedras con lagartijos*" ["on rocks with lizards"], 143–45), a small victory for illegal farm workers exploited by "*el sonavabitche*" (146–51). These are homages to the hardworking mexicanos/as cheated or abused by the likes of the violent, swindling white male narrator of "We Call Them Greasers" (156–57). They are dedicated to the poet's mother, to *mojaditos*, to "those who have worked in the fields" ("*Mar de repollos*/A Sea of Cabbages," 152–55).

Both of the first two poetry sections carry Mexican song lyrics as epigraphs, suggesting a cultural context for reading and understanding the poems that places them squarely in a Chicano/a tradition, even as the text wrings changes on that same tradition. "*Más antes en los ranchos*" carries a lyric from a Mexican song titled "*La Llorona*" that suggests deep sorrow is sometimes borne silently:

> *Dicen que no tengo duelo, Llorona,*
> *porque no me ven llorar.*
> *Hay muertos que no hacen ruido, Llorona . . ."*
> [They say that I have no grief, Llorona,
> because they do not see me cry.
> There are the dead who make no noise, Llorona . . .] (123)

Anzaldúa's verses weep aloud for the dead who do not or cannot speak for themselves, at least not in a monolingual, racist, sexist dominant culture— the long suffering grandmother of "Immaculate, Inviolate: *Como Ella*" ("Like Her," 130–33),[7] the animals who are hunted for sport ("White-Wing Season," 124–25), murdered out of necessity ("Cervicide," 126–27), and maimed ("horse," 128–29), and the people who suffer their losses in forced silence. The title page of "*La Pérdida*" carries a verse that speaks of nostalgic longing for the homeland, from the *corrido* "*Canción Misteca*" ("Mixteca Song," 137). As important as the sentiment is the fact that the song is a corrido. These "songs of love and death on the Texas Mexican borderlands," which Anzaldúa grew up hearing, are "usually about Mexican heroes who do valiant deeds against the Anglo oppressors" (83). Corridos, marked by "a strong narrative or dramatic line . . . strongly influenced the course of Chicano poetic expression" during El Movimiento (Pérez-Torres, *Movements*, 6). Both influences show up in Anzaldúa's narrative poems valorizing the lives and struggles of everyday heroes who prevailed or survived (the labor organizer and farm workers in *"El sonavabitche,"* "She" in *"sus plumas el viento"*), and those who did not (the mojado narrator of *"sobre piedras con lagartijos,"* the "troublemakers" in "We Call Them Greasers").

In keeping with the Spanish-language corrido tradition and the Chicano movement's assertion of Spanish as a valid language, most of Anzaldúa's poems include at least some Spanish words or phrases. Anzaldúa's willingness to serve as "bridge" or translator to Anglos and other non-Spanish speakers is well documented (e.g., Anzaldúa, "Bridge, Drawbridge," *Borderlands/La Frontera*, 107), but she insists on her right to speak and write her many languages as well—including Nahua, six forms of Spanish, two of English, and infinite combinations (*Borderlands/La Frontera*, 77–78). "Ethnic identity is twin skin to linguistic identity—I am my voice," Anzaldúa writes (81). Aware like Lorde of "the Tradition of Silence," Anzaldúa explains how sexism silences girls and women in Chicano culture (76) and how "Linguistic Terrorism" silences Chicanos/as in the dominant culture (75–81). "I will have my voice," she asserts in response to both (59). In the poems of the book's second half, Anzaldúa's voice takes on a variety of linguistic forms. Only five of the thirty-eight poems are written entirely in English. Twenty-six include scattered words, phrases, or lines in some form of Spanish, with English glossaries appended to only about a quarter of them. While some reviewers disliked the inconsistent translation, Anzaldúa explained in an interview that what seemed "haphazard" to one reviewer (Kaye/Kantrowitz, "Crossover Dreams," 238) mirrors "the kind of border dialect that I grew up with." Further, she purposely set out to challenge "the myth of a monocultural U.S. . . . I wanted to force that awareness that this country is not what those in power say it is" (Perry, "Interview," 22).

A dozen of *Borderlands/La Frontera*'s poems are written entirely in Spanish, but only two are translated into English, *"Mar de repollos/A Sea of Cabbages,"* which honors the hard work, faith, and desperate hope of poor farmers, and *"No se raje, chicanita/*Don't Give In, *Chicanita,"* an inspirational poem dedicated to Anzaldúa's niece that ends the book, assuring her,

> *Sí, se me hace que en unos cuantos años o siglos*
> *la Raza se levantará, lengua intacta*
> *cargando lo mejor de todas las culturas.*
> *Esa víbora dormida, la rebeldía, saltará.*
> *Como cuero viejo caerá la esclavitud*
> *de obedecer, de callar, de aceptar.*

Como víbora relampagueando nos moveremos, mujercita.
¡Ya verás! (ll. 36–43)

Yes, in a few years or centuries
la Raza will rise up, tongue intact
carrying the best of all the cultures.
That sleeping serpent,
rebellion-(r)evolution, will spring up.
Like old skin will fall the slave ways of
obedience, acceptance, silence.
Like serpent lightning we'll move, little woman.
You'll see. (ll. 37–45)

Anzaldúa's Spanish tongue is intact in the ten untranslated poems, which either require work for the nonfluent Spanish speaker (and even for the Spanish speaker unfamiliar with Anzaldúa's blend of dialects) or lock out the non-Spanish speaker altogether, teaching an object lesson in monolingualism. Anzaldúa's choices to use Spanish and not to translate are not arbitrary, however. The untranslated poems take up some of her most intimate themes. In "*Compañera, cuando amábamos*" ("*Compañera,* when we were loving," 168–69), dedicated to Juanita Ramos "and other spik dykes," Anzaldúa recalls intense emotional intimacy and sensual pleasure:

¿Volverán, compañera, esas tardes sordas
Cuando nos amábamos tiradas en las sombras bajo otoño?
Mis ojos clavados en tu mirada
Tu mirada que siempre retiraba al mundo
Esas tardes cuando nos acostábamos en las nubes (ll. 1–5)
[Will they return, *compañera*, those deaf afternoons
When we loved each other in the shadows of autumn?
My eyes fixed on your gaze
Your gaze that always swept away the world
Those afternoons when we lay in the clouds]

¿Te acuerdas cuando te decía ¡tócame!?
¿Cuando ilesa carne buscaba carne y dientes labios
En los laberintos de tus bocas?
Esas tardes, islas no descubiertas
Cuando caminábamos hasta la orilla.
Mis dedos lentos andaban las lomas de tus pechos,

Recorriendo la llanura de tu espalda
Tus moras hinchándose en mi boca . . . (ll. 17–24)
[Do you remember when I said, take me!?
When untouched flesh searched for flesh and teeth lips
In the labyrinths of your mouths?
Those afternoons, undiscovered islands
When we walked to the edge.
My slow fingers traveled the hills of your breasts,
Wandering the plains of your back
Your dark blackberries swelling in my mouth . . .][8]

In *"En el nombre de todas las madres que han perdido sus hijos en la guerra"* ("In the Name of All Mothers Who Have Lost Sons in the War," 182–85), Anzaldúa plumbs the depths of a mother's pain for her children lost to a nationalist, racist border "war":

Le cubro su cabecita,
mi criatura con sus piesecitos fríos.
Aquí lo tendré acurrucado en mis brazos
hasta que me muera. (ll. 1–4)
[I cover its little head,
my baby with its cold, tiny feet.
Here I will curl it up in my arms
until I die.]

Madre dios, quiero matar
a todo hombre que hace guerra,
que quebra, que acaba con la vida.
Esta guerra me ha quitado todo.
¿Qué han hecho con nuestra tierra?
¿Pa' qué hacemos niños?
¿Pa' qué les damos vida?
¿Para qué sean masacrados?
¿Para qué los güeros
se burlen de la gente?
En sus ojos nosotros los indios
somos peores que los animales. (ll. 115–26)
[Mother of God, I want to kill
every man that makes war,
that smashes, that puts an end to life.

This war has taken everything from me.
What have they done with our land?
Why do we make children?
Why do we give them life?
So that they can be massacred?
So that the *güeros*[9]
can ridicule the people?
In their eyes we the *indios*
are worse than the animals.]

Anzaldúa reports in an interview that "the more spiritual stuff" is difficult for her to translate, so poems like *"Cagado abismo, quiero saber"* (lit., "Shit-scared Abyss, I want to know"), *"mujer cacto"* ("cactus woman"), and *"Sobre piedras con lagartijos"* go untranslated (Perry, "Interview," 23–24). These poems may make many readers feel like Anzaldúa did as a Spanish-speaking child in an English-speaking educational system, when she was "supposed to pick up a little bit of English in Beginners I and II" (Perry, "Interview," 23)—a frustrating endeavor that requires rereading, hard work, and may cause a reader to throw up her hands in defeat.

Near the end of *Borderlands/La Frontera*, Anzaldúa includes a stirring, militant anthem, all in Spanish but five lines. Titled *"Arriba mi gente"* ("Arise My People," 214–15, it is a call to mobilize the legions of *"hijas de la Chingada"* ("daughters of the Fucked One"). *La Chingada* (a derogatory name for Malinche/Malintzín) is a common Mexican curse word; she is the legendary traitor who supposedly sold out the Mexican people to the Spaniards by sleeping with Cortés and literally giving birth to the mestizo "race." Anzaldúa offers an alternative explanation of the fall of the Aztecs in chapter 3, "Entering the Serpent." She explains that the conquered tribes hated their Aztec rulers long before the Spaniards arrived because the Aztecs changed "the egalitarian traditions of a wandering tribe to those of a predatory state." The "class split" caused by the Aztec practices of conquer, rape, and taxation made the oppressed Tlaxcalans "bitter enemies" of the Aztecs. As a result, they aided the Spanish; "the Aztec nation fell not because *Malinali (la Chingada)* interpreted for and slept with Cortés, but because the ruling elite had subverted the solidarity between men and women and between noble and commoner" (56).[10] Anzaldúa concludes, "Not me sold out my people but they me" (43–44); not women nor queers sell out la Raza, but through the image of la Chingada (the Fucked One, the traitor, the bad mother), her people harm her.[11]

In the poem Anzaldúa calls for *las Hijas de la Chingada* to reclaim their names,

> *Hijas de la Chingada,*
> born of the violated *india,*
> *guerrilleras divinas—*
> *mujeres de fuego ardiente*
> *que dan luz a la noche oscura* (ll. 24–28)
> [Daughters of *la Chingada,*
> born of the violated *india,*
> divine guerillas—
> women of ardent fire
> that give light to the dark night]

In a refrain she calls on *las Hijas de la Chingada* to wage a liberation struggle:

> *Retornará nuestra antigua fe*
> *y levantará el campo.*
> *Arriba, despierten, mi gente*
> *a liberar los pueblos.* (ll. 36–39)
> [Our ancient faith will return
> and will cause the countryside to rise up.
> Arise, awaken, my people
> to liberate the towns.[12]]

The goal of Anzaldúa's call to arms is the search for *el Mundo Zurdo,* "the Left-handed World," where people who "do not fit" in dominant society come together in a "Balancing Act" to "change the world" ("*La Prieta,*" 208–9): *Toda la gente junta / en busca del Mundo Zurdo* (All the people together / in search of *el Mundo Zurdo,* ll. 1–7).

The "*gente*" that "*arriba*" here are not exactly the same as the *gente que arriba* in any analogous Movimiento anthem. As Pérez-Torres notes, Anzaldúa's book is instrumental in "the transformation of 'Aztlán' from homeland to borderland signif[ying] an opening with Chicano cultural discourse. It marks a significant transformation away from the dream of origin toward an engagement with the construction of cultural identity" (96). As the title of *Borderlands/La Frontera*'s first chapter, "The Homeland Aztlán/ *El Otro México*" ("The Other Mexico") serves as Anzaldúa's starting point. The text immediately makes clear, in prose and poetry, that she has wrought changes on the Chicano/a identity politics theme.

Otros "Movimientos de Rebeldía": *Feminism, Lesbian Feminism, and* Borderlands/La Frontera

Other *"Movimientos de rebeldía"* ("Movements of Rebellion")—the title of *Borderlands/La Frontera*'s second chapter—demand Anzaldúa's attention as they play equally important roles in forming her mestiza existence. In the chapter titled *"La concienza de la mestiza/*Towards a New Consciousness," Anzaldúa declares that "the struggle of the mestiza is above all a feminist one" (106). She does not prioritize gender over race, class, and sexuality, but seeks to show the connections between the types of oppression and to establish feminism as a multi-issue fight against all of them. In so doing, she strikes themes present in lesbian feminism from its early days, even if they had been drowned out by the more limited vision that later came to dominate the movement in some quarters. By this last prose chapter of the text, Anzaldúa has built a strong case against racism and explored the forms it takes against Chicanos/as specifically; she has uncovered sexism and homophobia in Chicano/a culture, as in the dominant culture. Here she calls on the new mestiza to embrace all border crossers—even the queers, the most reviled *atravesados* of all—to join forces in a feminist movement to change the world:

> Being the supreme crossers of cultures, homosexuals have strong bonds with the queer white, Black, Asian, Native American, Latino, and with the queer in Italy, Australia and the rest of the planet. We come from all colors, all classes, all races, all time periods. Our role is to link people with each other. (106)

By queering the mestiza, Anzaldúa performs a maneuver akin to Sedgwick's "universalizing" move, even as she harks back to Judy Grahn's folkloric study *Another Mother Tongue.*

While the themes and time frame of *Borderlands/La Frontera,* and Latina lesbian identity poetics more generally, seem to fit perfectly with the postmodernism of multiple identities, they also are remarkably similar to earlier lesbian-feminist forms, which took their cue from other, earlier (and to some degree simultaneous) civil rights and cultural nationalist movements. The lesbian-feminist poetic project shares some of the hallmarks of "classic Chicano poetics" as described by Pérez-Torres: giving voice to silenced communities, revealing and criticizing oppressive assumptions and practices, and "foreground[ing] issues of identity formation" including self-naming and revisionary mythmaking (*Movements,* 6, 16, 17). Both poetries are "intimately linked to the political struggles" of a people (12). Pérez-Torres notes the influence of feminism on the shift from the polemical, and typically narrative, Movimiento poetry of the 1960s to the more local and intimate (often lyric) poetry of the eighties and nineties. The rising prominence of public "Chicana self-identification" has been part of the localization of politics,

> often crystallizing around sexual and gender issues, worker's rights and environmental issues, worker safety and immigration laws. The poetry evokes political discourses crossed at the site of the individual. . . . The later poetic work articulates on a personal level the disenfranchisement of and potential hope available to members of a dispossessed margin. (*Movements*, 13)

Borderlands/La Frontera is most often lauded for its mixed-genre first half and, partly because of its form, frequently categorized as a poststructuralist hybrid work of theory. The predominance of poetry in the text—an entire book's worth as the second half of the volume, and continually intruding on the prose first half—links it to both the lesbian-feminist movement (so prominently marked by its poet-theorists) and to the identity politics of El Movimiento. Poetry has fueled both movements from their inceptions, and it has remained important to them even if Pérez-Torres is right that the general audience for poetry in the United States has shrunk. As he notes, "Within the 'marginal' realms of Chicana and other multicultural literatures, the import and effect of poetry cannot be easily dismissed" (*Movements*, 20).

The evolution of *Borderlands/La Frontera* as a text shows its anchor in lesbian feminism and its evolution into poststructuralist queer theory, the aspect of the book that has received most attention. Originally, *Borderlands/La Frontera* was conceptualized as a straightforward volume of poems, with a ten-page prose introduction, but the ten pages grew to ninety-three plus endnotes (Adams, "Northamerican Silences," 134; Pinkvoss, personal communication, 1999).[13] The importance of genre is reflected in Anzaldúa's various biographical notes. Although *Borderlands/La Frontera* is her only published volume of poetry, and despite critics' nearly exclusive focus on the book's first half, Anzaldúa describes herself as "poet" in all of her own books and in most of the volumes in which her work (prose or poetry) appears. In *Borderlands/La Frontera*'s roots as a volume of poetry and in Anzaldúa's naming herself "poet" (even "lesbian-feminist" poet in some instances),[14] the book and its author belong squarely in the evolving tradition of Grahn, Parker, Lorde, and Rich.

It is not merely form but theme that links Anzaldúa to her lesbian-feminist predecessors and *comadres*. Like them, Anzaldúa is centrally concerned with the task of self-naming. That her project goes beyond the singular nomenclature "lesbian" reflects, as with Lorde, both her sense of self and her affinity with the postmodernism of multiple identities. If most attention has been paid to Anzaldúa's self-naming in the first half of *Borderlands/La Frontera,* it is in part because the poems are less straightforwardly concerned with defining terms, though still focused on defining a self to which the terms are applicable. Anzaldúa announces herself as a lesbian in "*Compañera, cuando nos amábamos*" and "Interface" (170–74), which both describe physical intimacy and emotional intensity between women. The lover in "Interface" is a "noumenal" being, called "a lez" by the narrator's brother, who cannot understand the spiritual depths of the lovers' relationship. In "*Canción de la diosa de la noche*" ("Song of the goddess of the night," 218–21), Anzaldúa describes a goddess-centered spiritual worldview fueled by that which the dominant culture discards, including its gay and lesbian members.

> Now, I drum on the carcass of the world
>   creating crises to recall my name.
> The filth you relegate to Satan,
> I absorb. I convert.
> When I dance it burgeons out
>   as song.
>   I seek *la diosa*
>   darkly awesome.
>   In love with my own kind,
>   I know you and inspirit you.
> All others flee from me. (ll. 65–75)

As she names herself spiritually, she names herself lesbian, "in love with my own kind."

Anzaldúa proudly names herself Chicana throughout *Borderlands/La Frontera,* a self-naming as politically charged as "lesbian." Alarcón explains,

> The name Chicana, in the present, is the name of resistance that enables cultural and political points of departure and thinking through the multiple migrations and dislocations of women of "Mexican" descent. The name Chicana is not a name that women (or men) are born to or with. . . . It serves as the point of redeparture for dismantling historical conjunctures of crisis, confusion, political and ideological conflict, and contradictions of

the simultaneous effects of having "no names," having "many names," not "know[ing] her names," and being someone else's "dreamwork." ("Chicana Feminism," 374)[15]

In step with Alarcón's definition of "Chicana" as implying a multifaceted critique and involving self-identification, two of Anzaldúa's poems explicitly delineate her difference within a larger Chicano context. "*Cihuatlyotl,* Woman Alone" (195) is Anzaldúa's declaration of independence from the oppressive expectations of "*Raza* / father mother church" (ll. 1–2) whose "soft brown / landscape, tender *nopalitos*" ("prickly pears," ll. 12–13, a commonplace in South Texas Mexican diet, and a recurrent image in Anzaldúa's poems) are "beckoning beckoning" (l. 12) but carry a price too high for her to pay: "No self, / only race *vecindad familia*" ("community," lit. "neighborhood," "family," ll. 21, 22). The right and left justification of the poem's margins on the page echo the narrator's justification of her break with her people:

> ... My soul   has always
> been yours   one spark   in the roar of your fire.
> We Mexicans are   collective animals.   This I
> accept   but my life's work   requires autonomy
> like oxygen. (ll. 22–26)

Her "life's work" is both the creation of art and her self-creation, what she calls "making soul" in the title of and introduction to her anthology *Making Face, Making Soul/Haciendo Caras*. In "*Cihuatlyotl,* Woman Alone," Anzaldúa is not only "woman" alone but all of the entities that make up her mestiza "soul. I remain who I am, multiple / and one of the herd, yet not of it" (ll. 30–31). Spinning a twist on the liberal Christian theologian Paul Tillich, who wrote of God as "the ground of all being," Anzaldúa asserts,

> ... I walk
> on the ground of my own being   browned and
> hardened by the ages. I am fully formed carved
> by the hands of the ancients,   drenched with
> the stench of today's headlines.   But my own
> hands whittle   the final work   me. (ll. 31–36)

Anzaldúa turns neither to Tillich's God nor the Catholic God of her own upbringing (indeed in several poems she invokes *la diosa,* the goddess), but to her hard-won, evolving sense of self.

Nopalitos, the food that beckons the narrator of *"Cihuatlyotl,* Woman Alone" to her home culture, is the title of another poem of self-definition wrought in contrast to her family and community of origin. The first six stanzas of *"Nopalitos"* (134–35) set a languorous South Texas stage, full of the smells, tastes, and sights of Anzaldúa's beloved homeland on a shimmering hot, late afternoon. The last sentence of stanza 6 shifts the poem from a pastoral reminiscence to a melancholy recognition—completed, as the sentence is finished, in stanza 7—that she no longer fully belongs. The tone pivots on the first word of the sentence, "Though," as the poem turns from a vivid tableau into a more abstract explanation of the narrator's position:

> Though I'm part of their *camaradería*
> am one of them
>
> I left and have been gone a long time.
> I keep leaving and when I am home
> they remember no one but me had ever left.
> I listen to the *grillos* [cicadas] more intently
> than I do their *regaños* [scoldings].
> I have more languages than they,
> am aware of every root of my *pueblo* [people];
> they, my people, are not.
> They are the living, sleeping roots. (ll. 48–58)

The narrator mourns the necessary loss that leads to her self-actualization as an artist, a lesbian, an individual. She, like Cihuatlyotl, may be independent, educated, and strong, but she is also alone and sad: "I sweep up mesquite leaves, / thorns embedded in my flesh, / stings behind my eyes" (ll. 59–61).

"To live in the Borderlands means you" (216–17) explains that she is embattled as well. The poem exemplifies Anzaldúa's mestiza existence as neither one thing nor another, but a mixture of "*hispana india negra española* / . . . *mestiza mulata,* half-breed / caught in the cross-fire between camps" ("Hispanic, Indian, black, Spanish / . . . *mestiza,* mulatto, half-breed," ll. 1–3). The poem's first seven stanzas describe the splits, estrangements, and border wars that threaten the mestiza, but the eighth and final stanza delivers Anzaldúa's solution to the conflict: "To survive the Borderlands / you must live *sin fronteras* [without borders] / be a crossroads" (ll. 40–42). Figured elsewhere as a "bridge" (Anzaldúa, "Bridge, Drawbridge"; Moraga and Anzaldúa, *This Bridge*), here as throughout *Borderlands/La Frontera* Anzaldúa shares her vision of la mestiza ushering in a new age of alliance. In the chapter "*La conciencia de la mestiza*/Towards a New Consciousness" she implores Chicanos/as "to acknowledge the political and artistic contributions of their queer. People, listen to what your *jotería* [queers/faggotry] is saying" (107). Similarly, though she acknowledges that some people of color do not want to work with white people on racism, she writes that "I, for one, choose to use some of my energy to serve as mediator. I think we need to allow whites to be our allies. . . . They will come to see that they are not helping us but following our lead" (107).

One of the few critics to write extensively about Anzaldúa's poetry, Ann E. Reuman focuses on the "intense and unrelenting threats of violence" confronting Anzaldúa "as a poor Mexican-American, a woman, a lesbian, and a writer" ("'Wild Tongues,'" 306). While Reuman's readings of the poems are astute, the picture she paints is incomplete until the second half of her essay, when she shows how Anzaldúa's poems serve in the healing process, fighting back against the violence they describe. Reuman remarks upon Anzaldúa's poems of sometimes literal physical dismemberment (e.g., "Holy Relics," 176–81, inspired by Grahn's "Marilyn Monroe Poem" [Perry, "Interview," 25], "The Cannibals' *Canción*," 165); crucially, the new mestiza re-members, reassembling all her parts into a new whole, often using memory, history, and legend as ingredients. She speaks, to quote Adrienne Rich, "a whole new language" as she "re-visions" past, present, and future in her prophetic text. In this sense she shares a great deal with Lorde, another poet of many "crossroads."[16]

Especially powerful in narrative mode, Anzaldúa describes herself through stories of spiritual, emotional, and political journeys. "I Had to Go Down" (189–91), for example, is a classic Jungian dream sequence in which the narrator is drawn to the dark, creepy basement of an old house to confront her fears and finds only herself:

> Then I heard the footsteps again
> making scuffing sounds
> on the packed dirt floor.
> It was my feet making them.
> It had been my footsteps I'd heard. (ll. 88–92)

In "*Antigua, mi diosa*" (Ancient, my goddess, 210–11), she describes being filled with the light of her goddess, like an ax blow, resulting in a lifelong journey following in her footsteps, searching her out: "*Descalza, gateando a ciegas voy / sigo tus huellas ligeras y tu linaje viejo"* ("Barefoot, crawling blindly I go / I follow your light tracks and your ancient lineage," ll. 1–2); *"ahora por todas las tierras vulneradas te busco"* ("now through all the damaged lands I search for you," l. 48).[17]

"That dark shining thing" (193–94) shows most clearly the confluence of Anzaldúa's spiritual and political identities as well as her chosen role as activist bridge builder or crossroads. Anzaldúa addresses herself to those "Colored, poor white, latent queer / passing as white" (ll. 10–11) who choose "that closet" (l. 3) of internalized oppression but who simultaneously "elected me to pry open a crack / . . . choose me to pick at the masks" (ll. 5, 16). The narrator describes herself as the visible token, "the only round face, / Indian-beaked, off-colored / in the faculty lineup, the workshop, the panel / and reckless enough to take you on" (ll. 17–20). For her troubles, she is abused, but much as she wants to she cannot turn her back, because she remembers her own self-hatred and process of rebirth, helped along by midwives like the one she has become. Anzaldúa highlights the importance of naming to the process of giving birth to "that dark shining thing,"

> . . . the numinous thing
> it was black and it had my name
> it spoke to me and I spoke to it.
>
> Here we are four women stinking with guilt
> you for not speaking your names
> me for not holding out my hand sooner.
> I don't know how long I can keep naming
> that dark animal
> coaxing it out of you, out of me
> keep calling it good or woman-god
> while everyone says no no no. (ll. 48–58)

Anzaldúa's narrator acknowledges and embraces "that Beast" (l. 59) within herself that represents all she has been told to fear and despise; she recognizes that owning it, looking at "the pain . . . the fear / that all my life had walked beside me" (ll. 46–47) is a matter of *"vida o muerte,* life or death" (l. 67).

The narrator's acceptance of "the Beast" and "that dark shining thing" resolve, to some extent, Anzaldúa's struggles with dark and black aspects of herself, which recur in poems such as *" Cagado abismo, quiero saber,"* *"Matriz sin tumba,"* ("Womb without a grave," 158–60), and *"Canción de la diosa de la noche,"* three poems set in *"una noche oscura"* ("a dark night," *"Matriz sin tumba,"* l. 11). Anzaldúa fights the cultural pressure to consider that which is dark evil, harmful, or fearful, but she acknowledges that she has been taught to do so; darkness in her poems often signals emotional and spiritual turmoil that must be traveled through, or repressed states that must be reclaimed, like the "Shadow-Beast" of chapter 2, the internal image of the lust and desire that we have been taught to loathe:

> To avoid rejection, some of us conform to the values of the culture, push the unacceptable parts into the shadows. Which leaves only one fear—that we will be found out and that the Shadow-Beast will break out of its cage. Some of us take another route. We try to make ourselves conscious of the Shadow-Beast, stare at the sexual lust and lust for power and destruction we see on its face, discern among its features the undershadow that the reigning order of heterosexual males project on our Beast. Yet still others of us take it another step: we try to waken the Shadow-Beast inside us. . . . A few of us have been lucky—on the face of the Shadow-Beast we have seen not lust but tenderness; on its face we have uncovered the lie. (42)

This is the positive potential of "the Beast" that the narrator of "that dark shining thing" urges others to embrace, but the dominant culture coerces most of us to silence the Beast, to refuse our names.

Reading Queerly: The Postmodernism of Borderlands/La Frontera

"Mestiza" is the name Anzaldúa most consistently applies to herself in *Borderlands/La Frontera.* Anzaldúa's multiple sense of self, her frequent use of the term *queer* and the prominence of her writings in the late 1980s and early 1990s make it tempting to place her in the rising tide of queer theory—and several commentators have done so. Anzaldúa's work has had an important influence on the rise of queer theory, and many people who write about her call her work poststructuralist or queer theory; at the same time, however, most people who write about queer theory ignore her, as they ignore the work of most lesbians of color. Critics who with hindsight place *Borderlands/La Frontera* squarely in the poststructuralist camp ignore Anzaldúa's simultaneous self-naming as lesbian, lesbian feminist, and dyke[18]—and sometimes remove her work from its Chicano/a context in order to discuss it primarily as queer.[19] One of the better critical essays linking a lesbian of color to the foundational ideas of queer theory, Ian Barnard's "Gloria

Anzaldúa's Queer *Mestizaje*," nevertheless paradoxically misses half the story, that Anzaldúa's work illuminates the points of connection between lesbian-feminist identity politics and poststructuralist queer theory, not merely (nor even necessarily) the differences.

Barnard's essay comes out aggressively pro-queer and disparagingly anti-gay-and-lesbian from its first pages. Oddly, Barnard then praises queer theory and politics for possessing one of identity politics' primary strengths, its emphasis on reclaiming derogatory terms for politicized self-naming (37). Like many others who build the (not insignificant) case for Anzaldúa's relevance to queer theory, Barnard notes Anzaldúa's invocation of *queer* and conveniently, if disingenuously, ignores her several uses of *lesbian*. The use of *queer* in *Borderlands/La Frontera* certainly predates its widespread adoption as the basis of a movement, political or academic (Barnard, "Gloria Anzaldúa's," 38), but her use of *lesbian* and *feminist* in the same text are no less significant and are made possible by the groundwork laid by lesbian feminism, a movement in which Anzaldúa participated.[20] Barnard's blind spot is all the more curious given his perception that Anzaldúa adroitly combines her queer "contestatory politics" with "lived experience," that is, at least in some respect, a politics of identity (44). For Barnard, Anzaldúa's positioning is exemplary queer theory; he misses the connection of her "complex identity narration" (to cite an apt term coined by Diane Fowlkes) to her identity politics and lesbian feminism. Barnard terms Anzaldúa's mestiza "metaphoric" (44), and perhaps that is where his analysis ultimately goes astray. Anzaldúa is not *really* just one side of her multifaceted racial identity, sexuality, or geographic home base. She is not *really* queer as opposed to lesbian; she states again and again that she is *really mestiza,* both/and/neither: "To live in the Borderlands," she writes, "means you / are neither *hispana india negra española / ni gabacha, eres mestiza mulata, half-breed*" ("neither Hispanic, Indian, black, Spanish / nor white, you are *mestiza,* mulatto, half-breed").

Barnard also cites Anzaldúa's 1991 essay "To(o) Queer the Writer" as an example of queer theory written by a person of color (38). It is true that Anzaldúa rejects the label *lesbian* in favor of *queer* in the essay; as she explains in a 1993 interview,

> When everybody says "lesbian," a word connected with Sappho and the island of Lesbos, that automatically means that your forefathers and fore-mothers are European, that George Washington is the father of our country and Columbus discovered America—all false assumptions. The word

"lesbian" was sufficient when I first came out: Being a lesbian meant that I had a community, albeit a *gringa* community. (Perry, "Interview," 32)

However, in "To(o) Queer the Writer" Anzaldúa clearly is hostile toward appropriation of the work of people of color by white activists and theorists, both "lesbian" and "queer." For a queer theorist to claim Anzaldúa's allegiance is a misreading of the content and tone of her essay. Anzaldúa makes this clear in another 1993 interview in which she refers to "To(o) Queer the Writer":

> I think that the white dykes really want a community that's diversified. Sometimes they want it so badly that they want to put everybody under this queer umbrella: "We're all in this together and we're all equal." But we are not equal. . . . The greater our numbers the more power we have as queers. Bringing us under this queer umbrella is a kind of survival tactic. But often in order to bring us under the queer umbrella they ignore differences, collapse the differences, not really deal with the issue. . . . I wrote an essay called 'To(o) Queer the Writer' that deals with these concerns. (*Interviews*/Entrevistas, 208)

In any event, Anzaldúa does not entirely foreswear use of the word *lesbian*; in the interview in which she explains her preference for *queer*, she refers to herself as lesbian five times (she employs *dyke*, a term reclaimed by lesbian feminists, four times), while only using *queer* when explaining why she prefers it to *lesbian* (Perry, "Interview"). In interviews ranging from 1982 to 1999, Anzaldúa uses *queer, lesbian*, and *dyke* more or less interchangeably. Phelan reminds readers of *Borderlands/La Frontera* that Anzaldúa's "we"

> shifts from page to page, meaning sometimes queers, sometimes Chicanos/Chicanas, sometimes feminists. Her contextualization of this shifting "we" removes the possibility of reading her statements as simple calls for unity, instead calling on us to acknowledge all of her locations at once and equally. (66)

Anzaldúa's text is not unproblematically part of a queer theory canon, nor should her work be dismissed as irrelevant to or entirely divorced from it. (The same, as I have been arguing, must be said for her relationship to lesbian feminism.) The two inform one another, in some cases, and without question overlap in substance and concept if not always form. Phelan deftly captures the "specificity" of Anzaldúa's work with respect to poststructuralism, explaining that Anzaldúa's shifting positionality does not mean that Anzaldúa "is postmodern," or that every aspect of the mestiza is replicated and captured by poststructuralist theory. The belong-ingness of the mestiza for Anzaldúa is not simply a matter of choice, of vol-untary affiliation, but of history and social density. In that evocation of history and rebellion, and in her political commitment, she is allied with Michel Foucault. She is not simply "Foucauldian," however, as if reading Foucault would tell us what Anzaldúa thinks. (*Getting Specific,* 66–67)

Phelan's contribution warns against Barnard's variety of co-optation of Anzaldúa to queer theory. Another version goes beyond conflating the two, seemingly reversing the chronology of published ideas if not direct theoreti-cal influence. Jennifer Browdy de Hernández, for example, has queer theory influencing Anzaldúa and Lorde, whose referenced work prefigures it:

In *Gender Trouble* [published in 1990], [Judith] Butler argues that identity can be 'proliferated' subversively, in a way that breaks out of binary oppo-sitions. . . . Anzaldúa and Lorde take Butler's oppositional strategy even further, proliferating identity not only in terms of gender but also in terms of race, class, ethnicity, and other even more marginalized affinities, such as Anzaldúa's Chicana mysticism and Lorde's Afrocentrist mysticism. ("Mothering," 253)[21]

In the same essay Browdy de Hernández terms Anzaldúa and Lorde "queer theorists *avant-la-lettre,*" at least putting things in correct historical order (244–45). Pérez-Torres links the material to the theoretical, perhaps nailing most accurately the connection between the two, as he contradicts Browdy de Hernández French term for term: "Chicanos have [not] formed a postmodern culture *avant la lettre.* . . . Chicanos have lived and survived (which is a form of triumph over) the disparities made plain by the critical light of postmodernism" (*Movements,* 4). That Anzaldúa theorizes and versifies from the basis of that theorizably postmodern experience makes her what we might perhaps best call a materialist poet-theorist, a practitioner of identity poetics.

Shifting Genres: From Poetry to Theory

Since the birth of lesbian feminism in the early 1970s, and through the 1980s, a cultural shift of emphasis has taken place within feminism—certainly

within the academy—to theory and away from poetry. Theory as a language
has gained cultural capital as the study of women writers has declined from
the heyday of rediscovering authors in the late 1970s. This period of the
growth of cultural studies and queer theory also has seen the decline of ven-
ues for lesbian poetry such as feminist bookstores, lesbian coffeehouses, lesbian-feminist newspapers, and independent lesbian and feminist publishing
houses. The story of the theory section of *Borderlands/La Frontera* growing
out of an otherwise self-sustaining volume of poetry provides a neat metaphor
for the shift from the poetry-centered lesbian-feminist movement (in which
Anzaldúa has roots) to the prose-theory-centered queer movement (which has
taken her up and which she, to some extent, now embraces). The evolution
of the book echoes Audre Lorde's explanation of the evolution of poetry into
theory into activist movement—which in light of the shift of genre central to
the movement could be seen as prophetic. The evolution of *Borderlands/La
Frontera* also plays out at least one of Anzaldúa's description of how she works:

> First there has to be something that is bothering me . . . . Then I start med-
> itating on it. . . . Usually I come up with something visual of what I am
> feeling. . . . So behind this feeling there is this image, this visual, and I have
> to figure out what the articulation of this image is. That's how I get into
> the theory. I start theorizing about it. But it always comes from a feeling.
> (Ikas, "Interview," 236)

If feeling and image are more traditionally associated with poetry, then this
passage reads very similarly to Lorde's from "Poetry Is Not a Luxury":
"[Poetry] forms the quality of the light within which we predicate our hopes
and dreams toward survival and change, first made into language, then into
idea, then into more tangible action. Poetry is the way we help give name to
the nameless so it can be thought" (*Sister*, 37). Anzaldúa similarly indicates
that poetry and theory are two different, equally viable forms for expressing
ideas, if perhaps to different audiences.

> When I start with an idea . . . I want to be able to unravel it for different
> readers—for the academic professors and students as well as for children
> and the average person. I want to do it through different media, through
> poetry, fiction and through theory because each of these genres enriches
> the others. (Ikas, "Interview, 235–36)

Academics have devoted reams to *Borderlands/La Frontera*'s theorizing, and
nearly all account for the genre mestizaje that produces what they frequently

call "poetic prose," but almost no one writes about Anzaldúa's poems. In an essay titled "Crossing Borders: An Aesthetic Practice in Writings by Gloria Anzaldúa," Monika Kaup typically refers to Anzaldúa's "diverse centers of consciousness—both poetic and academic," setting up the traditional binary split. Kaup goes further, noting the division of the book into "two parts, the first consisting of cultural description, the second poetry, the first concerned with fact, the second with fiction" (105). To focus on the prose writing of the book's first half, Kaup must intentionally dismiss the fact that even the first chapter of the first half begins with a poem, introducing her analysis with the direction to ignore the primary placement of poetry, "In these first sentences of the book (if we leave aside an introductory poem)" (107), as if the conspicuous prioritizing of poetry in the text were somehow negligible.

Anzaldúa's poems fare little better in the hands of a multitude of other scholars. María Lugones's frequently quoted essay, "On *Borderlands/La Frontera*: An Interpretive Essay," ignores the poems of the second half of the text, mentioning only an untitled poem in chapter 4. In "Texas Border Literature," Héctor Calderón makes no mention of the poetry, treating *Borderlands/La Frontera* as straightforward *testimonio,* or prose autobiography. Browdy de Hernández actually asserts that "*Borderlands* ends" on page 91, with the end of the prose chapters ("Mothering," 259). A few critics provide suggestions, but almost no one actually explicates the poetry at any length. Even the introduction to the second edition spends four times the number of pages discussing the prose section as the poetry section.

It is somewhat ironic, given the book's striving against academic co-optation—its resistance, at least, to traditions of genre and its rewriting of colonialist history—that there is so much scholarly writing about *Borderlands/La Frontera* as a theoretical text. The best of this scholarship takes into account the genre mix of the "theory half" of the book, but virtually all of it acts as though that is the only text that exists, or matters. By the early 1990s, when the fifteenth-anniversary retrospective issue of the lesbian-feminist journal *Sinister Wisdom* was published, Anzaldúa was calling herself a "Chicana *tejana* dyke-feminist poet-writer-*theorist*" (emphasis added) in her contributor's note. Clearly influenced by the changing winds in feminism and the academic reception of her *Borderlands/La Frontera,* by 1998's *Living Chicana Theory* Anzaldúa termed herself "a queer Chicana Tejana feminist patlache poet, fictionist, and cultural theorist" (Trujillo, *Living*). The second edition of *Borderlands/La Frontera,* published in 1999, announces the book's adoption as an academic text in a number of ways, including a critical introduction attentive to its reception and its place in theoretical debates and an interview with

Anzaldúa that highlights the importance of the author as a theorist to contend with. Promotional copy on the back cover also testifies to the book's incorporation into academia. The label "Chicana Studies/Women's Studies" in the upper right corner categorizes it as a text for classroom use (though curiously not for American literature classes). Cover copy also positions the text academically as "a book that speaks across fields." The publisher prominently announces the inclusion in the new edition of a "critical introduction" written by Sonia Saldívar-Hull, "Associate Professor of English at UCLA and author of *Feminism on the Border*," understood to be scholarly and validating Chicana feminist studies as an accepted field of scholarship. Indeed, the multiple printings of *Borderlands/La Frontera's* first edition and the publication of a second edition were made possible by its widespread classroom use.

Borderlands/La Frontera in its academic setting is read largely as a work of cultural theory by feminists, Chicano/a studies scholars, cultural studies scholars, and queer theorists, as the multitude of critical articles and the introduction to the second edition make clear:

> While *estudios de la frontera* (border studies) certainly were not invented by Gloria Anzaldúa in *Borderlands,* this book signaled a new visibility for academic programs on the study of the U.S.-Mexico border area. . . .
>
> This *transfrontera*, transdisciplinary text also crossed rigid boundaries in academia as it traveled between Literature (English and Spanish), History, American Studies, Anthropology and Political Science departments, and further illuminated multiple theories of feminism in women's studies and Chicana studies. (Saldívar-Hull, "Introduction," 12–13)

While the poets in this study, including Anzaldúa, and the lesbian-feminist movement generally see their poetry as integrally, activistly theoretical, academics do not. By most scholarly lights, if the critical writing on Anzaldúa is any guide, poets are allowed to write (prose) theory (though usually not what is termed "high theory"), but their poetry is not acknowledged as theory in its own right.

The "poetry half" of *Borderlands/La Frontera* presents other problems that perhaps lie behind critics' neglect of it. Anzaldúa herself hints at two of them in the interview appended to the second edition. First, she suggests that audience varies for different genres of writing. She does not seem to expect "academic professors" to turn to literature for theoretical ideas (Ikas, "Interview," 235), an insight perhaps born of her experience as a doctoral student. In another interview, Anzaldúa explains this concept further, at least by implication. "High theorists," she says, are intolerant of discussions about spirituality, at least as much as they seem averse to poetry. And Anzaldúa's poetry is rife with references to her abiding spiritual worldview. "They equate . . . essentialism with spirituality," Anzaldúa explains, "and I don't" (Keating, "Writing," 114). While there exist some fine examples of critical writing about Anzaldúa's prose writing on spirituality,[22] most academics focus on Anzaldúa's racial and sexual politics, the innovations of her particular conceptions of mestiza and queer, and her relevance to poststructuralist, postcolonialist, and/or queer theory.

Anzaldúa asserts that it is her anger that is ignored by many scholars, and she considers their aversion to discussing aspects of the text with which they cannot identify racist (Ikas, "Interview," 232; Perry, "Interview," 31). Certainly, several of the poems express, provoke, or seek to inspire anger (e.g., "*sus plumas el viento,*" "Cultures," "We Call Them Greasers," "Corner of 50th St. and Fifth Av.," "Cuyamaca"). But anger is not the only difficulty that is being avoided. Poetry, itself, is difficult—a code to be cracked, a nonlinear and emotive discourse. Like Lorde's poetry, Anzaldúa's presents the additional barrier of cultural difference for the non-Chicana reader through its Chicano, mexicano, and *nahuatl* references. Though foregrounded by the exposition of the first half of the book, the images still require work on the reader's part. The additional difficulty for English-only readers of Anzaldúa's liberal use of Spanish likely also contributes to the neglect of the poems. (Could it be this making critics angry, rather than Anzaldúa's anger making critics avoid the poems? Both?) If the abstract concept of mestizaje can be appropriated by white readers and readers of color alike, the specific imagery of poetry cannot. Anzaldúa's verse resists appropriation, is perceived as being of no use to dominant academic theories, and is therefore ignored—considered "literature," perhaps, but of no consequence to theorists who trade in a different medium. (Judith Roof observes that "difference is erased as difference and made the same in the name of theory"; i.e., the difference that matters, when constructing a theoretical narrative, is whether something is "theory" or "nontheory" [*Lure,* 226].)[23]

Anzaldúa's tendency to work on several projects, in several genres, at once (Ikas, "Interview," 244–45) and the genre mestizaje within *Borderlands/La Frontera* are analogous to the multiple identities embodied by Anzaldúa as mestiza and in that sense clearly aligned with a poststructuralist reading of her self-concept and her work. The second half of the book, a straightforward (one might even say "old-fashioned") collection of poems, belongs more obviously to the lesbian-feminist tradition of Grahn and Parker (not known as essayists) and Lorde and Rich (essayists known separately as poets). The first half of the book looks like theory, sounds like theory—and sexy, postmodern theory, at that—so it must be theory, and therefore worthy of comment. The poetry requires literary decoding, embodies the wrong genre, and therefore is assumed to be of little importance to the queer theoretical project, its content never considered, though it so clearly mirrors the concerns of the rest of the book.

The most generous reading of the incorporation of Anzaldúa's "poetic" text into the theoretical cannon is that the estimation of literature as theoretical—that is to say, as existing shoulder to shoulder with the genre currently most valued by academics—is being accorded to *Borderlands/La Frontera*. The selective attention to sections of *Borderlands/La Frontera* and the neglect of Anzaldúa's poems leads to a more parsimonious assessment. In addition to calling for placing Anzaldúa's poems, like the other four poets' here, in an activist theoretical tradition, I also protest, with postcolonialist critic Vilashini Cooppan, that "We must do resistance literature the honor of treating it as literature" ("Writing").

Obviously, focusing *only* on Anzaldúa's poetry is as problematic as ignoring it outright. I do not intend to contribute to the notion that women of color don't, or can't, "do theory," but only do literature and/or experience.[24] I am arguing that poetry is theory, but that it is also literature and should be discussed as such—that we do it a disservice to leave the available critical tools unused when the poetry (or fiction, for that matter) seems to carry other than purely "literary" (read white, male, pre-postmodern?) content. I am arguing more broadly that activist theory—what the anthropologist Kath Weston calls "street theorizing"—is theory ("Theory," 145). That finally the categories break down, Anzaldúa's point all along.

Chapter Seven

Around 1991: The Rise of Queer Theory and the Lesbian Intertext

Historians and other commentators on feminism and gay liberation widely acknowledge the influence of the civil rights movement on other liberation movements that followed. The standard chronology states that the civil rights movement made possible the black power movement, the antiwar movement, the women's liberation movement, and gay liberation.[1] Commentators rarely extend the litany beyond the early 1970s, treating the five movements as definitive of an era of direct-action politics. Typical of the American tendency to see things, as it were, in black and white, the Chicano power movement, American Indian movement, and other ethnic and racial identity movements often are ignored. Lesbian feminism, the multicultural women/lesbian of color movement of the 1980s, Queer Nation, and other more recent struggles don't make the cut-off, either because they are too recent or perhaps in some cases insufficiently direct-action oriented to neatly fit the category.[2] Related to the problem of historical periodization is the issue of genre. Historians who chronicle political movements rarely address parallel developments in academic writing, and academic theorists are none-too-consistent about acknowledging the influence of direct-action politics on their scholarship. The problem has been dubbed "the activist-academic split."

If it is reasonable to assume that the same civil-rights-black-power-anti-war-women's-liberation-gay-liberation legacy extends to lesbian feminism and the multicultural women/lesbians of color movement, then it ought to be a short step to acknowledging that contemporary poststructuralist theories of sexual identity—"queer theory"—belong to the same historical lineage. With few exceptions, queer theorists have obscured this genealogy, however, by emphasizing their academic predecessors—among them Continental postmodernist philosophies, psychoanalysis, poststructuralism, and cultural studies. Poststructuralism, deconstruction, and postmodernism all took hold within academic feminism in the U.S. after the literature, theory, and activism of lesbian-feminist/working-class/women of color had established difference as an unavoidable, integral topic of U.S. feminism on all levels. However, as Chela Sandoval argues in "U.S. Third World Feminism," white hegemonic feminism is most comfortable acknowledging its institutionally powerful (white, heterosexual, middle-class) roots. Insurgent, activist feminisms—including lesbian feminism and the poetry that constitutes some of its key early political theory—played as important a role in recent U.S. feminist and queer academic trends as did European developments in linguistics, psychoanalysis, and the like.

"The Race for Theory": Privileging Postmodernism and Poststructuralism

Queer theory certainly is not the first or only scholarly movement participating in the general trend toward poststructuralism that gathered steam in the humanities in the 1980s. Barbara Christian questions the motivations for the theoreticization of literary studies in her well-known essay "The Race for Theory" (1987). She worries that theory, which "has become a commodity that helps determine whether we are hired or promoted in academic institutions—worse, whether we are heard at all" (67), has "influenced, even co-opted" "black, women, Third World" critics "into speaking a language and defining their discussion in terms alien to and opposed to our needs and orientation" (68). Christian's argument is not with the practice of theory per se, but with "its academic hegemony" (69). At issue is not what theory includes but what it precludes, whom it silences. "Since I am slightly paranoid," Christian writes, "it has begun to occur to me that the literature [of radical people of color] being produced *is* precisely one of the reasons why this philosophical-literary-critical theory of relativity is so prominent" (73). It "surfaced, interestingly enough, just when the literature of peoples of color, black women, Latin Americans, and Africans began to move to 'the center'" (71).

While Michel Foucault, Jacques Derrida, and Jacques Lacan are the major "New Philosophers" whom Christian implicates and indicts, famous white men are not the only culprits she names. She sees a parallel, hegemonic force in the Black Arts movement, which "resulted in a necessary and important critique both of previous Afro-American literature and of the white-established literary world," but in the process "became much like its opponent, monolithic and downright repressive" ("Race for Theory," 74). In the late eighties, Christian identified white, middle-class feminists "eager to enter the halls of power" as the most recent participants in "the race for theory" (75).[3] In other words, the Black Arts movement excluded women, poststructuralist feminist criticism ignores women of color, and both movements deny histories of literature and literary criticism that do not fit their totalizing theories.

Sagri Dhairyam cites "The Race for Theory" in her essay "Racing the Lesbian, Dodging White Critics" (1994), in which she makes a similar point, specifically about queer theory:

> Though academic analyses locate identity as a contingent filiation of discourses and help to destabilize a regime of heterosexual sameness, in the process, these analyses run the danger of erasing the experiential and affective realities of alternative sexualities and/or raced communities, which must constantly struggle not only to affirm their pleasure but to describe their terrors." (33–34)

The irony of Dhairyam's assimilation of academic theory and language into her critique of the same is not lost on the author, who apologizes early in the essay for "the turgid intellectualism of these speculations [which] minimizes the risks of speaking a lesbian body in professional space as they underwrite [her] stake in disciplinary, and in this case academic, power" ("Racing," 26). Sharon Holland sees a similar power dynamic at play and calls for "*moving to close the gap between 'politics' and 'theory,' 'literature' and 'experience'*" ("(White) Lesbian," 254). Like Dhairyam, Shane Phelan cites Christian in her analysis of a "two-tier system of citizenship in feminist theory" and calls for "challenging the lines between philosophy, politics, and literature" (Phelan, *Getting Specific*, xix).

While Christian's essay is often cited with (at least tacit) approval, the congratulations have not been universal. In the introduction to the special issue of *Cultural Critique* in which "The Race for Theory" first appeared, the editors disavow what they consider Christian's opposition to "theoretical reflection" (JanMohamed and Lloyd, 7, 8–12). In the introduction to *Changing Our Own Words: Essays on Criticism, Theory, and Writing by Black Women* editor Cheryl A. Wall notes that "undoubtedly [Christian's] words touch a responsive chord in many of [her] readers" (8) but argues that the time has come (in 1989) to participate in "the move to theory" (7). Similarly, in 1987 Hazel V. Carby approvingly cites Deborah McDowell's call for black feminist and lesbian criticism to "expand to embrace other modes of critical inquiry," which would challenge what she sees as naive, essentialist black feminist criticism of the 1970s—the decade during which Christian and others established the field.[4] By 1991 Nancie E. Caraway saw the need to defend Christian and other "Black feminists [who] have questioned the emphasis of many feminist theorists" against the charge that they are "anti-intellectual scolds" ("Challenge and Theory," 112). Without naming names, bell hooks grants that an antipoststructuralist stance similar to Christian's can be "an apt and oftentimes appropriate comeback," but argues that "it does not really intervene in the discourse in a way that alters and transforms" ("Postmodern," 28).[5] Many other critics challenge Christian's argument indirectly by ignoring it, that is, by forging ahead in a highly theoretical, poststructuralist/postmodernist discourse. Hooks states her strategy plainly: "To change the exclusionary practice of postmodern critical discourse is to enact a postmodernism of resistance. Part of this intervention entails black intellectual participation in the discourse" ("Postmodern," 30).

Hooks's critique occupies a unique moment; her essay exists on the border between skepticism toward postmodernism and commitment to challenging theory from the inside. Jane Gallop points out a similar moment in lesbian criticism, citing two versions of Bonnie Zimmerman's often anthologized essay, "What Has Never Been: An Overview of Lesbian Feminist Criticism." In the original essay, published in 1981, Zimmerman writes,

> To me *it seems imperative* that lesbian criticism develop diversity in theory and approach. Much as lesbians, even more than heterosexual feminists, may mistrust systems of thought developed by and associated with men and male values, *we may, in fact,* enrich our work through the insights of Marxist, structuralist, semiotic, or even psychoanalytic criticism. Perhaps "male" systems of thought are incompatible with a lesbian literary vision, but *we will not know until we attempt* to integrate these ideas into our work. (cited in Gallop, *Around 1981*, 177; emphasis added)

The passage is reprinted identically in Elaine Showalter's 1985 anthology, *The New Feminist Criticism,* in which most of the essays were originally published in 1980–81 (Gallop, *Around 1981*, 178, 21). In a revised version of the essay, also published in 1985,[6] Zimmerman rewrites the passage:

> Increasingly, lesbian criticism *has developed* diversity in theory and approach, [i]ncorporating the insights of Marxist, structuralist, semiotic and even psychoanalytic criticism. Although lesbians, perhaps more than heterosexual feminists, may mistrust systems of thought developed by and

associated with men and male values, our work *is in fact* richer and subtler for this incorporation. (cited in Gallop, *Around 1981*, 178; emphasis added)

As Gallop points out, by 1985 the incorporation of theory "has become a *fait accompli*" (*Around 1981*, 178).

"Around 1981": The Institutionalization of Feminist Theory

Gallop traces the incorporation of feminist criticism into the American academy in *Around 1981: Academic Feminist Literary Theory*, a study of twelve anthologies of "mainstream . . . American academic feminist literary criticism" (2) published between 1972 and 1987. Unlike Christian, Gallop argues that exclusion is the by-product of institutional acceptance. In other words, Christian (among others)[7] argues that feminist criticism went mainstream in order to silence radical voices; Gallop argues that feminist criticism ignored dissident, non- or "anti-theoretical" voices in order to go mainstream. Gallop interrogates but ultimately and pragmatically embraces the institutionalization of feminist criticism:

> My focus is the institutionalization of feminist criticism; what, it might be asked, do I think about that? I think it is a fact. . . . I do not want to celebrate our being in. . . . But I do not want to bemoan it either. I want to understand why we are located here, how we got here, what we sacrificed to get here, what we gained. . . . How do we do the most good . . . speaking from this location. (*Around 1981*, 4–5)

At stake, according to Gallop, is the very definition of the subfield of feminist criticism. She explains that "there is an at least figurative nationalism at work in any definitional fencing off of literary territory" (37), and "such nationalism, whether now literal or figurative (as in the Lesbian Nation), involves a theoretical definition of the 'national' character which not only excludes foreigners but searches to purify the interior by expelling the alien within" (30).

"The alien within" is not only the radical, unruly feminist of color suggested by Christian but also the white feminist critic of the 1970s whose "Images of Women" criticism is scorned by the feminist theorist of the eighties. By 1981, the academic critic was no longer reading Susan Koppelman Cornillon's *Images of Women in Fiction,* the first anthology of feminist literary criticism, published in 1972 (Gallop, *Around 1981*, 78, 77). Gallop explains,

> Usually cited as the first phase of feminist literary study, considerations of Images of Women in literature are generally treated as juvenalia, of archival value at best. . . . Just two decades old, we already have a myth of our early years: a heroic, simpler time, when we were bold but crude. (79)

Michèle Barrett and Anne Phillips echo Gallop on this point. In the introduction to *Destabilizing Theory: Contemporary Feminist Debates*, they write that the consensus among feminists in the 1970s on the nature of "relevant questions" to ask "should not be regarded as a symptom of underdevelopment—a 'prehistory' now well transcended in the sophistication of contemporary thought—for many of the issues posed in that period return to haunt the present" (2).

By 1984 Showalter proclaimed that a "second wave" had hit feminist criticism, comprised of academics who had come from "psychoanalytic, poststructuralist, or deconstructionist theory, rather than via the women's movement and women's studies."[8] According to Gallop, Showalter's 1985 anthology *The New Feminist Criticism* showcases the "rise of theory, which includes its usurpation of the place of the women's movement" in feminist criticism (*Around 1981*, 22). Where earlier feminist critics had struggled to resolve the conflict between politics and aesthetics, by the mid eighties the "new feminist critics" were torn between the poles of politics and theory. "Where once [the academic feminist] looked to Emily Dickinson" as a canonically recognized writer, "now she pins her hopes on Julia Kristeva, 'for in her can truly be found the female intellectual, demanding comparison with Derrida and Lacan.'"[9]

Gallop points out that although theory has become the dominant interest of feminist criticism, *Images of Women in Fiction* is still in print, suggesting that "for some readers this is not the remote past but the present" (*Around 1981*, 79). This is so not only because some teachers, students, and critics still find discussions of portrayals of women relevant but also because that is not all the anthology contains. Reading *Images of Women* for the first time in 1987, Gallop is surprised to find herself "excited by and enjoying some of the more sophisticated essays," even as she is "embarrassed by some of the articles" that fit the stereotypical definition of "crude" earlier work (80).

Similarly, were contemporary queer theorists to pay attention to early lesbian-feminist literature and theory, they might be surprised to find sophisticated representations of lesbian identity and politics. Examples from Pat Parker's and Judy Grahn's work include Parker's critique of identity labels in "Where Will You Be?" the "genderfuck" (to employ a popular "queer" term) of "My Lady Ain't No Lady," the incipient constructionism of "Child of Myself," the challenge to heterosexism of "For the Straight Folks," the response to racist essentialism in "Movement in Black," Grahn's send-up of psychoanalytic discourse in "The Psychoanalysis of Edward the Dyke," the eroticism of "in the place where" and "fortunately the skins," the interrogation of representation in "The Woman in Three Pieces," and the sense of play running through both poets' oeuvres.

Around 1991: The Rise of Queer Theory

The parallels between Gallop's institutional history of feminist theory and the story of lesbian criticism and queer theory are inescapable. Classics of Images of Lesbians criticism include Jeannette Foster's *Sex Variant Women in Literature* (1956, reprinted in 1975 and 1985), Barbara Grier's book-length bibliography, *The Lesbian in Literature* (1967, reprinted in 1975 and 1981), and Jane Rule's *Lesbian Images* (1975). Lesbian critical "juvenilia" apparently lacks the staying power (that is, the market viability) of earlier straight feminist criticism; of the three, only *Sex Variant Women in Literature* is currently in print, published by a lesbian press committed to keeping lesbian classics available. There is a crucial difference between Images of Women criticism and early Images of Lesbians work; whereas Images of Women criticism like Kate Millett's *Sexual Politics* was looking for and finding evidence of male writers' misogyny, early Images of Lesbians criticism was rejoicing in virtually any evidence of lesbian existence, even if the examples were deeply misogynist and antilesbian. Pleased to lay claim to woman-identified heroes in history and literature, Foster's and Grier's works do not hesitate to chronicle lesbians carefully wherever they appeared in fiction, from pulp novels to the so-called great works. Grier uses an elaborate rating system to indicate whether entries in her bibliography include "major Lesbian characters and/or action," "minor Lesbian characters and/or action," "latent, repressed Lesbianism or characters who can be so interpreted. This type of behavior is properly termed 'variant behavior'; or 'trash.'"[10]

Zimmerman's call to incorporate "the insights of Marxist, structuralist, semiotic, or even psychoanalytic criticism" into lesbian criticism was first sounded in 1981, the year in which Gallop places the institutionalization of straight feminist criticism. A decade later, "around 1991," queer theory similarly ascended to a position of recognized (if marginalized) institutional power, eclipsing earlier varieties of both Images of Lesbians criticism and lesbian-feminist political and critical theory which had gained some prominence within women's studies. As had been true of the rise of feminist theory, the rise of queer theory concentrated on work by white, middle-class academics and drew heavily on white male philosophers and social theorists. Just as the collective voice of lesbians of color was achieving prominence within and around the lesbian-feminist movement, queer theory eclipsed lesbian feminism in the academy.

What has come to be considered the first national lesbian and gay studies conference was held by the Yale University Lesbian and Gay Studies Center in 1986, but the first to gain national attention took place at Yale in 1989, when over five hundred people attended; the size and scope of the conference expanded greatly in 1990, when the fourth conference was held at Harvard. By the time the sixth national conference (held in 1994) was announced, organizers used the word queer in the title: "InQueery In Theory Indeed." The first Out Write lesbian and gay writers' conference was held in San Francisco in 1990. City College of San Francisco set up the first department of gay and lesbian studies in the U.S. in 1989 and created the first full-time tenure-track position in the field in 1991. The Center for Lesbian and Gay Studies at the Graduate School of the City University of New York put out the first issue of its newsletter in 1991.

The *Chronicle of Higher Education* reported in late 1990 that "the gay-studies movement is gaining acceptance in academe . . . with a surge in sophisticated scholarship"—by which the writer meant queer theory, naming Eve Sedgwick as the "lightning rod for [those] working in gay studies" (cited in Morton, "Politics," 121–22). Three of the germinal queer theory texts were published in 1990 and 1991: Judith Butler's *Gender Trouble* (1990), Sedgwick's *Epistemology of the Closet* (1990), and Diana Fuss's anthology, *Inside/Out: Lesbian Theories, Gay Theories* (1991), which opens with an essay by Butler. The "Queer Theory" issue of *differences,* cited by Robyn Wiegman as the first use of the term *queer theory* in an academic journal or book (Wiegman 171*n*), was published in 1991 and includes some of the proceedings of the "Queer Theory" conference held at UC Santa Cruz in 1990. The *Socialist Review* published its "Queer Innovation" issue at the beginning of 1992. Conferences, caucuses, and organizations had been set up earlier, but critical mass was reached around 1991, with the ascendancy of queer theory and the movement for lesbian/gay studies centers and programs at many colleges and universities.[11]

When the massive, 666-page *Lesbian and Gay Studies Reader* was published by Routledge in 1993, its editors professed their affinity for the term *queer studies*. They explained that they used "lesbian and gay" in the title of the book only as a nod to "the force of current usage" (xvii). The anthology includes a range of writers—some contemporary queer theorists, others associated with older (though still current) lesbian, gay, or bisexual movements. The table of contents, however, is organized in sections whose titles echo contemporary queer theoretical language and concerns: "Politics and Representation," "Spectacular Logic," "Subjectivity, Discipline, Resistance." An alternative organization of the essays along traditional disciplinary lines is provided in a "User's Guide." The inclusion of both organizational strategies points out the tensions in lesbian/gay/queer studies as well as the increasing interdisciplinarity of the humanities and social sciences. The inclusion of such lesbian-feminist classics as Adrienne Rich's "Compulsory Heterosexuality and Lesbian Existence" and Audre Lorde's "Uses of the Erotic" signals the editors' recognition of the range and history of lesbian/gay/queer studies. It also indicates more of a continuity than a paradigm shift between lesbian-feminist and queer theories, despite the presentist inclinations of some queer theorists.[12] Nevertheless, two-thirds of the essays reprinted in the *Lesbian and Gay Studies Reader* were originally published between 1988 and 1993, the period of the ascendancy of queer theory.

Sheila Jeffreys, a British lesbian-feminist critic known for her uncompromising opposition to queer theory, lambastes the *Reader* for treating feminism "as a minor theme within lesbian and gay studies . . . [a] slightly quirky minority perspective" ("Queer," 467). In *The Lesbian Heresy: A Feminist Perspective on the Lesbian Sexual Revolution* (1993) Jeffreys links queer theory to a "backlash" within "the lesbian community" in the 1980s and nineties against lesbian-feminist politics, parallel to "the backlash against feminism in general [that] has been powerfully documented by Naomi Wolf and Susan Faludi" (x). Jeffreys fires a number of well-placed salvos at queer theory, taking aim at "the disappearance of lesbians" and "women's bodies" in much of the work and at the claims of gender neutrality for the term *queer* ("Queer," 459, 471, 460). At times on the mark, elsewhere Jeffreys misstates some of queer theory's basic precepts. (For example, she asserts that "queer politics accepts and celebrates the minority status of homosexuality" [469], ignoring or unaware of Sedgwick's treatise on the "universalizing" rather than "minoritizing" discourse of queer studies [Sedgwick, *Epistemology*].) Her particular doctrinaire brand of lesbian feminism, more characteristic of England and Australia than the United States in the 1990s, has led one queer critic to write that if Jeffreys "did not exist, Camille Paglia would have had to invent her. [*The Lesbian Heresy* confirms] the worst paranoid fantasies of the feminist baiters and the lesbophobes."[13]

Other lesbian critics who are more difficult to dismiss criticize queer theory for reasons similar to Jeffreys's. Zimmerman notes the "imperative" that "each generation of scholars . . . establish its credentials against those of the preceding generation" ("History," 5), a practice that applies equally to the overlapping categories of activist and academic theory. She continues, "The work of first-generation feminist and lesbian scholars is . . . re-read or misread in order to provide a space in which younger scholars can develop their own theories and interpretations free from the stifling 'anxiety of influence' identified fifteen years ago by Sandra Gilbert and Susan Gubar."[14] Invoking similar generational imagery, Lillian Faderman notes that "Queer Theory came out of the womb of gay and lesbian scholarship whose own parent was the identity politics born of the Stonewall Riots. But Queer Theory was fathered by postmodernist theory. And like the goddess Athena, its first allegiance appears to be to the father" ("Preface," 12–13). The split between lesbian-feminist or lesbian/gay studies and queer theory is often described by both queer theorists and their detractors. Queer theorist Michael Warner writes that "the idea of queer theory may involve some generational mythmaking" and makes reference to "the queer generation" ("From Queer," 18, 19).

There are many exceptions to this sort of generalization, however; chronologically, *Identity Poetics* and I as its author should belong to the queer era, but obviously this volume harbors some reservations and illustrates a longer lesbian-historical memory than much of queer theory, even as it reflects a clear, queer influence. To the extent that lesbian feminism informs queer theory—and, more important, that the work of working-class/lesbians of color prefigures postmodern insights about positionality, coalition, and multiply located, shifting "identity"—the neat divide by generation quickly breaks down. (That is, for example, to the extent that it is accurate to call Lorde's work "postmodern" or "queer," nevertheless one could not argue that it is part of a younger queer generation.) It should be obvious that queer theory was not institutionalized by young graduate students (though the enthusiasm and hard work of many helped to propel it) but rather by tenured scholars with access to the instruments of academic power—academic journals, fellowships, professorships. While queer theory arose after lesbian feminism did, it is not necessarily true that all young lesbians call themselves "queer" while all older scholars and activists prefer "lesbian-feminist." (And what would be the dividing line? Thirty-five years old? Forty-five? Sixty?) While queer may have more cachet, both strains of thought—dare I say, both *identities*—coexist, sometimes within the same person, and they inform one another as lesbian theory continues to develop.

In "Against Proper Objects," Judith Butler explores the danger of opposing lesbian and gay studies to feminism, as she analyzes the way the editors of *The Lesbian and Gay Studies Reader* seek to define the new field against the older one:

> The second term (gay and lesbian studies) is distinguished from the first (feminist studies) through a separation of the kinds of objects they pursue. . . . And though the language of the editorial introduction to the volume appears to appreciate the feminist precedent, this is an idealization which is perhaps not without its aggression. . . . The institution of the "proper object" takes place, as usual, through a mundane sort of violence. Indeed, we might read moments of methodological founding as pervasively antihistorical acts, beginnings which fabricate their legitimating histories through a retroactive narrative, burying complicity and division in and through the funereal figure of the "ground." (4, 6)

Sue-Ellen Case's astute, humorous account also merits quoting at length, as she describes the misrepresentation of various lesbian styles to fit the dismissable stereotype of lesbian feminism that was in widespread circulation by the early 1990s:

> From the developing perspective of queer, lesbian became conflated with what was once more specifically identified as radical feminist politics. . . . Soon, in queer quarters, it seemed that all lesbian feminists had been wearing Birkenstocks and ripping off their shirts at the Michigan Womyn's Music Festival. Some of us chortled at the revisionist image of bar/butch/feminist dykes listening to acoustic guitars. . . . Slapping each other on the back, we joked, "was lesbian s/m invented by Gayle Rubin and Pat Califia in an argument with antiporn advocates?" . . . What a surprise . . . to learn that queer dykes associated . . . sexual promiscuity as more narrowly particular to a gay male culture that they would then need to assimilate and imitate. Butch feminists, it seemed, had been having

monogamous, vanilla, Saturday-morning slight sex since the 1970s. We snickered. Then it wasn't funny anymore. ("Toward," 209–10)

The issue of historicity is especially of concern to second-wave feminists who remember that an important project of the movement has been to recover lost or suppressed historical information. Citing Adrienne Rich's watershed 1976 MLA address, "It Is the Lesbian in Us . . . ," Zimmerman comments that queer theory "either render[s] invisible, unknown, 'unspeakable' the history of lesbian (and, equally, feminist) theory, scholarship, and criticism—or, perhaps more important, distort[s] it in such a way as to render it unrecognizable" ("History," 7). Her and other critics' concern resonates with many feminist critics' skepticism toward the larger project of poststructuralist theory; in Wiegman's words, "For a number of feminists who have approached the question of the postmodern, it is [postmodernism's] circumvention of historical metanarrativity that defers any kind of positive embrace of the postmodern" ("Introduction," 12–13). Stated more simply by Jeffreys, "The reader [of queer theory] can feel as though a women's liberation movement and lesbian feminism never existed" ("Queer," 462). Barbara Smith, whose many years of writing and organizing have been committed to coalition politics, comments, "Unlike the early lesbian and gay movement, which had both ideological and practical links to the left, black activism, and feminism, today's 'queer' politicos seem to operate in a historical vacuum" ("Queer Politics," 13).

In *The Apparitional Lesbian: Female Homosexuality and Modern Culture*, Terry Castle takes exception with queer theory not in the name of lesbian-feminist history but in defense of lesbian itself as a category. Calling herself "flagrantly out of step with current thinking" (13), Castle writes that she has "resisted placing [her] version of lesbian phenomenology under the currently fashionable rubric of queer theory" because of queer theory's tendency to privilege gay men and erase lesbians under "pseudo-umbrella terms" (12). Castle indicts Sedgwick, "currently the most eloquent proponent of 'queer theory' in the academic world," for her exclusive focus on men (13, 66–91), and disagrees with such queer theorists as Judith Butler—"lesbian and gay scholars trained in Continental philosophy [among whom] it has recently become popular to contest, along deconstructionist lines, the very meaningfulness of terms such as *lesbian* or *gay* or *homosexual* or *coming out*" (13–14). Butler "goes farther in this direction than any other major queer theorist," according to Warner ("From Queer," 19), and is the queer theorist most closely associated with a postidentity stance. An excerpt from the first paragraph of Butler's "Imitation and Gender Insubordination," the lead essay in

Diana Fuss's *Inside/Out: Lesbian Theories, Gay Theories,* exemplifies queer theory's critique of identity categories:

> To write or speak *as a lesbian* appears a paradoxical appearance of this "I," one which feels neither true nor false. For it is a production, usually in response to a request, to come out or write in the name of an identity which, once produced, sometimes functions as a politically efficacious phantasm. I'm not at ease with "lesbian theories, gay theories," for as I've argued elsewhere,[15] identity categories tend to be instruments of regulatory regimes, whether as the normalizing categories of oppressive structures or as the rallying points for a liberatory contestation of that very oppression. This is not to say that I will not appear at political occasions under the sign of lesbian, but that I would like to have it permanently unclear what precisely that sign signifies. (13–14)

It is perhaps the usefulness of identity categories as "rallying point" that most concerns queer theory's lesbian and gay critics. Simon Watney, a prominent AIDS activist, asks, "If the rejection of identity politics is what 'queer theory' means . . . then who needs it?" (quoted in Warner, "From Queer," 19). Warner, who in at least two essays has taken up the job of defining and defending queer theory, responds that Watney has misread Butler (19). And, indeed, if in "Against Proper Objects" Butler does not promote identity politics, she certainly stands up for feminist analysis. Wiegman seems to shore up Watney, however, when she explains in *The Lesbian Postmodern* why that book's title is an unsolvable paradox:

> So what is the lesbian postmodern? The language itself constrains, acting too much like a category, too much like a name. . . . Quite rightly, or so it seems to me, the lesbian postmodern slips and shifts Monique Wittig's decidedly modernist proclamation: not just that the lesbian is "not a woman" but the lesbian is not—cannot continue to be—"the lesbian" either. (16)

Faderman views queer theory's postidentity stance "with some alarm,"

since the concept of gay identity was crucial to ["the older generation of scholars"], whether or not they believed that homosexuality was a social construct. Because we had defined a gay and lesbian identity (as fictive and limited as it may have been), and an identity politics that grew out of it, we were able to form our caucuses in professional organizations, agitate to teach gay and lesbian courses, and initiate gay and lesbian scholarship. We saw our construction of gay and lesbian identity as the sine qua non that would lead to our successes. ("Preface," 11)

Faderman partially seems drawn to queer theory, recognizing that the insights of "the older generation" have some limitations. But she reasserts the importance of the construction—not the unquestioning assumption—of identity politics as a crucial "political tool," harking back to the original Combahee River Collective formulation.

Yet a fair amount of queer theory's considerable intellectual fire power is aimed at its political and academic predecessors, particularly the many forms of lesbian-feminist and lesbian and gay theory, misread as naive expressions of essentialist identity politics. Teresa de Lauretis writes in the introduction to the "Queer Theory" issue of *differences* that the term *queer theory* is intended to "transgress and transcend . . . or at the very least problematize" the terms *gay* and *lesbian* (v). In that benchmark 1991 essay, de Lauretis envisions queer theory succeeding where Terry Castle sees it fail, arguing that queer theory must interrogate the silencing of lesbians under the rubric of "lesbian and gay," which implies but then "covers over" gender differences (v–vii). Since de Lauretis's declaration, a raft of lesbian and feminist critics have called the term *queer* a false generic that erases the existence of lesbians and the insights of feminism. It is worth noting that the activist group the Lesbian Avengers organized at least in part as a response to the male bias of and the invisibility of lesbians within Queer Nation. Julie Abraham devotes an entire *Village Voice* essay to exposing the male-centered canonicity of queer studies ("I Know"); Butler herself cautions against the "masculinist" and " 'gayocon' sensibility" that "has arrived in queer studies" via the relegation of gender (and thereby women) to feminism ("Against," 22). Farwell pens her study of lesbian narrative in the face of queer criticism's focus on "gay male literary themes" (*Heterosexual Plots*, 5), and Zimmerman poses the "urgent question . . . how to maintain the specificity of lesbian textuality, culture, identity, community—in short, existence—within the claim of generic gayness or queerness" (Zimmerman, " 'Confessions,' " 166). Although much prominent queer theory is written *by* women, it is most often not written *about* lesbians.

In "Queer Theory," de Lauretis expresses hope that queer theory can avoid the racism, as well as the sexism, of lesbian and gay studies: "Can our queerness act as an agency of social change, and our theory construct another discursive horizon, another way of living the racial and the sexual?" (x–xi).

Given the presumption that "critical dialog alone can provide a better under-standing of the specificity and partiality of our respective histories"—and given that the queer "critical dialog" has been almost exclusively among white academics—it is not surprising that queer theory, like so many other discourses, largely has failed to meaningfully address race and class. A num-ber of critics have commented on the racist and classist implications of queer theory, from Abraham noting that the field's focus on the canon "give[s] us again the Greeks, the English Renaissance, the American Renaissance, Oscar Wilde" ("I Know," 21) to Sagri Dhairyam's observation that " 'queer theory' comes increasingly to be reckoned with as a critical discourse, but concomi-tantly writes a queer whiteness over raced queerness; it domesticates race in its elaboration of sexual difference" ("Racing," 26). "I did read recently that there's a queer book coming out in which race is central," Beverly Guy-Shef-tall reports dryly. "But," she adds, "most of queer theory is very insensitive to race" ("New Directions," 31).[16] No wonder, then, that by her 1997 essay, "Fem/Les Scramble," de Lauretis voices her disappointment that some took the " 'gender and race neutrality' " of the term *queer theory* to be "a plus" (4).

When de Lauretis wrote in 1991 that "racial as well as gender differences are a crucial area of concern for queer theory" ("Queer Theory," xi), she was either inaccurately portraying the movement, stating a goal as an accom-plished deed, or applying the label *queer theorist* to a great many lesbians and gay men of color not usually considered (by themselves or others) as such. Some critics argue, like Harriet Malinowitz, that postmodernism "is of par-ticular importance to subjugated peoples" as it "puncture[s] the master cul-tural narratives that swallow up anarchic and infinitely complicated human difference" ("Lesbian Studies," 265). Others question, like Case,

> If queer . . . claims to cut across differences . . . and all the "antinormal" could be included in its embrace, and if it also claims multicultural repre-sentation at its base, then why do we read things like the following? Cher-ríe Moraga, the lesbian Chicana poet and dramatist writes:
>
> We discussed the limitations of "Queer Nation," whose leather-jack-eted, shaved-headed white radicals and accompanying anglo-centricity were an alien-nation to most lesbians and gay men of color (*The Last Gen-eration* 147). (Case, "Toward," 216–17)

While Malinowitz's analysis of modernist master narratives hits its mark, while the potential of queer theory may be there, it most often fails to deliver on the promise of providing a useful liberatory analysis of class and race.

Like de Lauretis's early defense of queer theory's activist applicability, Butler in her essay "Critically Queer" defends theorists "who have questioned the presentist assumptions in contemporary identity categories" against the charge that they are "depoliticizing theory." Butler, who writes some of the densest academic prose in the field of queer theory, asserts that "the critique of the queer subject is crucial to the continuing *democratization* of queer politics" because at its best queer theory both affirms "outness" and questions who can afford to be "out" in a sexist, racist, classist society. She writes, "The genealogical critique of the queer subject . . . constitutes a self-critical dimension within activism, a persistent reminder to take the time to consider the exclusionary force of one of activism's most treasured contemporary premises," that is, the importance of coming out ("Critically Queer," 227). Butler makes this statement without irony, failing to consider the problem of audience created by her own highly exclusionary prose. First published in the inaugural issue of the scholarly *GLQ: A Journal of Lesbian and Gay Studies,* the essay claimed a relatively small academic readership. To her credit, Butler recognizes the democratizing potential of the critique of the provisional term *queer,* noting that it could "initiate a resurgence of both feminist and anti-racist mobilization within lesbian and gay politics" (228–29), presumably by people who feel left out by the false generic, if in Butler's view historically temporary, term *queer.*

Like de Lauretis, in "Critically Queer" Butler sounded less convincing than optimistic that queer studies would interrogate the intersections of race and sexuality (229). The following year, in "Against Proper Objects," she productively took up the issue herself. She explains that the establishment of lesbian and gay studies (sexuality studies) as distinct from women's studies (gender studies) renders impossible or invisible "the various anti-racist positions developed within feminist frameworks for which gender is no more central than race, or for which gender is no more central than colonial positionality or class—the domains of socialist feminism, postcolonial feminism, Third World feminism" (15–16). Specifically, the polarization of queer theory and feminist theory "denies the emergence of a feminism specific to women of color in the U.S. who have sought to complicate the feminist framework to take account of relations of power that help to constitute and yet exceed gender, including race and racialization, as well as geopolitical positionality in colonial and postcolonial contexts" (17)—writers such as Norma Alarcón, Cherríe Moraga, Chandra Mohanty, Valerie Smith, Hortense Spillers, Gayatri Chakravorty Spivak, and others (5).

Wheras Butler's understanding of the limits of queer studies leads her to point to the "contingency" of the term *queer,* in *Tendencies* (1993) Sedgwick claims "that something about *queer* is inextinguishable" (xii). She asserts that "lesbian or gay" must stand at the "definitional center" of the term *queer* (8), but throughout her introductory chapter she uses *queer* to signify a diffuse "condition in which things 'can't be made to line up neatly together'" (Mohr, 24, "When Men," citing Sedgwick, *Tendencies,* 3, 6, 13). Sedgwick explains that she prefers the "experimental" and radically contextual/connotative word *queer* to the denotative " 'gay' and 'lesbian' [which] present themselves (however delusively) as objective, empirical categories governed by empirical rules of evidence (however contested)" (*Tendencies,* 9).

Sedgwick's parenthetical swipes at lesbian and gay meaning provide a good example of why Castle insists on naming her own work "lesbian" instead of "queer":

> I believe that we live in a world in which the word *lesbian* still makes sense, and that it is possible to use the word frequently, even lyrically, and still be understood. . . . And indeed, I still maintain, if in ordinary speech I say, "I am a lesbian," the meaning is instantly (even dangerously) clear: I am a woman whose primary emotional and erotic allegiance is to my own sex. (*Apparitional,* 14–15)

Castle insists on placing definition in the everyday world, in which shared, sometimes dangerous meanings can be painfully obvious.

One of the projects of queer theory, with its goal of "queering" all inquiry—its "aggressive impulse of generalization" (Warner, *Fear,* xxvi)—has been to come full circle and engage in "images of" criticism, with a twist. Rather than looking for instances of homophobia in straight literature, or isolated examples of putative queer heroes, some theorists argue that the canon of Western civilization is itself queer. As Abraham quips, "We were everywhere. Now we are the world" ("I Know," 20). In this respect, Castle is more in line with queer theory than she might like. (Castle does note, however, that "the canny reader will find the volatile traces" of Sedgwick's influence throughout *The Apparitional Lesbian* [13].) The project of *The Apparitional Lesbian* is to make visible the "ghosted" lesbian characters in Diderot, James, the opera, the *New Yorker*—indeed throughout modern Western civilization.

For Sedgwick the traditional literary canon provides infinite possibilities for queer studies, defined in part as "the process of making salient the homosocial, homosexual, and homophobic strains and torsions in the already existing master-canon" (*Epistemology,* 51). While feminist critics had to muster a separate female canon to answer the question "Where is your Shakespeare?" queer scholars can point to the pervasively queer (if male) character of the traditional canon.

> Has there ever been a gay Socrates?
> Has there ever been a gay Shakespeare?
> Has there ever been a gay Proust?
> Does the Pope wear a dress? If these questions startle, it is not least as tautologies. A short answer, though a very incomplete one, might be that not only have there been a gay Socrates, Shakespeare, and Proust but that their names are Socrates, Shakespeare, Proust. (Sedgwick, *Epistemology*, 52)

Lesbian feminists addressed the question imaginatively, if less concretely, on a poster for the Third Annual Lesbian Writers Conference in Chicago (1976), which reads, "And the men ask, 'Where is your Shakespeare?' She was a Lesbian, and you burned her books." Sedgwick's approach not only resurrects queer heroes but also asserts that the canon can never "be treated as the repository of reassuring 'traditional' truths that could be made matter for any settled consolidation or congratulation" (*Epistemology*, 54).

In "Fear of a Queer Planet," Michael Warner writes that he sees a parallel between Sedgwick's queer work (around 1991) and earlier feminist criticism (around 1981), which "open[ed] up when feminists began treating gender more and more as a primary category for understanding problems that did not initially look gender-specific" (xiv). Warner is one of the only queer theorists who speaks of a connection between earlier lesbian or feminist theory and queer theory—but he confuses history at times, even when he is trying to honor it. The subtitle of his essay, "From Queer to Eternity: An Army of Theorists Cannot Fail," is a clear play on the 1970s slogan "An Army of Lovers Cannot Fail." Warner appears eager to give credit where credit is due, but he does not seem to know what the term *lesbian feminist* means. He calls Monique Wittig, Luce Irigaray, Julia Kristeva, Teresa de Lauretis, Judith Mayne, Sue-Ellen Case, Judith Roof, Judith Butler, and Diana Fuss—with the exception of Wittig, all academic poststructuralist theorists—"this tradition of lesbian feminism," because they are "women who write about women" ("From Queer," 18). On the other hand, Warner does acknowledge that many lesbian scholars (and here he means lesbian feminists) have worked "without recognition or reward for years—some as independent scholars, others as academics who often suffered in their careers for doing lesbian work—only to see a younger generation cashing in for having the same interests" ("From Queer," 18). Amid the differences Warner finds a remarkable "continuity of interests" between the republished gay liberation anthology *Out of the Closets* (1992) and the *differences* "Queer Theory" issue (1991): interest in racial difference, how power relationships shape sexuality, the interdependence of feminist and gay resistance, and a "sense of alienation from most available ways of affirming identity" ("From Queer," 18–19).

Others who have pointed out queer theory's debt to feminism and gay liberation—such as Abraham, Lisa Duggan, Faderman, Rosemary Hennessy, Jeffreys, and Zimmerman—have been more critical of queer theory than Warner. Margaret Homans sees queer theory as a direct descendant of feminist criticism:

> 1970s feminist criticism made possible the lively discussion of the construction of gender going on nowadays, and even the work going on under the rubric of queer theory, with its occasional rejection of gender as a useful category of analysis. We could not be talking about gender or sexuality in any of the ways we do now if [it] weren't for the feminist reformation of literary history. (Feminist Criticism, 3–4)

Homans calls queer theory one of the "new fields of inquiry that feminist literary history has vanished into" (8).

Situated within the academy—which serves as both audience and source of legitimation—queer theory seems to have little use for activist movements preceding ACT-UP and Queer Nation that helped create the social space for antihomophobic academic work. A handful of critics who are not typically associated with lesbian feminism—including Judith Halberstam, Harriet Malinowitz, and Tania Modleski—have published essays that in various ways include lesbian feminism as part of queer theory's genealogy (Halberstam, "Queering," 260–61; Malinowitz, "Lesbian Studies," 268; Modleski, "White Negress," 79). But Zimmerman accurately assessed the lay of the land, speaking on the same MLA panel as Homans in 1994: "One could conclude from contemporary writing [i.e., queer theory] that lesbian theory emerged full-grown from the head of Lacan or Foucault around 1989. The depth and richness of lesbian criticism and theory from the early 1970s on is being ignored and lost" ("History," 2).

The phenomenon is not without precedent, of course. Lesbian feminists in the 1970s repudiated the essentialist position of both homophile activists and butch-femme bar culture (which were often at odds with each other in the 1950s and sixties), but in the 1980s and nineties historians have argued persuasively that lesbian and gay culture in the 1950s enabled the lesbian-feminist and gay liberation movements to arise and flourish.[17] Although Margaret Cruikshank explains in *The Gay and Lesbian Liberation Movement* that "lesbian feminism originated in the women's movement rather than in the homophile movement" (167), she states that Daughters of Bilitis, the first lesbian organization in the United States (founded in 1955), "laid the ground-work for lesbian feminism of the next decade" (148).

Historian John D'Emilio explains that in the 1970s

> young gay radicals exhibited as little respect toward the homophile move-ment as they did toward the institutions of American society. They scorned its moderation and reformist politics. . . . Many of the shifts that occurred in [the 1970s] were due to the weakening of traditional centers of power caused by the protest movements of the 1960s, but the relative ease with which gay liberationists accumulated victories can only be explained by the persistent, plodding work of the activists who preceded them. The homophile movement deserves kinder treatment than it has received. The popular wisdom of gay liberation needs to be reevaluated. (D'Emilio, *Sexual Politics*, 240)

Audience and the Problem of "Citationality"

I am arguing that the "popular wisdom" of queer theory "needs to be reeval-uated," in part because queer theory suffers from an apparent problem of what Butler (following Derrida) in a different context has called "citational-ity" (*Bodies*, 13). In "Critically Queer," Butler explains that "citation of a prior, authoritative set of practices" or discourse gives "binding power" to a performative speech act (227, 225). (For example, a judge's verdict relies on citation of socially sanctioned legal precedent.) Queer theory as it is usually practiced indeed "accumulates the force of authority" (Butler, *Bodies*, 227) from its choice of academic citations.

In Butler's *Bodies That Matter*, in which "Critically Queer" is reprinted, citations to works by people of color occur almost exclusively in chapters specifically devoted to people of color and/or the construct of race. While Butler's attention to an African American writer (Nella Larsen, in chapter 6) and a film about African American drag queens (*Paris Is Burning*, produced and directed by white lesbian filmmaker Jennie Livingston, in chapter 4) is laudable, if unusual, for queer theory, her citational practice appears oddly segregationist—an apt metaphor, since the only people of color she discusses are African American. Judith Roof notes a similar phenomenon in predominantly white, heterosexual feminist anthologies of literary criticism published in the 1980s, in which black and lesbian function as "the excess that disrupts the disrupters, but they also . . . are kept separate but equal" (*Lure*, 224). Do lesbian and gay men of color contribute nothing historically or presently to queer theory itself, as their absence as citational reference points in "Critically Queer" implies? Do white queers not have race?

Butler anticipates this sort of criticism in her introduction, and seeks to deflect it by maintaining that, as the saying goes, you can't please all of the people all of the time:

> On the one hand, any analysis which foregrounds one vector of power over another will doubtless become vulnerable to criticisms that it not only ignores or devalues the others, but that its own constructions depend on the exclusion of the others in order to proceed. On the other hand, any analysis which pretends to be able to encompass every vector of power runs the risk of a certain epistemological imperialism which consists in the presupposition that any given writer might fully stand for and explain the complexities of contemporary power. (*Bodies*, 18–19)

Thus, Butler circumnavigates the "simultaneous nature of . . . oppression" described in 1977 by the Combahee River Collective, and by many others since. Butler points out that she does pursue "the political problematic of operating within the complexities of power" in two chapters and part of a third (*Bodies*, 19). The number of chapters is not the issue here but rather the relegation of expertise according to a sort of identity politics that Butler and other constructivist queer theorists disdain. Ultimately, Butler defends herself with the idea that others will take up where she left off—or out:

> Taking the heterosexual matrix or heterosexual hegemony as a point of departure will run the risk of narrowness, but it will run it in order, finally, to cede its apparent priority and autonomy as a form of power. This will happen within the text, but perhaps most successfully in its various appropriations. Indeed, it seems to me that one writes into a field of writing that is invariably and promisingly larger and less masterable than the one over which one maintains a provisional authority, and that the unanticipated reappropriations of a given work in areas for which it was never consciously intended are some of the most useful. (19)

To discuss topics ranging from film to literature to queer theory itself, in *Bodies That Matter* Butler lines up a dazzling series of theoretical heavy hitters: Aristotle, Nietszche, Foucault, Plato, Irigaray, Freud, Žižek, Spivak, Althusser, Derrida, and Lacan. With such impressive academic credentials, it is small wonder that queer theory, not lesbian feminism, gained the power position "around 1991." Lesbian feminists in the 1970s attempted to rid their communities of the taint of patriarchy; queer theory embraces some of its most prominent academic spokesmen (and token women), if for stated antiestablishment ends.

Is exclusion the by-product of institutional acceptance, as Gallop argues in the case of feminist theory? Or is mainstreaming a means to excluding nonacademically acceptable voices, as Christian would have it? Without lesbian feminism, women-of-color feminism, and gay liberation (among other movements) there would be no "free spaces" for queer theory.[18] Yet, Butler's "Against Proper Objects" notwithstanding, queer theory often leaves out recognition of lesbian-feminist/working-class/women-of-color forerunners and contemporaries. Phelan's work on "postmodern lesbian politics," on the other hand, is a good example of academic theory that acknowledges its affinity with the work of lesbian feminists, lesbians of color, *and* queer theorists— proof positive that a provocative, sophisticated, and scholarly book does not need to ignore the diversity of lesbian intellectual and activist history.

While queer theory is often perceived and presented as the avant-garde, an intertextual historical reading illuminates similarities between queer theory and other lesbian/gay movements and genres. Frequently the message of queer theory (indeed, of much poststructuralist theory) is not as new as it appears to be in its academic context. What is often different is the intended audience: then, a marginalized activist readership, now, an academic one steeped in the high theoretical traditions of Continental philosophy. One reason for the difference is that some of the earlier activist writers were creating the academic fields that later writers took for granted. Often lacking the privilege of academic positions, activist writers did not (and many still do not) have any stake in pleasing an academic readership. This is not to say that there are no real disagreements among various lesbian, gay, and queer thinkers but rather to suggest that many of the arguments have been around for a long time, like the social-constructionist/essentialist argument lesbian feminists had with "gay women" in the late sixties and early seventies.

A difference of language usually accompanies the difference in perceived audience for queer and lesbian-feminist theories. Faderman contends that the poststructuralist jargon of Queer Theory . . . ignores and even cuts out much of the audience that needs to be served by gay and lesbian studies—undergraduate students, non-academic gays and lesbians, and the non-academic world in general, whose prejudices and ignorance about homosexuality need to continue to be challenged in language that addresses them clearly." ("Preface," 12).

Lisa Duggan noted the tendency of presenters at the Rutgers Lesbian/Gay Studies conference in 1991 to "reference Lacan, Foucault, and Bourdieu while neglecting (relatively) the contributions of the activist writers, independent scholars, and cultural producers who created the conditions for theoretical commentary. . . . Different languages and audiences bring very diverse (read: 'unequal') access to resources and rewards" (27). Or, as Papusa Molina put it at the 1995 National Women's Studies Association conference lesbian caucus meeting, "It's a class issue."[19] These criticisms mirror Parker and Grahn's concerns with accessible language—in Parker's words, "to put the poetry in the language that we speak," a rejection of academic and traditional poetic language that Parker knew would "get [her] in trouble" with critics outside the activist women's movement (Rushin, "Pat Parker," 28). Indeed, Rich's evocation of "a common language" and "a whole new poetry" got her in trouble aplenty.

In her essay "A Manifesto for Cyborgs," Donna Haraway argues for the necessity of political coalition as analogous to science fiction "cybernetic organism[s] . . . creatures simultaneously animal and machine" (191). Haraway, a postmodern critic who like Phelan cites her sources, draws on writings about coalition politics by lesbian and straight women of color, including works by Chela Sandoval, Trinh T. Minh-ha, and Bernice Johnson Reagon. Of the three, whom Haraway cites together in one footnote, Reagon's "Coalition Politics: Turning the Century" is the farthest removed from the academy; the essay is the transcript of a talk presented in more or less conversational language at a women's (predominantly lesbian-feminist) music festival. Sandoval and Trinh write from and into an academic context.

Both Haraway and Reagon situate the necessity for feminist, antiracist, antiheterosexist coalition in a technologically complex world. Haraway sees the identity category "women of color" as emblematic of postmodern cyborg consciousness, built on what Sandoval calls "oppositional consciousness" and Haraway defines as "a kind of postmodernist identity [constructed] of otherness, difference, and specificity" ("Manifesto," 197). All of us, according to Haraway, must embrace "permanently partial identities" (196) in a postmodern world in which we are all "cybernetic organisms" plugged into the political and technological "integrated circuit," a construct and a reality that can either destroy us or work for us. Haraway discusses the fragmentation of feminism along identity lines and the possibilities for reunification through coalition:

> It has become difficult to name one's feminism by a single adjective—or even to insist in every circumstance upon the noun. Consciousness of exclusion through naming is acute. Identities seem contradictory, partial, and strategic. . . . Painful fragmentation among feminists (not to mention among women) along every possible fault line has made the concept of woman elusive, an excuse for the matrix of women's dominations of each other. . . . The recent history for much of the U.S. Left and the [*sic*] U.S. feminism has been a response to this kind of crisis by endless splitting and searches for a new essential unity. But there has also been a growing recognition of another response through coalition—affinity, not identity. ("Manifesto," 196–97)

Reagon warns her women-only, mostly white audience that in the age of communications technology "we've pretty much come to the end of a time when you can have a space that is 'yours only.' . . . There is no hiding place. There is nowhere you can go and only be with people who are like you. It's over. Give it up" ("Coalition," 357). Reagon distinguishes between affinity based on identity—the periodically necessary resting place she calls "home"—and coalition based on shared goals: "You don't go into coalition because you just *like* it. The only reason you would consider trying to team up with somebody who could possibly kill you, is because that's the only way you can figure you can stay alive" ("Coalition," 356–57). Reagon's "home" is the space of identity-through-similarity that Haraway considers obsolete in a cyborgian, coalitional world.

Haraway's analysis of the breakdown of Aristotelian hierarchical dualism ("Manifesto," 205) echoes Reagon's primary admonition:

> It is very important not to confuse them—home and coalition. . . . The women's movement has perpetuated a myth that there is some common experience that comes just cause you're women. . . . If you're the same kind of women like the folk in that little barred room [marked "women only"], it works. But as soon as some other folk check the definition of "women" that's in the dictionary . . . they decide that they can come because they

are women, but when they do, they don't see or hear nothing that is like them. Then they charge, "This ain't no women's thing!" . . . And you try to figure out what happened to your wonderful barred room. It comes from taking a word like "women" and using it as a code [for "woman-iden-tified" or "lesbian feminist"]. ("Coalition," 360)

According to Haraway, "the self feminists must code" is the cyborg, a "dis-assembled and reassembled, postmodern collective and personal self" plugged into the political "integrated circuit" of progressive coalition ("Man-ifesto," 205). Reagon prefigures the coalitional cyborg with a simple expla-nation of "why we have to have coalitions. Cause I ain't gonna let you live unless you let me live. Now there's danger in that, but there's also the possi-bility that we can both live—if you can stand it" ("Coalition," 365). Any brief comparison between two long works is of course reductive, but Reagon's and Haraway's similar content and distinct language is so striking as to be worth comparison. Haraway addresses the academy; Reagon (although the text of her speech has made its way into some women's studies classrooms) addresses lesbian-feminist activists gathered at a separatist cultural event. The audi-ences may overlap, but not by much.

As a component of institutional acceptance, academic lesbian (and gay) theory has shifted away from its origins, and away from any attempt to gain a mass movement audience. As the location, language, and audience shift, the past is often disregarded, nonacademic voices are marginalized, and read-ership shrinks to a small, highly educated group. Although queer theorists cannot—and should not—be required to write in the vernacular of Reagon or others, something is awry when queer theory both appropriates and erases earlier lesbian and gay theory and political literature. One consequence, for example, is the claim that queer theorists invented the notion of the lesbian (or queer) as significant because she disrupts gender norms, when the idea of lesbian as metaphor is a staple of 1970s activist thought (Zimmerman, "Les-bians," 12; Farwell, *Heterosexual Plots*, 8). Farwell comes right out and accuses queer theory of appropriating the work of Audre Lorde, particularly *Zami*, by claiming it as postmodern rather than exploring how queer theory is indebted to the work of a black lesbian feminist (*Heterosexual Plots*, 94).[20] Phelan recognizes the potential for co-optation of Anzaldúa's work and cau-tions against it: "Appropriating *mestizaje* does not serve to build alliances; it serves to convince mestizas that white women don't get it, that white women are blind to their own privilege and oblivious to the force of history. Our alliances cannot be built by grafting ourselves onto others' identities"

(*Getting Specific*, 72). Faderman goes as far as saying that queer theorists "sometimes seem to be reinventing the theoretical wheel, painting it in mauve and fuchsia, then passing it off as entirely original" ("Afterword," 225).

In *The Highest Apple* Judy Grahn notes several examples of lesbian-feminist poets "surfac[ing] with the key words and phrases that later became full-blown movement issues and obsessions" (71), including "compulsory heterosexuality"—a term introduced by Adrienne Rich in 1980 and used without citation by Butler in 1993 (*Bodies*, 18). Perhaps "compulsory heterosexuality" had entered the queer public domain by then, but it is significant that Butler's only citations to Rich in *Bodies That Matter* refer to an essay about Willa Cather, reinforcing a split between lesbian literature (Rich as poet) and lesbian theory (Butler as theorist) that is belied by lesbian history. Lesbian-feminist poets appear to be nowhere—and everywhere—in queer theory; to paraphrase Homans, lesbian-feminist literature and theory have vanished into queer theory.

Queer theory currently claims the limited space the academy is willing to cede to the sexually marginalized and is struggling with its own status as authority figure. It is not the existence of queer theory but rather its hegemony within the academic position of celebrity other to which its lesbian and gay critics object. Berlant and Warner caution against making "one corpus of work (often Eve Sedgwick's or Judith Butler's) . . . a metonym for queer theory or queer culture building itself, exemplary either for good or for bad" ("What Does," 345). The fact remains that Sedgwick, Butler, and their followers do occupy star positions "on the academic stage" (Berlant and Warner, 348), possessing "the authority of a critical intellectualism capable of provoking yet legislating what is dangerous in philosophical thought" (Dhairyam, "Racing," 29). "Academia encourages hegemony," as Faderman argues, and

> Queer Studies seems at present to have wrested the hegemonic mantle from gay and lesbian studies because it comes closer to employing the language and perspective of poststructuralism that has currency in the academy. Therefore, it is likely that graduate students with an interest in the discipline will feel constrained to do Queer Theory rather than any other approach to gay and lesbian studies. ("Preface," 12)

As the marginal moves to the center, dissident voices are once again suppressed. By this I mean not only lesbian feminism, or "lesbian and gay studies," but also the variety of "non-theorists"—working-class/lesbians of color, poets, community organizers—whose presence disrupts both the rise to institutional power and the false dichotomy queer/lesbian-feminist that functions as definitional to queer theory and politics. Farwell points out the irony in a postmodern criticism seeing itself as part of "a grand . . . narrative of liberation that obscures lesbian-feminist thought" (*Heterosexual Plots*, 107); a simple deconstruction exposes a similar irony in positing only two, dramatically opposed, possibilities for lesbian theory.

Queer theorists seem uncomfortable with the move from being disrupters (Roof, *Lure*, 224) of "normal business in the academy" (Warner, "From Queer," 18) to their "'virtual deification'" (Watney on Butler, in Warner, "From Queer," 19). Butler attempts to shed the mantle of academic power that has been bestowed upon her:

> I do not understand the notion of "theory," and am hardly interested in being cast as its defender, much less in being signified as part of an elite gay/lesbian theory crowd that seeks to establish the legitimacy and domes-tication of gay/lesbian studies within the academy. Is there a pregiven dis-tinction between theory, politics, culture, media? How do those divisions operate to quell a certain intertextual writing that might well generate wholly different epistemic maps? (Butler, "Imitation," 14)

But it should be no surprise that choosing to cite primarily theorists with a great deal of institutional currency lands queer theory squarely within the academic "elite."

The problem, then, is how to chart an effective middle ground for les-bian/gay/queer studies. As Lisa Duggan asks, "How can we criticize our infant field of study without engaging in mindless theory bashing and anti-intellectual posturing, or positing a moral universe in which the academy is always bad and the community (whatever that is) by definition good?" ("Scholars," 27). Duggan proposes the sort of confluence of activist and aca-demic, queer and lesbian-feminist, "high" and "low" theory that *Identity Poetics* attempts to model, an interdisciplinary, multi-issue approach that looks responsibly to the past, even as it is "radically anticipatory" (Berlant and Warner, "What Does," 344) of a different world and academic order. This is largely a problem of citation, of widening one's field of vision to acknowledge a variety of perspectives without co-opting or silencing them in the name of a "monolithic and all-subsuming paradigm [that] denies differ-ence except as it can be supportive, aligned with the pattern" (Roof, *Lure*, 226). As long ago as 1994 Butler herself proposed that

Perhaps the time has arrived to encourage the kinds of conversations that resist the urge to stake territorial claims through the reduction or caricature of the positions from which they are differentiated. . . . There is more to learn from upsetting such grounds, reversing the exclusions by which they are instated, and resisting the institutional domestication of queer thinking. For normalizing the queer would be, after all, its sad finish. ("Against," 22)

In "The Theoretical Subject(s) of *This Bridge Called My Back* and Anglo-American Feminism," Norma Alarcón argues that "Anglo-American feminist theory . . . takes for granted the linguistic status which founds subjectivity. In this way it appropriates woman/women for itself" (363). In other words, by privileging an academic discourse that is more readily accessible to white, middle-class women than to working-class/women of color (because in the United States white, middle-class women are more likely to go to college and to earn advanced degrees), feminist theory can simultaneously make reference to and exclude the words of many women who do not fit the Enlightenment mold of the "autonomous, self-conscious" and highly educated "individual" (Alarcón, "Theoretical Subjects," 363). Alarcón argues that the citation of "other" women's voices is often an appropriation of them in the service of an essentially white, middle-class, gender-standpoint epistemology. She concludes that radical works by lesbian and straight women of color have resulted in merely "cosmetic" changes in Anglo-American feminism ("Theoretical Subjects," 357).

Erin Carlston sees a somewhat different dynamic at work in the uses of Audre Lorde's "biomythography" *Zami,* which she views as "an early, important attempt to articulate a politics of location in a work of fiction," similar to but "rather more subtle than Reagon's 'Coalition Politics,'" particularly in its treatment of identity" ("*Zami,*" 226). Carlston explains that in *Zami* Lorde portrays identity as "positionality," that is, "identity as an unstable construct, constantly (re)produced both by and within the social matrix, and by the subject's conscious creation of her self." Carlston notes that "in this regard, Lorde prefigures more recent theoretical work by writers like Chandra Mohanty, Gayatri Spivak, and Trinh Minh-ha," three women of color whose work has been influential in poststructuralist feminist criticism (Carlston, "*Zami,*" 226).

Carlston invokes critic Linda Alcoff to explain what she perceives to be a weak point in Lorde's presentation of identity, the essentializing of her lesbianism. Carlston implies Lorde's naïveté relative to Alcoff's superior theoretical insight: "It could be argued that Lorde is less persuasive when she is most essentialist, namely, in her treatment of female sexuality, which she describes, as Alcoff would say, as a 'place where meaning can be discovered'" ("*Zami,*" 234). In a footnote the careful reader discovers that Carlston finds in Alcoff a "cogent analysis . . . of the kind of strategies Lorde deploys in *Zami*" ("*Zami,*" 236*n3*). Carlston quotes Alcoff at length, revealing that the idea of "positionality" comes from Alcoff's 1988 essay, "Cultural Feminist Versus Post-Structuralism: The Identity Crisis in Feminist Theory." In this context, Alcoff's essay may be viewed, at least in part, as a theoreticization of the ideas Lorde (and others) had put forth by 1984. Elsewhere, Carlston's description of *Zami*'s politics of location is reminiscent of Haraway's postmodern cyborg: "The experience of being marginalized within every group with which she identifies becomes a constant in Audre's story, until she finally claims and transforms that experience as the basis of her politics of location" (Carlston, "*Zami,*" 231).

Perhaps the influence of women of color on Anglo-American feminism is not as superficial as Alarcón suggests. Alarcón clearly illustrates that Anglo-American gender-standpoint feminism acknowledges women of color only to "proceed to negate that difference by subsuming women of color into the unitary category of woman/women" ("Theoretical Subjects," 358). But what of postmodern feminist theory, and perhaps especially that postmodern feminist (or queer) theory that rarely cites women of color at all? Has lesbian-feminist/working-class/lesbian of color theory "vanished into" queer theory? A more thorough historical and intertextual reading of contemporary theory might reveal that marginalized activist writings are foundational to many of postmodern feminist and queer theory's most powerful ideas. In the case of lesbian/gay/queer studies, such an undertaking could begin to heal the antagonisms between factions by illustrating the relationships between the works of writers as diverse as Grahn, Parker, Lorde, Rich, Anzaldúa, Butler, Sedgwick, and de Lauretis.

"Scratching the Surface:" Exposing the Intertext

Identity Poetics attempts to contextualize queer theory, and both benefit from the same concatenation of historical, political, literary, and theoretical sources, if to differing degrees of influence. In calling for an expanded citationality, I rely particularly on the literary critical concept of "intertextuality" to illustrate the connections between queer theory and writing by working-class/lesbian-feminist/women of color. Introduced by M. M. Bakhtin (and later employed influentially by Julia Kristeva [1969], Roland Barthes [1977], and Michael Riffaterre [1984]), intertextuality refers to "the sum of knowledge that makes it possible for texts to have meaning" (Culler, *Structuralist Poetics*, 104, paraphrasing Kristeva). "Every text takes shape as a mosaic of citations, every text is the absorption and transformation of other texts" (Kristeva 146, cited in Culler, *Structuralist Poetics*, 139). In short, intertextuality is "the way any text refers to others" (de Beaugrande, *Critical*, 272), thereby creating meaning for the reader who is on some level aware of the references being made (Suleiman, *Subversive*, 218n7). *Text,* in the sense it is used here, refers not only to books and essays but to any type of discourse or locus of meaning. Thus Linda Hutcheon discusses "history as intertextual" (*Poetics,* 142), Thaïs Morgan writes that "*culture* itself . . . *is radically intertextual*" ("Space," 246), and so forth. Critics allow that extraliterary discourse as intertext informs lesbian literature.[21] When read against contemporary poststructuralist lesbian/queer theory, the political content of the poetry under study here suggests that the opposite is also true. Literature can provide an intertext for theory, as surely as social commentary, historical circumstance, and "culture" may inform literature. Further, theories—even political ideologies themselves—can be understood intertextually.

If one takes seriously Hutcheon's proposition of "history as intertext" (*Poetics,* 142), or Morgan's "*culture* itself [as] *radically intertextual*" ("Space," 246), then it is possible to see in the succession of civil rights movements since the 1960s the allusion, repetition, even (at worst) parody that mark intertextual interplay. Certainly, the rhetoric of contemporary civil rights movements has been (at times quite consciously) intertextual: from Indian Nation to Lesbian Nation, "U.S. out of Vietnam" to "U.S. out of my uterus." Contemporary queer theory and politics are no less historically influenced and intertextually informed. The controversial adoption of the label *queer* (from Lesbian Nation to Queer Nation, from the concept of the lesbian continuum to queer) is one among many examples.

Lesbian feminism provides an intertext for queer theory in a variety of ways—on a broad conceptual level in some cases, in more detailed allusions in others. Butler's analysis of "gender performativity" and drag—which she accomplishes via deconstruction, psychoanalytic theory, and philosophy—is not the first lesbian analysis of the production of gender through socially enforced heterosexuality. Her theory resonates with lesbian-feminist analyses of feminine "drag" as symptomatic of patriarchy, with the lesbian-feminist ideal of gender subversion through androgynous behavior and appearance,

and not least with Rich's notion of compulsory heterosexuality (itself intertextual with the work of lesbian-feminist theorist Charlotte Bunch, among
others). Butler also echoes Grahn's descriptions in *Another Mother Tongue* of
butch and femme lesbians playing with gender in the 1950s (Grahn, *Another*,
31, 156, 221, 222). Grahn describes the rituals of the working-class lesbian
gender performance called "butch" and analyzes its significance:

> Our point was not to be men; our point was to be butch and get away with
> it. We always kept something back: a high-pitched voice, a slant of the
> head, or a limpness of hand gestures, something that was clearly labeled
> female. I believe our statement was "Here is another way of being a
> woman," not "Here is a woman trying to be taken for a man." (31)

Essays by the French lesbian-feminist writer Monique Wittig resonate in
works by both Butler and Sedgwick. Echoing Simone de Beauvoir, Wittig
wrote in 1981 that "one is not born a woman" but becomes one, because gender categories are "political and economic categories not eternal ones" (Wittig, *Straight Mind*, 15). Butler writes that "ontology is . . . not a foundation,
but a normative injunction" (*Gender Trouble*, 148). Wittig's analysis of how
one "becomes" one's gender differs from Butler's, but the two theorists' radical constructionist stances are similar. Lesbians, according to Wittig, refuse
to become "women" in that "the refusal to become (or to remain) heterosexual always meant to refuse to become a man or a woman, consciously or not"
(*Straight Mind*, 13). In her famous formulation, "Lesbians are not women,"
because women are defined in relationship to men; gender is socially constructed and performed, and can be politically deconstructed—this is what
"lesbian society accomplishes practically" and "materialist analysis," that is,
theory, "does by reasoning" (Wittig, *Straight Mind*, 32, 9). In "The Point of
View: Universal or Particular" (1983) and "The Mark of Gender" (1986),
Wittig employs the concept of a "minority" (and therefore ghettoizing) vs. a
"universal" lesbian/gay point of view; in the introduction to *Epistemology of
the Closet*, Sedgwick acknowledges the necessary existence of both "minority-
model and universalist-model" political strategies. Like Wittig, Sedgwick
"privilege[s] constructivist over essentialist, universalizing over minoritizing"; but when she privileges "gender-transitive over gender-separatist
understandings of sexual choice," Sedgwick parts company with Wittig
(*Epistemology*, 13).[22]

Malinowitz reports that many lesbian feminists see allegedly queer-theo-
retical preoccupations with

analyzing decentered subjectivity, critiquing the ways hegemonic structures reproduce themselves, and examining the ways that the notion of difference organizes society and epistemology [as] some of the most basic concerns that have guided their own work. And in truth, contemporary queer theory, though appearing to some as an extraterrestrial landing and threatening to wreak perverse acts on an undefended populace, *does* count feminism as a substantial part of its mixed lineage. ("Lesbian," 265)

Faderman points to several similarities between lesbian-feminist and queer thought: androgyny as a type of "gender fuck," feminist formulations of gender as socially constructed, a sort of early performance theory, an inclusive theoretical conception of women, opposition to sexual "puritanism through a valorization of nonmonogamy" ("Afterword," 222–24). Zimmerman notes the decades-long tradition of defining lesbian as disrupter of the heterosexist order, similarities between the early nineties poststructuralist work of Elizabeth Meese and the seventies lesbian-feminist work of Rich, Bunch, and Marilyn Frye, and, in what she terms her "old-fashioned way," relates the Lacanian concept of phallogocentrism to "what feminists have always called 'patriarchy' " (Zimmerman, "Lesbians," 5). Perhaps it is not such a stretch, then, to speculate with Dana Heller that "feminism was queer studies before queer studies was queer studies, although feminism still remains to be productively expanded by lesbian, gay, and queer studies" (*Cross Purposes*, 11).

Theory is shaped by which questions are asked, which in turn is often shaped by which texts one reads. Phelan points out that for white feminists in the seventies "[Shulamith] Firestone was the theorist, the author cited in discussions of radical feminism. She had to be dealt with in white women's education in feminism" (*Getting Specific*, 28). In the mid eighties the authors were Audre Lorde, Gloria Anzaldúa, Adrienne Rich, the texts *Sister Outsider* and *This Bridge Called My Back*. And in the nineties they were Butler's *Gender Trouble* and Sedgwick's *Epistemology of the Closet*. Which texts will we read or teach in the coming decades? To return to Holland's question, *how* will we employ them? The answers to these questions, of course, have a great deal to do with who the "we" of lesbian theory will be. The cross-genre writings of working-class/lesbians of color must be central to theorizing in order to overcome the debate which is not one and to build lesbian theories that are coalitional, dynamic, and broadly influential in both academic and activist spheres.

A rigorous intertextual reading, a more explicit, accountable practice of citationality, could go far in creating the sort of textual and activist alliances that are so urgently needed but so rarely forged. "Lesbian, gay, and queer studies" must open up to working-class/lesbians of color instead of continuing to either swallow them up or ignore them (or both, since one sometimes looks like the other). Who knows what fascinating and productive turns theoretical discussions would take then? One thing is clear: the debates, publications, conferences, and departments would not look the same as they do now, and that's a positive step out of an old exclusionary rut.

Afterward, the Dy$_2$ke March: June 24, 2000, San Francisco

There we were on the eve of Gay Pride, ten or twenty (the organizers said fifty) thousand "dykes" gathered in Dolores Park for one of the largest lesbian-separatist events this side of the Michigan Womyn's Music Festival in its heyday. No one cried "essentialist," though, or dismissed the event as hopelessly "lesbian-feminist." No one seemed to mind. It was Dy$_2$ke, San Francisco's eighth annual Dyke March, and the folks who might have leveled those charges in another arena seemed to be everywhere, enjoying themselves, even running the show. A more vibrant mass example of contemporary identity poetics I have never seen.

Walking up 18th Street to the park, the first seeming anachronism I noticed was the presence of neon-bright Queer Nation-style stickers on some young women's jeans. They were everywhere. What was odd, and wonderful, was the range of seventies, eighties, nineties, and Y2K slogans on them. From the contemporary—*Digital Queer, Tranny Dyke*—to the sex wars—*Leather Dyke*—to some old chestnuts I would never have imagined seeing on those orange and magenta rectangles: *Vagitarian, Butch on the Streets Femme on the Sheets, Clean and Sober Dyke, A Lesbian a Day Keeps the Patriarchy at Bay*. Even, and perhaps of course, *Woman-Loving Woman* and, simply, *Sappho*. Things appeared to be coming full circle.

The sound system was decked with posters picturing a female figure dancing on a casket beneath the caption "Death to the Patriarchy." Had I entered the twilight zone?

Rallying the assembled masses for the march, an enthusiastic young woman announced that this was a march for women only. A separatist event, in the year 2000? Of course, "dyke" and "woman" look somewhat different in San Francisco in 2000 than, say, in Michigan twenty years ago, but nevertheless. And that's what made Dy$_2$ke both queer and lesbian feminist.

A lesbian march in 1975 would have been largely ignored by gay men. In 2000, it inspired banners hung from apartment windows: *We Love the Daughters of Sappho. You Go Girl.* The building that won the most enthusiastic response from the marchers sported the camp slogans *Leave It to Beaver, Muff Is Enuf,* and *I Love Lezi.*

When the announcer proudly proclaimed that the Dyke March, unlike the official march, had no corporate sponsors and "no titty policy," something was clearly up. For one thing, this march was staking a claim to a certain kind of radical nonassimilationist politics. The "titty policy" comment led to some confusion among my group of friends. One heard it as an anti-tranny comment (perhaps my friend had seen the woman carrying the angry sign reading, "This Ain't No Faux-Gina"); another heard it as a pro-tranny comment (i.e., no titties required). It turned out to mean that the marchers weren't going to police who took their shirts off.

Plenty of women did. But unlike marches in years past, when we took our shirts off as a protest against gender inequality (if men can do it, we should be able to), this breast baring, at least for some, was mainly sexual. The Sex Wars had happened, and sex clearly had won. As we marched through the Mission District, women in their apartment windows took off their shirts and shimmied for the delighted crowd—a politicized, hooting and hollering ooze of celebratory sexuality. (The free sex show caused some of my friends in their forties and fifties to ask each other with quizzical looks, "This is what we fought for?" but they were enjoying themselves too.) When we reached our destination, Market and 17th Streets in the Castro, and a young woman danced a striptease on a floodlit billboard, well, we weren't in Kansas anymore, Toto.

And yet.

There were NOW "Lesbian Rights" signs. There was a group marching behind a "Women of Color Unite" banner. But the identity politics the banner signified were transformed by the exuberant chaos of the march, leading to a postmodern moment of recognition for me when I realized that my group of mostly white friends was marching with the contingent.

The melding of queer and lesbian-feminist politics and cultures was astoundingly obvious and correspondingly hopeful. The identity poetics on parade was marked, not surprisingly, by a clear diversity of participants. Race, class, age, family, disability—all were addressed in some way by the rally or the organizers. The two featured speakers at the rally, Dorothy Allison and Jewelle Gomez, were billed as "authors and activists." One white and working class, the other African American—and both, among other things, poets.

Notes

Introduction: Race, Class, and Generations

1. I employ the hybrid category "working-class/lesbians of color" to indicate two overlapping identities that often have been treated separately. The shorthand "lesbian" may imply, but often excludes, women of color and/or working-class women. I mean to signify lesbians of color *and/or* working-class identified lesbians.

2. For "purists," see Farwell, *Heterosexual Plots*, 96. For " 'deploying' or 'activating' essentialism," see Fuss, *Essentially Speaking*, 20.

3. I use the shorthand *LGBT* in place of the more cumbersome *lesbian, gay, bisexual, and transgender*. Other terms currently in use include *lesbian and gay, lesbigay,* and *queer*. The choice of terminology, including the order in which the terms appear, is often a point of contention within the academy and in activist groups. Teresa de Lauretis's discussion is a benchmark in the discipline-naming controversy. See her "Queer Theory," especially iii–vii. For further discussion, see chapter 7 of this volume.

4. Thanks to Vilashini Cooppan for recommending that I read Hall's essay "Minimal Selves."

1. The Social Construction of Lesbian Feminism

1. For more on the medicalization of female homosexuality, see Chauncey, "From Sexual Inversion to Homosexuality"; Faderman, "Morbidification"; and Faderman, *Odd Girls*, 37–61.

2. Hall's main character, Stephen Gordon, is closely based on a case history described by sexologist Richard von Krafft-Ebing. I am indebted to Kim Emery for her clear explication of Hall's sexological model, in "Teaching Writing and the Lesbian Subject," 6–8.

3. For an extensive treatment of various versions of Sappho's life—lesbian, decadent, virginal, and otherwise—see DeJean, *Fictions of Sappho*.

4. See Martin and Lyon, *Lesbian/Woman*, 238; for a discussion of Louÿs's Sappho, see DeJean, *Fictions of Sappho*, 276–79.

5. More thorough discussions of the pro- and antihomosexual uses of the congenital theory are available in Steakley, *The Homosexual Emancipation Movement*, and in Carlston, "'A Finer Differentiation.'" Eve Kosovsky Sedgwick theorizes the difference between "minoritizing" and "universalizing" strategies of homosexual identity in *Epistemology of the Closet*, 40. Phelan suggests adopting "a version of postmodern lesbianism" that would subvert the essentialist/constructionist dichotomy in part by recognizing both positions as strategies. Postmodern lesbianism in Phelan's terms would undermine "enlightenment standards of truth" that keep the dichotomy in place and ultimately result in the oppression of lesbian and gay people (Phelan, "(Be)Coming Out," 769–73).

6. Phelan, on the other hand, considers "The Woman-Identified Woman" to be exemplary of an essentialist strain in lesbian feminism that seeks to find "the 'meaning' of lesbianism" (Phelan, *Getting Specific*, 49–50). Elsewhere, however, she acknowledges that the manifesto "articulated lesbianism as a political identity, as 'woman-identification' rather than 'simply' a sexual identity. This founding gesture of lesbian feminism in some sense made lesbianism into something it had not previously been and located lesbians as political radicals regardless of their particular individual political consciousnesses" (Phelan, *Getting Specific*, 21).

7. See Atkinson, *Amazon Odyssey*, 131–89.

8. See Whisman, "Identity Crises," 47–60; Goldsby, "Queen for 307 Days," 110–28; Allison, "A Question of Class," 133–55; and Hall, "Bitches in Solitude," 218–29.

9. Deborah Price, in "Patchwork," outlines Faderman's working-class background and her contributions to lesbian studies.

10. Kennedy and Davis make a similar point; commenting on the changing social life of butch lesbians in bars in the 1930s, forties, and fifties, they argue that "the use of decades as a marker in lesbian history is a somewhat arbitrary imposition" (*Boots of Leather*, 402).

11. Most of Morgan's anthology is written about women "as women," in much the same manner criticized by Spelman, but this early collection is notable for its inclusion of two essays by and about lesbians, and a section by and about "Women in the Black Liberation Movement." This is clearly the ampersand problem in action, but even a segregated section for women of color and/or lesbians was unusual in a mainstream press publication in the early 1970s.

12. According to Kranich, in "Catalysts for Transforming Ourselves," the following women of color periodicals were available in the 1970s. (Kranich indicates that periodicals may have continued to publish after the dates listed):

Al Dia, New York City, 1976–
Asian American Women, Stanford University, 1976
Asian Women, Berkeley, 1971
Asian Women's Center Newsletter, Los Angeles, 1973–74
Black Women's Log, Springfield, Mass, 1974

Brown Sister, Wellesley, 1977
Charisma, Cincinnati, 1977; newsletter of Black Career Women
Comisión Femenil Mexicana Report, Los Angeles, 1971–73
CSAC News, Los Angeles, 1973–74; newsletter of the Chicana Service Action
    Center
Hijas de Cuantemor, Long Beach, Calif., 197? [date partially obscured]
In Touch, New York, 1979; newsletter of Asian Women United
La Razon Mestiza II, San Francisco, 1974–75
National Black Feminist Organization Newsletter, 1975
Ohoyo, Wichita Falls, Texas, 1979–1983; newsletter by/for indigenous women
Shenabe Quai, Turtle Lake, Wisconsin, 1979; North American Indian
    Women's Council on Chemical Dependency
Sojourner: Third World Women's Research News, Detroit, 1977–1982
Triple Jeopardy, New York City, 1971–75
Wisconsin Tribal Women's News Najinokwe, Madison, 1974–76

2. Putting the Word Dyke on the Map: Judy Grahn

1. At a 1988 benefit for Pat Parker, who was living with breast cancer, Judy Grahn began her reading by walking up to the microphone, looking directly into the audience, and saying, "I want to be remembered as someone who helped put the word *dyke* on the map." The reading took place at Ollie's, a lesbian bar in Oakland, California.

2. For an introduction to socialist feminism, see Jaggar, *Feminist Politics and Human Nature.*

3. For information regarding the contents of early lesbian newspapers, I am indebted to Clare Potter for compiling and editing *The Lesbian Periodicals Index.* Many of the periodicals indexed by Potter are available in the Herstory Microfilm Collection distributed by UMI. Bound copies of periodicals are difficult to find, but various lesbian and gay archives have substantial holdings of unbound periodicals. Two of the largest collections belong to the Lesbian Herstory Archives (Brooklyn) and the Gay and Lesbian Historical Society of Northern California (San Francisco).

4. Correspondence with Judy Grahn.

5. Backus cites Schenck, *Mourning and Panegyric.*

6. I am indebted to Jan Montefiore, whose quotation of this passage in her book *Feminism and Poetry* (71), led me to a rereading of Bulkin's essay.

7. One "dumb blonde joke" turns the tables on the genre: Q: "Why are dumb blonde jokes so short?" A: "So men will understand them."

8. I include *bulldagger,* a variation of *bulldyke,* from "I am the wall."

9. Throughout this chapter, traditional interpretations of symbols are drawn from Cooper, *An Illustrated Encyclopaedia of Traditional Symbols.*

10. Grahn's project is not unproblematic. See Phelan, *Playing with Fire,* for a trenchant analysis of the cultural appropriation performed by Grahn in *Another Mother Tongue* as she searches cross-culturally and transhistorically for "a culture and a history . . . as part of the project of 'ethnicizing' sexuality" (80).

3. *"I Have a Dream Too": Pat Parker*

1. The first three editions of Parker's *Movement in Black* are identical with respect to poem titles, punctuation, capitalization, line breaks, and spacing. Changes were made in the 1999 edition, published after Parker's death. The 1999 edition includes several "Celebrations/Remembrances/Tributes," including Smith's. References to these are cited parenthetically in chapter 3 as *Movement* 1999 followed by page number. References to the poems are to the 1983 Crossing Press edition and are noted in the text as *Movement* followed by page number. (As the 1983 Crossing Press and 1989 Firebrand Books editions are facsimiles of the first edition, all three editions are identical, including page numbers.)

2. The room was ultimately named after Audre Lorde, whose name was the "most popular request," in part because Parker "was problematic" for some people who did not share her politics (Wolfe, "Interview," 16–17; Maxine Wolfe, Lesbian Herstory Archives, personal communication, 1997).

3. Callaghan focuses on Parker's "My lover is a woman" (*Movement,* 98–100), which "brings the contradiction of politics and postmodernity to a crisis." Curiously, Callaghan does not choose to focus on Parker's poems or statements that critique imperialism, some in the context of the Vietnam War; e.g., "Revolution: It's Not Neat or Pretty or Quick" (in *This Bridge Called My Back*), "i wonder" (*Movement,* 60), "Where do you go to become a non-citizen?" (*Movement,* 61–62), and "Tour America!" (*Movement,* 69).

4. Grahn's introduction appears in all editions of *Movement in Black* up to the 1999 edition, where it is replaced by an introduction by Cheryl Clarke. Page numbers to Grahn's introduction refer to the 1983 Crossing Press edition.

5. I was first made aware of Parker's role in Lorde's decision to come out publicly in an off-the-record remark made by someone who knew both poets. This history was later confirmed by someone who had been Parker's housemate at the time (personal communication, 2000).

6. David Lionel Smith notes the continuing influence of the Black Aesthetic on Houston Baker's work, which also "has absorbed deconstruction," and contrasts Baker to Henry Louis Gates Jr., whose "harsh" rejection of the Black Aesthetic "reflects the bitter conflict between movement critics and conventional academics." Smith argues that "despite this antagonism, Gates' own criticism," particularly *The Signifying Monkey,* "has been deeply influence by Black Aesthetic theory" (Smith, "Black Arts," 105–6).

7. I am indebted to my students in "The Politics of Poetry" at Stanford University in 1989 for pointing out this pun to me.

8. Judy Grahn, personal communication, November 1, 1999.

4. "High Over the Halfway Between Your World and Mine": Audre Lorde

1. From Lorde's acceptance speech when she was named state poet of New York for 1991–1993. See Michelle Parkerson and Ada Gay Griffin's video documentary about Lorde's life and work, *A Litany for Survival,* available from Third World Newsreel, 335 W. 38th Street, 5th Floor, New York, NY 10018–2916, (212) 947–9277. In various essays, interviews, and speeches Lorde refers to herself with some combination of the same string of identifiers; see *Sister Outsider.*

2. Fraser and Nicholson presumably paraphrase Lorde's better-known and more succinct rhetorical flourishes, such as her query "What is the theory behind racist feminism?" (Lorde, "Master's Tools," 112).

3. The term is used by Hammond in her "Audre Lorde: Interview," conducted October 1978.

4. See, for example, Carruthers, "Revision"; Farwell *Heterosexual Plots,* 7, 64, 87; Grahn, *Highest Apple;* Yorke, "Primary Intensities," 159; Clarke, *Movement,* 15–22; Davis, *Movement,* 28; Parkerson, *Movement,* 34; Smith, *Movement,* 39.

5. *Sister Outsider* is the title of Lorde's first collection of essays and of a poem published in *The Black Unicorn.*

6. For "differences within women," see de Lauretis, "Feminist," 14. See Alarcón's criticism of de Lauretis and others in "Theoretical Subject(s)," especially 364–65.

7. Jonathan Rollins, in the video *A Litany for Survival.*

8. "Transformation" was first published in *Sinister Wisdom* 6 (1978), and subsequently in Lorde's *Cancer Journals.* Page numbers in the text are from *Sister Outsider.*

9. Gloria (Akasha T.) Hull's "Poem (for Audre)" responds to the power of the proclamation: "What you said / keeps bothering me / keeps needling, grinding." The poem's placement as the frontispiece for *Conditions: five, The Black Women's Issue,* dedicated to Mabel Hampton and Audre Lorde, attests to the statement's resonance among black feminists, as Hull asks Lorde to "please keep on / teaching us" the vital lesson "how / to speak."

10. In a 1962 statement for *Sixes and Sevens: An Anthology of New Poetry,* Lorde wrote,

> I am Black, Woman, and Poet—all three are facts outside
> the realm of choice. My eyes have a part in my seeing;
> my breath in my breathing; and all that I am in who I am.
> All who I love are of my people; it is not simple.
> (cited in Cornwell, *Black Lesbian,* 35)

McLaurin-Allen, "Audre Lorde," 219, discusses the importance of "Martha" as "the first poetic expression of Lorde's homosexuality."

Various sources state that "Love Poem" was first published in *Ms.* magazine in 1971, probably because that is what Lorde is quoted as saying in "An Interview: Audre Lorde and Adrienne Rich" (*Sister,* 98; first published in *Signs* 6:4 [Summer 1981]). In fact, the poem was first published in *Ms.* in February 1974. *Ms.* did not commence publication until 1972.

The reference to Fall 1977 is an interview conducted by Anita Cornwell in 1975 and first published in *Sinister Wisdom* 4 (1977), reprinted in Cornwell, *Black Lesbian,* 35–50.

11. All five essays are reprinted in Lorde, *Sister Outsider.* All page references are to *Sister Outsider.*

12. Lorde's statement has occasioned accusations of racial and gender essentialism. See her discussion in "An Interview: Audre Lorde and Adrienne Rich," 100–2.

13. Dhairyam, "Artifacts," 240–41, cites Avi-Ram.

14. Kate Walter's *Village Voice* review of *Sister Outsider* begins, "Hey, hey, ho, ho, patriarchy's got to go! That's the gist of *Sister Outsider,* Audre Lorde's collection of 15 essays and speeches from the past eight years. . . . When she lets rip, it's hard to argue." Cited in "Audre Lorde," 245.

15. Various reviewers and critics have commented on the significance of *The Black Unicorn*'s cover illustration. Dhairyam, for example, begins her essay "'Artifacts for Survival'" with a discussion of the elements of the book jacket (229). Shariat's review of *The Black Unicorn* begins with an excerpt from Randall's poem, which questions the eurocentrism of "universal themes" such as "the white unicorn." See also reviews by Bethel, "Review"; and Rushing, "Creative Use."

16. See Avi-Ram for a discussion of Lorde's frequent use of *apo koinu,* "a figure of speech, a variety of zeugma, in which a single word or phrase is shared between two distinct, independent syntactic units" (193).

17. My thanks to Sharon Holland for sharing with me some of her lecture notes from her course "Politics and Poetry" (Stanford University, winter 1994).

18. For a discussion of Lorde's use of pre-Christian notions of the unicorn as a Mother Goddess figure, see Dhairyam, "Artifacts," 237.

19. Davies sees Lorde's term *zami* as a "revision of the term 'lesbian' of Greek origin," an expression "of the way in which her various identities converge, but also of how European language and definition do not capture her identities" (*Black Women,* 18):

The name *zami* becomes a renaming of the self as "Black lesbian" (i.e., lesbian as a white-identified, Greek-originated term has to be qualified with the adjective "Black" or latina or Asian, for example, or renamed). The deploying of the etymology and meaning of *Zami* is a similar move to find new language and new starting-points from which to express a reality, as is, for example, Alice Walker's definition of "womanist" as another term of meaning for 'Black feminist' or *'khush'* as a starting-point for gay identity in Indian cultures. (121–22)

20. Many sources on Yoruba and Dahomey are in print, but I have limited my research to three sources that Lorde lists in the bibliography at the end of *The Black Unicorn:* Bascom, *The Yoruba of Southwestern Nigeria;* Courlander, *Tales of Yoruba Gods and Heroes;* and Herskovits, *Dahomey,* vols. 1–2. I was unable to locate the fourth source in Lorde's bibliography, Yoruba Temple, *The Gods of Africa.*

21. Shakur was a leader of the radical activist Black Liberation Army in the early 1970s. Arrested and convicted in connection with the shooting of a police officer in New Jersey in 1973, she has always maintained her innocence. She escaped from prison in 1979 and has been living in exile in Cuba since 1984. There have been periodic attempts to extradite her to the United States, most recently in 1998. *New York Times,* May 1, 1998. See also Shakur, *Assata.*

22. Lorde may have chosen Yaa Asantewa because she was an African nationalist freedom fighter in present-day Ghana, home of the much celebrated pan-Africanist leader Kwame Nkrumah. Nkrumah's rise to leadership in Ghana and his ouster by military coup in 1966 was an important chapter in African nationalist politics, and it was closely followed by black nationalist activists in the United States. There is widespread speculation that the coup that ousted Nkrumah was supported or engineered by the CIA; both Nkrumah and Shakur were seen as targets of the racist U.S. government by leftists and black nationalists. See Nkrumah,"On the Coup"; DuBois, "Kwame Krumah."

23. The frontispiece of *Movement in Black* pictures two symbols, *Aya,* "the fern, a symbol of defiance," which appears next to the title of each poem, and *Nkyimkyim,* "twisted pattern, changing one's self or playing many parts," which heads each section of the book.

24. For further discussion of the Kitty/Afrekete character in *Zami,* see Keating, "Making"; and Provost, "Becoming."

25. Several critics have written about the importance of Lorde's mother to her work. See, for example, Browdy de Hernández, "Mothering"; Chinosole, "Audre Lorde"; Georgoudaki, "Audre Lorde"; and Worsham, "Poetics."

26. See *Zami,* 9, for one example of the contrasting consequences of her father's dark skin and her light-skinned mother's ability to pass.

27. On "pro-s/m, 'politically incorrect' sexual discourse that marked the sex-radical 1980s and queer 1990s," see, for example, Allison, "Public Silence, Private Terror" in Allison, *Skin;* and Phelan, "Sadomasochism and the Meaning of Feminism," in Phelan, *Identity Politics,* 99–133. The proceedings of the Barnard College conference that became ground zero of the "sex wars," the 1982 Scholar and Feminist IX Conference, are published in Vance, *Pleasure and Danger.*

For more on Lorde's relationship to the "sex wars" of the 1980s, see Phelan, *Identity Politics*, 113–15; Lorde and Star, "Interview with Audre Lorde"; Stein, *Sisters, Sexperts*, 17–18.

28. Lorde was a founding member of Kitchen Table Women of Color Press, which published *Home Girls* as one of its early titles.

29. "Sister Outsider" is the title of a poem in *The Black Unicorn*, but is better known as the title of Lorde's collected essays. As such, it is a title that became a signifier of Lorde's identity. For a brief discussion, see Hull, "Living," 154.

30. For news coverage and commentary about the conference, see Felman, "I Am Your Sister"; Folayan, "I Am Your Sister"; Stato, "I Am Your Sister." I draw on personal notes and the conference program for information.

5. An Uncommonly Queer Reading: Adrienne Rich

1. Quotations are from Meese's response to Jan Montefiore's *Feminism and Poetry: Language, Experience, Identity in Women's Writing*; Meese, *(Ex)tensions*, 171–72.

2. The three nearly identical references to Rich's lesbian continuum idea appear in Stein, *Sex and Sensibility*, 38, 108, 112. Two of the three employ the blurring metaphor.

3. "Teaching Language in Open Admissions" is a discussion of Rich's involvement in the SEEK Program at the City College of New York, a program in which now prominent poet-teachers such as Rich, Toni Cade Bambara, and June Jordan taught writing "to black and Puerto Rican freshmen entering [the college] from substandard ghetto high schools, where the prevailing assumption had been that they were of inferior intelligence" (*On Lies*, 55); the essay is also a meditation on the meaning of the college experience for poor students versus wealthier, elite-university students. In "Toward a Woman-Centered University" Rich draws parallels between the projects of and resistance to Women's Studies and Ethnic Studies. "Motherhood" includes sustained analysis of the oppression of women of color through attacks on funding for birth control and abortion, and through forced sterilization and restriction of access to health care, drawing connections between racism, classism, sexism, and homophobia. "Disloyal to Civilization" is Rich's first essay to take as its main subject the racism and antiracist activism within the women's movement, past and present. The published version of the essay is an expansion of her speech for the MLA panel, "The Transformation of Silence into Language and Action," for which Lorde delivered her essay of the same name. Other essays in *On Lies, Secrets, and Silence* make at least passing reference to race and class; the earliest to do so is "When We Dead Awaken," first published in 1971, the second essay in the volume (*On Lies*, 38).

4. Alcoff, in fact, inaccurately conflates the radical feminisms of Daly and Rich. For an explication of the differences between the two, see Hedley, "Surviving."

5. For example, the two poets appeared together in 1980 as part of The Poetry Series at the Manhattan Theatre Club; the advertisement highlights *The Work of a Common Woman* (noting Rich's introduction to it) and *The Dream of a Common Language*. A 1984 appearance by Rich at the University of Nebraska-Lincoln was titled "To Dream a Common Language." Advertisements can be found in the subject files of the Lesbian Herstory Archives, Brooklyn, New York.

6. Leila Rupp explores the implications of the debate for historians in her essay "Finding the Lesbians in Lesbian History"; for reference to Rich, see 154.

7. I was reminded of the exchange of letters in *LGSN* by Terry Castle, who commented on it when she lectured as part of the Jing Lyman Lecture Series on "Gay/Lesbian/Queer Studies: An Emerging Discipline," sponsored by Stanford's Institute for Research on Women and Gender (IRWG), winter 1994.

8. Personal communication, 1994.

9. *Necessities of Life* was Rich's first book published by Norton; *Coal* was Lorde's. Both poets continued to publish broadsides and special limited editions with small literary and feminist presses after they began publishing with Norton.

10. Rich's statement on the "erotic feelings between women" resonates in Lorde's essay "Uses of the Erotic." My point here is not to suggest that Rich's and Lorde's work is redundant, but that they are part of the same political project, a multifaceted movement called lesbian feminism whose tenets and contributions resound in contemporary theory.

11. Catherine Stimpson even notes that "rhetorically, she is more like—well, Robert Lowell—than Gertrude Stein," 250, an observation that others have made as well. For other comparisons to Robert Lowell, see McDaniel, *Reconstituting*, 8; Ostriker, *Writing*, 105. Among the wide array of influences on Rich that critics have noted are several both more and less "avant-garde," to use Stimpson's term: W. H. Auden (Ostriker, *Writing*, 104, 115–16 and *Stealing*, 4), John Berryman (McDaniel, *Reconstituting*, 8), Elizabeth Bishop (Brogan, "Planets," 266, 269), William Blake (McCorkle, *Still Performance*, 92; Ostriker, *Writing*, 124), Hart Crane (Martin, "Another View," 259), Emily Dickinson (Erkkila, "Dickinson and Rich"; Ostriker, *Writing*, 112; Runzo, "Intimacy," 75), T. S. Eliot (Erkkila, "Dickinson and Rich," 547; Martin, "Another View," 259), Robert Frost (Erkkila, "Dickinson and Rich," 547; Martin, "Another View," 259; McPherson, "Adrienne Rich," 438; Ostriker, *Writing*, 104, 124), H.D. (Friedman "I Go" and "Reply," 238; Martin, "Another View," 259; Rich, "Comment"), June Jordan (Brogan, "Planets," 270), Edna St. Vincent Millay (Erkkila, "Dickinson and Rich," 545–56), John Milton (Bundtzen, "Power," 51, 55–57), Sylvia Plath (McDaniel, *Reconstituting*, 8–9), Anne Sexton (McDaniel, *Reconstituting*, 8), Wallace Stevens (Brogan, "Planets"; Erkkila, "Dickinson and Rich," 547; Estrin, "Space-Off"; Karp, "Adrienne Cecile," 463), Walt Whitman (Bundtzen, "Power," 51), William Wordsworth (Bundtzen, "Power," 45, 48, 55), and William Butler Yeats (Erkkila, "Dickinson and Rich," 547; McPherson, "Adrienne Rich," 438).

6. "Caught in the Crossfire Between Camps": Gloria Anzaldúa

1. The title may also be translated "A Struggle of Borders," which captures the sense of the multiple borders that Anzaldúa straddles.

2. Unless otherwise noted, page references to Anzaldúa refer to *Borderlands/La Frontera*, 2d ed. My own translations of poetry extracts appear in square brackets; my translations in running text appear in parentheses.

3. A note on terminology: "Latino/a" is but one among several highly contested terms for people of Latin American and Caribbean descent living in the United States. Following Juanita Ramos's lead in titling her 1987 anthology *Compañeras: Latina Lesbians,* I use *Latina* as a generic name for women from a variety of national, ethnic, and racial heritages, recognizing the problems inherent in creating a generic category at all. I use *Chicana* for women of Mexican descent who claim this politically charged label associated with *El Movimiento,* the Chicano/a power movement of the 1960s. These and other related terms are discussed by Anzaldúa in *Borderlands/La Frontera* (84–85). Other useful discussions can be found in Pérez-Torres, *Movements,* 19; and Alarcón, "Chicana Feminism," 373–74.

4. On the use of the Spanish term *teoría* for theorizing by women of color, see Anzaldúa (*"Haciendo caras,"* xxv–xxvi); Espinoza, "Women of Color."

5. The essay was originally published in *The Oxford Companion to Women's Writing in the United States* as "U.S. Third World Feminism."

6. Several critics have commented on the role of Coatlicue to Anzaldúa's cosmology and creativity. See for example Keating, "Myth," 81–88; Yarbro-Bejarano, "Gloria Anzaldúa's," 14–15, 21; Lugones, "On *Borderlands/La Frontera,*" 33.

7. "*Ella,*" capitalized, refers to *La Virgen.*

8. This translation benefits from an earlier verbal translation by my graduate school classmate, Hilda Gutierrez-Baldoquín. Any mistakes are entirely my own.

9. White people, sometimes used pejoratively; though in the hierarchy of skin color among Chicanos/as, being *güero/a* can be viewed positively.

10. Anzaldúa cites June Nash, "The Aztecs and the Ideology of Male Dominance," *Signs* (Winter 1978):361–62.

11. In the essay "*La Prieta*" (The Dark One) Anzaldúa discusses her terror of being "hard on people of color who are the oppressed victims. I am still afraid because I will have to call us on a lot of shit like our own racism, our fear of women and sexuality. One of my biggest fears is that of betraying myself, of consuming myself with self-castigation, of not being able to unseat the guilt that has ridden on my back for years" (198).

12. *Los pueblos* can mean "the peoples" as well as "the towns." In Anzaldúa's vision *las hijas de la Chingada* will liberate both.

13. Joan Pinkvoss runs Aunt Lute, the press that published *Borderlands/La Frontera.*

14. Anzaldúa names herself "lesbian-feminist" or a "lesbian-feminist poet" in her biographical notes to Ramos, *Compañeras: Latina Lesbians* (1987), Anzaldúa, *Borderlands/La Frontera* (1987), and Anzaldúa, *Making Face, Making Soul/Haciendo Caras* (1990). This list does not account for some of the anthologies nor the many journals in which her essays and poems have been published.

15. Alarcón quotes a poem within chapter 4 of *Borderlands/La Frontera*, "La herencia de Coatlicue/The *Coatlicue* State," 65.

16. Several critics have drawn connections between Lorde and Anzaldúa. See, for example, Browdy de Hernández, "Mothering"; Fowlkes, "Moving," 109; Hedley, "Nepantilist," 44; Keating, "Myth"; Reuman, "'Wild Tongues,'" 308, 310, 311, 312, 317–18.

17. In the first edition of *Borderlands/La Frontera* the line reads, "ahora por todas las tierras vulnerada te busco," a typo. The line has been corrected to read "tierras vulneradas" in the second edition.

18. In *Borderlands/La Frontera* Anzaldúa alternately employs "lesbian" (41, 42, 102), "*lesbiana*" (106), "feminist" (44, 102, 106), "*femenista*" (106), and "queer" (40, 41, 94, 102, 104, 106, 107). One reason "queer" appears more often is that Anzaldúa is not always talking about women alone. For the same reason, she uses "homosexual" (41, 60, 106, 107), "gay" (when talking about men, 81, 106), and "*jotería*" (queers/faggotry; 107). In the interview appended to the second edition (published in 1999), Anzaldúa uses "lesbian" (242), "dyke" (229), and "queer" (242) an equal number of times.

In addition to the biographical notes in which Anzaldúa calls herself either a "lesbian-feminist" or a "dyke-feminist," a number of scholars discuss Anzaldúa's connections, albeit sometimes difficult, to lesbian feminism (Adams, "Northamerican Silences," 138; Fowlkes, "Moving," 105–6; Kaup, "Crossing," 100; Keating, "Myth," 73; Perry, "Interview," 20; Ramírez, "Review," 186.

19. Yarbro-Bejarano, "Gloria Anzaldúa's"; and Phelan, *Getting Specific*, 57–75, provide insightful discussions of the deracination and appropriation of Anzaldúa's mestiza concept.

20. This is evident in a number of ways, but perhaps most clearly through Anzaldúa's retelling of the genesis of *This Bridge Called My Back*, which grew out of her frustration with the monocultural assumptions of white women in the lesbian-feminist groups in which she was active; see Perry, "Interview," 20, 33–34; Keating, "Writing," 106.

21. Note, too, that the white academic Butler is presented as a rational theorist who argues; Anzaldúa and Lorde are figured as mystical women of color who, presumably, intuit.

22. See, for example, Keating, "Myth"; Yarbro-Bejarano, "Gloria Anzaldúa's."

23. Roof's observation is made with respect to Toril Moi's dismissal of Anglo-American feminist criticism in her 1985 book, *Sexual/Textual Politics*.

24. For a discussion of the tendency to imply tht only white lesbians "do theory," see Holland, "(White) Lesbian Studies," especially 250.

7. Around 1991: The Rise of Queer Theory and the Lesbian Intertext

1. See, for example, Cruikshank, *Gay and Lesbian,* 9, 62, 92, 149, 189; D'Emilio, *Sexual Politics,* 150, 153, 224–25; D'Emilio and Freedman, *Intimate Matters,* 310; Douglas, *Love and Politics,* 25; Echols, *Daring to Be Bad,* 23, 36–37, 53, 103–37, 222–23; Evans, *Personal Politics,* passim; Grahn, *Highest Apple,* xvii–xviii.

2. There are exceptions, of course. Cruikshank, for example, directly relates AIDS activism to the legacy of the civil rights movement; *Gay and Lesbian,* 189.

Activist Bernice Johnson Reagon is another exception. Addressing a mostly white, lesbian-feminist audience at a women's music festival in 1981, Reagon said:

> I'm going to start with the Civil Rights movement because of course I think that that was the first [liberation movement] in the era we're in. Black folks started it, Black folks did it, so everything you've done politically rests on the efforts of my people—that's my arrogance! Yes, and it's the truth; it's my truth. You can take it or leave it, but that's the way I see it. So once we did what we did, then you've got women, you've got Chicanos, you've got the Native Americans, and you've got homosexuals, and you got all of these people who also got sick of somebody being on their neck. And maybe if they come together, they can do something about it. And I claim all of you as coming from something that made me who I am. You can't tell me that you ain't in the Civil Rights movement. You are in the Civil Rights movement that we created that just rolled up to your door. ("Coalition Politics," 362)

3. Christian's original sentence reads, "In the race for theory, feminists, eager to enter the halls of power, have attempted their own prescriptions." I take her to mean primarily white, middle-class feminists because two sentences later she points out that "seldom do feminist theorists take into account the complexity of life—that women are of many races and ethnic backgrounds with different histories and cultures and that as a rule belong to different classes that have difference concerns." Most critical writing by working-class/feminists of color in the 1980s does account for differences among women and criticizes white feminists for failing to do so.

4. Carby, *Reconstructing Womanhood,* 13. Carby is quoting from McDowell, "New Directions," 196. Carby and McDowell both focus their critiques of black feminist criticism's essentialism on Smith's "Toward a Black Feminist Criticism."

5. Hooks paraphrases Christian's argument but does not make reference to the specific text: "Should we not be suspicious of postmodern critiques of the 'subject' when they surface at a historical moment when many subjugated people feel themselves coming to voice for the first time?" "Postmodern," 28.

6. The revised version appears in Greene and Kahn, *Making a Difference.*

7. See, for example, Nina Baym, "The Madwoman and Her Languages," and Jane Marcus, "Still Practice, A/Wrested Alphabet," in Benstock, *Feminist Issues in Literary Scholarship,* a volume accused of being "an attack on theory" (Gallop *Around 1981,* 208) for pointing out exclusionary trends in white feminist criticism. Gallop devotes a chapter of *Around 1981* to the volume and its detractors.

8. Showalter, "Women's Time, Women's Space: Writing the History of Feminist Criticism," cited in Gallop, *Around 1981,* 21.

9. Gallop, *Around 1981,* 136, citing Janet Todd, *Feminist Literary History,* 60–61.

10. Entries to Grier's bibliography originally appeared in the *Ladder,* the magazine of the homophile organization Daughters of Bilitis, in the 1950s and early sixties.

11. It should be noted, however, that the institutional future of lesbian/gay studies is far from secure; while there are university press series, study centers, and a few tenure-track jobs devoted to the field, lesbian/gay studies has not (yet?) reached the mainstream position achieved (at least in the field of literary studies) by feminist criticism. Both fields remain targets of right-wing, anti-intellectual attacks, with LGBT studies especially targeted for misrepresentation and ridicule. (A segment of *Sixty Minutes* that aired in spring 1998 is one example of television "investigative journalism" that purports to introduce the public to "queer studies" but focuses almost solely on disapproval of discussions of sadomasochism in the classroom—complete with the investigating journalist pulling faces in response to his interview subjects.)

12. I thank Ann Pellegrini for sharing her insights about the anthology (personal communication).

13. For critiques of Jeffreys' lesbian-feminist and often separatist ideas, see Findlay, "Forum"; Miller, "Forum"; Halberstam," "Forum"; and Tallen, "Forum"; all reviews of *The Lesbian Heresy.* Reviewers' opinions range from reserved praise— "There are some things about *The Lesbian Heresy* that . . . give me pause" (Tallen "Forum," 6)—to scorn—the Camille Paglia quotation in this chapter (Halberstam, "Forum," 4).

14. Zimmerman, "History," 5–6, cites Gilbert and Gubar, *Madwoman,* which draws upon Harold Bloom's concept of the "anxiety of influence."

15. Butler here cites her book, *Gender Trouble.*

16. For notable exceptions, see Hammonds, "Black (W)holes"; Harper, "Queer Transexions"; Ongiri, "We Are Family"; Pellegrini, "Women on Top"; and Pellegrini, *Performance Anxieties.*

17. See Cruikshank, *Gay and Lesbian;* D'Emilio, *Sexual Politics;* D'Emilio and Freedman, *Intimate Matters;* Faderman, *Odd Girls;* and Kennedy and Davis, *Boots of Leather.*

18. Shane Phelan attributes the concept of "free spaces" to Evans and Boyte, *Free Spaces.* See Phelan, "(Be)Coming," 785.

19. Papusa Molina, National Women's Studies Association conference lesbian caucus meeting, Norman, Oklahoma, June 21, 1995.

20. See Malinowitz for a description of Lorde as a figure who "brought feminist praxis toward a far more postmodern interpretive arena than that in which it had heretofore conducted its work" ("Lesbian Studies," 266). Malinowitz uses Lorde's work to illustrate both connections and rifts between lesbian feminism and queer theory (265–68).

21. Two essays about a specifically "lesbian intertextuality" have been published to date, Elaine Marks's "Lesbian Intertextuality" (1979) and Diana Collecott's "What Is Not Said: A Study in Textual Inversion" (1990).

22. Of course, lesbian feminism is also intertextual with texts whose politics it is supposed to repudiate. Susan Rubin Suleiman points out that Adrienne Rich's influential concept of "writing as re-vision . . . can itself be seen as an appropriation of earlier theoretical and historical work by male, nonfeminist (sometimes even misogynist) critics," especially Mikhail Bakhtin, whose work "chiefly inspired Julia Kristeva's theory of intertextuality" (142–43). Additionally, the influence on Rich's poetry of such canonical writers as William Butler Yeats is widely documented (and acknowledged by Rich herself).

Works Cited

Aal, Katharyn Machan. "Judy Grahn on Women's Poetry Readings: History and Performance." Part 1. *Sinister Wisdom* 25 (Winter 1984): 67–76.

— "Judy Grahn on Women's Poetry Readings: History and Performance." Part 2. *Sinister Wisdom* 27 (Fall 1984): 54–61.

Abbott, Sidney and Barbara Love. *Sappho Was a Right-On Woman: A Liberated View of Lesbianism.* New York: Stein and Day, 1972.

Abbott, Steve. "Judy Grahn: Creating a Gay and Lesbian Mythology." *Advocate*, September 4, 1984, 45–47.

Abelove, Henry, Michèle Aina Barale, and David M. Halperin, eds. *The Lesbian and Gay Studies Reader.* New York and London: Routledge, 1993.

Abraham, Julie. "I Know What Boys Like: Tales from the Dyke Side." *Village Voice Literary Supplement*, June 1992, 20–1.

Adams, Kate. "Northamerican Silences: History, Identity, and Witness in the Poetry of Gloria Anzaldúa, Cherríe Moraga, and Leslie Marmon Silko." In Elaine Hedges and Shelley Fisher Fishkin, eds., *Listening to Silences: New Essays in Feminist Criticism*, 130–45. New York and Oxford: Oxford University Press, 1994.

"Adrienne Rich." Videotape. Los Angeles: Lannan Foundation, 1992.

Alarcón, Norma. "Chicana Feminism: In the Tracks of 'the' Native Woman." In Carla Trujillo, ed., *Living Chicana Theory*, 371–82. Berkeley: Third Woman, 1998.

— "The Theoretical Subject(s) of This Bridge Called My Back and Anglo-American Feminism." In Gloria Anzaldúa, ed., *Making Face, Making Soul/Haciendo Caras: Creative and Critical Perspectives by Women of Color*, 356–69. San Francisco: Aunt Lute, 1990.

Alcoff, Linda. "Cultural Feminism Versus Post-Structuralism: The Identity Crisis in Feminist Theory." *Signs* 13:3 (Spring 1988): 405–36.

Alkalay-Gut, Karen. "The Lesbian Imperative in Poetry." *Contemporary Review* 242:1407 (April 1983): 209–11.

Allison, Dorothy. "A Question of Class." In Arlene Stein, ed., *Sisters, Sexperts, Queers: Beyond the Lesbian Nation*, 133–55. New York: Plume, 1993.

— *Skin: Talking About Sex, Class, and Literature.* Ithaca: Firebrand, 1994.

Annas, Pamela. "A Poetry of Survival: Unnaming and Renaming in the Poetry of Audre Lorde, Pat Parker, Sylvia Plath, and Adrienne Rich. *Colby Library Quarterly* 18:1 (March 1982): 9–25.

Anzaldúa, Gloria. *Borderlands/La Frontera: The New Mestiza.* San Francisco: Spinsters/Aunt Lute, 1987.

— "Bridge, Drawbridge, Sandbar, or Island: Lesbians-of-Color *Hacienda Alianzas.*" In Lisa Albrecht and Rose M. Brower, eds. *Bridges of Power,* 216–31. Philadelphia: New Society, 1990.

— "*Haciendo caras, una entrada.*" In Gloria Anzaldúa, ed., *Making Face, Making Soul/Haciendo Caras: Creative and Critical Perspectives by Women of Color,* xv–xxviii. San Francisco: Aunt Lute, 1990.

— "*La Prieta.*" 1981. In Cherríe Moraga and Gloria Anzaldúa, eds., *This Bridge Called My Back: Writings by Radical Women of Color,* 198–209. New York: Kitchen Table, 1983.

— "To(o) Queer the Writer—Loca, Escritora, y Chicana." In Betsy Warland, ed., *InVersions: Writing by Dykes, Queers, and Lesbians,* 249–63. Vancouver: Press Gang, 1991.

Anzaldúa, Gloria, ed. *Making Face, Making Soul/Haciendo Caras: Creative and Critical Perspectives by Women of Color.* San Francisco: Aunt Lute, 1990.

Arruda, Tiana. Interview. October 27, 1992.

Atkinson, Ti Grace. *Amazon Odyssey: The First Collection of Writings by the Political Pioneer of the Women's Movement.* New York: Links, 1974.

"Audre Lorde." *Contemporary Literary Criticism,* 230–64. Vol. 71. Detroit: Gale Research, 1992.

Avi-Ram, Amitai F. "The Politics of the Refrain in Judy Grahn's *A Woman Is Talking to Death.*" *Women and Language* 10:2 (Spring 1987): 38–43.

Backus, Margot Gayle. "Judy Grahn and the Lesbian Invocational Elegy: Testimonial and Prophetic Responses to Social Death in 'A Woman Is Talking to Death.'" *Signs* 18:4 (Summer 1993): 815–37.

Barale, Michèle. "In the House of Women." Review of Judy Grahn, *The Highest Apple. Women's Review of Books* 3 (October 1985): 10.

— "When *Lambs* and *Aliens* Meet: Girl-Faggots and Boy-Dykes Go to the Movies." In Dana Heller, ed., *Cross Purposes: Lesbians, Feminists, and the Limits of Alliance,* 95–106. Bloomington: Indiana University Press, 1997.

Barnard, Ian. "Gloria Anzaldúa's Queer *Mestisaje.*" *MELUS* 22:1 (Spring 1997): 35–53.

Barrax, Gerald. "Six Poets: From Poetry to Verse." Review of Pat Parker, *Movement in Black. Callaloo,* no. 26, 9:1 (Winter 1986): 248–69.

Barrett, Michèle and Anne Phillips, eds. *Destabilizing Theory: Contemporary Feminist Debates.* Stanford: Stanford University Press, 1992.

— "Introduction." In Michèle Barrett and Anne Phillips, eds., *Destabilizing Theory: Contemporary Feminist Debates,* 1–9. Stanford: Stanford University Press, 1992.

Barthes, Roland. *Image Music Text.* Trans. Stephen Heath. New York: Hill and Wang, 1977.

Bascom, William. *The Yoruba of Southwestern Nigeria.* New York: Holt, Rinehart and Winston, 1969.

Bass, Ellen and Louise Thornton, eds. *I Never Told Anyone: Writings by Women Survivors of Child Sexual Abuse.* New York: Harper and Row, 1983.

Baym, Nina. "The Madwoman and Her Languages: Why I Don't Do Feminist Literary Theory." In Shari Benstock, ed., *Feminist Issues in Literary Scholarship,* 45–59. Bloomington: Indiana University Press, 1987.

Beckett, Judith. "Warrior/Dyke." *Woman of Power* 3 (Winter/Spring 1986): 56–59.

Beemyn, Brett. "Bibliography of Works by and About Pat Parker." *Sage* 7:1 (Summer 1989): 81–82.

Benstock, Shari, ed. *Feminist Issues in Literary Scholarship.* Bloomington: Indiana University Press, 1987.

Bereano, Nancy. "Introduction." In Audre Lorde, *Sister Outsider: Essays and Speeches,* 7–11. Ithaca: Firebrand, 1984.

Bergman, David. "Something About Eve: Eve Kosofsky Sedgwick's Closet Drama." Review of Eve Kosofsky Sedgwick, *Epistemology of the Closet.Raritan* 11:1 (Summer 1991): 115–31.

Berlant, Lauren and Michael Warner. "Guest Column: What Does Queer Theory Teach Us About *X*?" *PMLA* 110:3 (May 1995): 343–49.

Bethel, Lorraine. "The Poetry of Adrienne Rich." Review of Adrienne Rich, *The Dream of a Common Language.Gay Community News* (September 16, 1978): 8–9.

— Review of Audre Lorde, *The Black Unicorn. Gay Community News Book Review* (February 1979?): 1+.

— "What Chou Mean *We,* White Girl? Or, the Cullud Lesbian Feminist Declaration of Independence (Dedicated to the Proposition That All Women Are Not Equal, i.e., Identical/ly Oppressed)." *Conditions: Five, The Black Women's Issue* 2:2 (Autumn 1979): 86–92.

Bethel, Lorraine and Barbara Smith, eds. *Conditions: Five, The Black Women's Issue* 2:2 (Autumn 1979).

Birtha, Becky. "Speaking Out Loudly Before the Madness." Review of Pat Parker, *Jonestown and Other Madness.off our backs* (November 1985): 17.

"Black Women Together Presents: A Memorial Tribute in Honor of Pat Parker." Program, Howard University, September 10, 1989. New York: Lesbian Herstory Archives.

Blain, Virginia, Patricia Clements, and Isobel Grundy, eds. *The Feminist Companion to Literature in English,* 833. New Haven and London: Yale University Press, 1990.

Bloch, Alice. Review of Judy Grahn, *She Who.Chrysalis* 5 (1978): 103–4.

Bloom, Harold. *The Anxiety of Influence: A Theory of Poetry.* New York: Oxford University Press, 1973.

Borghi, Liana. "Between Essence and Presence: Politics, Self, and Symbols in Contemporary American Lesbian Poetry." In Dennis Altman et al., eds., *Homosexuality, Which Homosexuality?* 61–81. Amsterdam: Uitgeverij An Dekker/Schorer, 1988; London: GMP, 1989.

Bowen, Angela. "Completing the Kente: Enabling the Presence of Out Black Lesbians in Academia." In Bonnie Zimmerman and Toni A. H. McNaron, eds., *The New Lesbian Studies: Into the Twenty-First Century*, 223–28. New York: Feminist Press at the City University of New York, 1996.

Bowles, Gloria. "Adrienne Rich as Feminist Theorist." In Jane Roberta Cooper, ed., *Reading Adrienne Rich: Reviews and Re-Visions, 1951–1981*, 319–28. Ann Arbor: University of Michigan Press, 1984 [1981].

Braxton, Joanne M. "Introduction." In Joanne M. Braxton and Andrée Nicola McLaughlin, eds., *Wild Women in the Whirlwind: Afra-American Culture and the Contemporary Literary Renaissance*, xxi–xxx. New Brunswick, N.J.: Rutgers University Press, 1990.

Braxton, Joanne M. and Andrée Nicola McLaughlin, eds. *Wild Women in the Whirlwind: Afra-American Culture and the Contemporary Literary Renaissance*. New Brunswick, N.J.: Rutgers University Press, 1990.

Brimstone, Lyndie. "Pat Parker: A Tribute." *Feminist Review* 34 (Spring 1990): 4–7.

Brogan, Jacqueline Vaught. "Planets on the Table: From Wallace Stevens and Elizabeth Bishop to Adrienne Rich and June Jordan." *Wallace Stevens Journal* 19:2 (Fall 1995): 255–78.

Browdy de Hernández, Jennifer. "Mothering the Self: Writing through the Lesbian Sublime in Audre Lorde's *Zami* and Gloria Anzaldúa's *Borderlands/La Frontera*." In Sandra Kumamoto Stanley, ed., *Other Sisterhoods: Literary Theory and U.S. Women of Color*, 244–62. Urbana: University of Illinois Press, 1998.

— "The Plural Self: The Politicization of Memory and Form in Three American Ethnic Autobiographies." In Amjrit Singh, Joseph T. Skerrett Jr., and Robert E. Hogan, eds., *Memory and Cultural Politics: New Approaches to American Ethnic Literatures*, 41–59. Boston: Northeastern University Press, 1996.

Brown, Rita Mae. *A Plain Brown Rapper*. Oakland: Diana, 1976.

Bulkin, Elly. "An Interview with Adrienne Rich." Part 1. *Conditions: One* 1:1 (April 1977): 50–65.

— "An Interview with Adrienne Rich." Part 2. *Conditions: Two* 1:2 (October 1977): 53–65.

Bulkin, Elly and Joan Larkin, eds. *Lesbian Poetry: An Anthology*. Watertown, Mass.: Persephone, 1981.

Bunch, Charlotte. "Lesbians in Revolt." 1972. In Charlotte Bunch, *Passionate Politics: Feminist Theory in Action, Essays 1968–1986*, 161–67. New York: St. Martin's, 1987.

— *Passionate Politics: Feminist Theory in Action, Essays 1968–1986*. New York: St. Martin's, 1987.

Bunch, Charlotte and Nancy Myron, eds. *Class and Feminism: A Collection of Essays from "The Furies"*. Baltimore: Diana, 1974.

Bundtzen, Lynda K. "Power and Poetic Vocation in Adrienne Rich's *The Dream of a Common Language*." In Suzanne W. Jones, ed., *Writing the Woman Artist: Essays on Poetics, Politics and Portraiture*, 43–59. Philadelphia: University of Pennsylvania Press, 1991.

Butler, Judith. "Against Proper Objects." *differences* 6:2–3 (Summer-Fall 1994): 1–27.

— *Bodies That Matter: On the Discursive Limits of "Sex."* New York and London: Routledge, 1993.

— "Critically Queer." In Judith Butler, *Bodies That Matter: On the Discursive Limits of "Sex,"* 223–42. New York and London: Routledge, 1993.

— *Gender Trouble: Feminism and the Subversion of Identity*. New York and London: Routledge, 1990.

— "Imitation and Gender Insubordination." In Diana Fuss, ed., *Inside/Out: Lesbian Theories, Gay Theories*, 13–31. New York and London: Routledge, 1991.

Calderón, Héctor. "Texas Border Literature: Cultural Transformation and Historical Reflection in the Works of Américo Paredes, Rolando Hinojosa, and Gloria Anzaldúa." *Dispositio* 16:41 (1991): 13–27.

Callaghan, Dympna. "Pat Parker: Feminism in Postmodernity." In Antony Easthope and John O. Thompson, eds., *Contemporary Poetry Meets Modern Theory*, 128–38. New York: Harvester, 1991.

Caraway, Nancie E. "The Challenge and Theory of Feminist Identity Politics: Working on Racism." *Frontiers* 12:2 (1991): 109–29.

Carby, Hazel V. *Reconstructing Womanhood: The Emergence of the Afro-American Woman Novelist*. New York and Oxford: Oxford University Press, 1987.

Carlston, Erin G. " 'A Finer Differentiation': Female Homosexuality and the American Medical Community, 1926–1940." In Vernon A. Rosario, ed., *Science and Homosexualities*, 177–96. New York and London: Routledge, 1997.

— "*Zami* and the Politics of Plural Identity." In Susan J. Wolfe and Julia Penelope, eds., *Sexual Practice, Textual Theory: Lesbian Cultural Criticism*, 226–36. Cambridge and Oxford: Blackwell, 1993.

Carman, John. "Network TV: An All-White Environment." *San Francisco Chronicle*, July 14, 1999, D1.

Carr, Brenda. " 'A Woman Speaks . . . I Am Woman and Not White': Politics of Voice, Tactical Essentialism, and Cultural Intervention in Audre Lorde's Activist Poetics and Practice." *College Literature* 20:2 (June 1993): 133–53.

Carruthers, Mary. "Imagining Women: Notes Towards a Feminist Poetic." *Massachusetts Review* 20:2 (Summer 1979): 281–307.

— "The Re-Vision of the Muse: Adrienne Rich, Audre Lorde, Judy Grahn, Olga Broumas." *Hudson Review* 36:2 (Summer 1983): 293–322.

Case, Sue-Ellen. "Judy Grahn's Gynopoetics: *The Queen of Swords*." *Studies in the Literary Imagination* 21:2 (Fall 1988): 47–67.

— "Toward a Butch-Feminist Retro-Future." In Dana Heller, ed., *Cross Purposes: Lesbians, Feminists, and the Limits of Alliance,* 205–20. Bloomington: Indiana University Press, 1997.

Castle, Terry. *The Apparitional Lesbian: Female Homosexuality and Modern Culture.* New York: Columbia University Press, 1993.

— "Gay/Lesbian/Queer Studies: An Emerging Discipline." Jing Lyman Lecture Series. Institute for Research on Women and Gender, Stanford University, Winter 1994.

Casto, Estella Kathryn. "Reading Feminist Poetry: A Study of the Work of Anne Sexton, Adrienne Rich, Audre Lorde, and Olga Broumas." Diss. Ohio State University, 1990.

Chauncey, George. "From Sexual Inversion to Homosexuality: Medicine and the Changing Conceptualization of Female Deviance." *Salmagundi* 58–59 (Fall 1982-Winter 1983): 114–46.

Chinosole. "Audre Lorde and Matrilineal Diaspora: 'Moving History Beyond Nightmare Into Structures for the Future . . .'" In Joanne M. Braxton and Andrée Nicola McLaughlin, eds., *Wild Women in the Whirlwind: Afra-American Culture and the Contemporary Literary Renaissance,* 379–94. New Brunswick, N.J.: Rutgers University Press, 1990.

Christian, Barbara. "The Race for Theory." 1987. In Gloria Anzaldúa, ed., *Making Face, Making Soul/Haciendo Caras: Creative and Critical Perspectives by Women of Color,* 335–45. San Francisco: Aunt Lute, 1990.

— "Remembering Audre Lorde." *Women's Review of Books* 10:6 (March 1993): 5–6.

Clarke, Cheryl. Review of Pat Parker, *Movement in Black. Conditions: Six* 2:3 (Summer 1980): 217–25.

Clausen, Jan. "A Movement of Poets: Thoughts on Poetry and Feminism." 1981 and 1982. In Jan Clausen, *Books and Life,* 1–44. Columbus: Ohio State University Press, 1989.

Cohen, Ed. "Are We (Not) What We Are Becoming? 'Gay' 'Identity,' 'Gay Studies,' and the Disciplining of Knowledge." In Joseph A. Boone and Michael Cadden, eds., *Engendering Men: The Question of Male Feminist Criticism,* 161–75. New York and London: Routledge, 1990.

Collecott, Diana. "What Is Not Said: A Study in Textual Inversion." *Textual Practice* 4:2 (Summer 1990): 236–58.

Combahee River Collective. "Combahee River Collective Statement." 1977. In Barbara Smith, ed., *Home Girls: A Black Feminist Anthology,* 272–82. New York: Kitchen Table, 1983.

Conditions: Five, The Black Women's Issue 2:2 (Autumn 1979).

Constantine, Lynne and Suzanne Scott. "Belles Lettres Interview." Interview with Judy Grahn. *Belles Lettres* 2:4 (March/April 1987): 7–8.

Cooper, J. C. *An Illustrated Encyclopaedia of Traditional Symbols.* London: Thames and Hudson, 1978.

Cooppan, Vilashini. "Writing after Liberation: Literature, Non-Racialism, and the 'New South Africa.'" MLA Convention, San Francisco, December 29, 1998.

Cornillon, Susan Koppelman, ed. *Images of Women in Fiction: Feminist Perspectives.* Bowling Green, Ohio: Bowling Green University Popular Press, 1973 [1972].

Cornwell, Anita. *Black Lesbian in White America.* Tallahassee: Naiad, 1983.

—— "Pat Parker: Poet from San Francisco." *Hera* 1:4 (Summer 1975): 40–1.

Cornwell, Anita. " 'So Who's Giving Guarantees?': An Interview with Audre Lorde." *Sinister Wisdom* 4 (Fall 1977): 15–21.

Courlander, Harold. *Tales of Yoruba Gods and Heroes.* New York: Crown, 1973.

Cruikshank, Margaret. *The Gay and Lesbian Liberation Movement.* New York and London: Routledge, 1992.

Culler, Jonathan. *The Pursuit of Signs.* Ithaca: Cornell University Press, 1981.

—— *Structuralist Poetics: Structuralism, Linguistics, and the Study of Literature.* New York: Cornell University Press, 1975.

Culpepper, Emily Erwin. "A Genius for Putting the Emphasis Where It Belongs." *Gay Community News*, September 3–9, 1989, 8.

Davies, Carole Boyce. *Black Women, Writing and Identity: Migrations of the Subject.* New York and London: Routledge, 1994.

de Beaugrande, Robert. *Critical Discourse: A Survey of Literary Theorists.* Norwood, N.J.: Ablex, 1988.

"Decade Dance: The '80s." *Lambda Book Report* 2:9 (March/April 1991): 10–13.

De Jean, Joan E. *Fictions of Sappho, 1546–1937.* Chicago: University of Chicago Press, 1989.

de Lauretis, Teresa. "Fem/Les Scramble." In Dana Heller, ed., *Cross Purposes: Lesbians, Feminists, and the Limits of Alliance,* 42–48. Bloomington: Indiana University Press, 1997.

—— "Feminist Studies/Critical Studies: Issues, Terms, and Contexts." In Teresa de Lauretis, ed., *Feminist Studies/Critical Studies,* 1–19. Bloomington: Indiana University Press, 1986.

—— "Queer Theory: Lesbian and Gay Sexualities—an Introduction." *differences* 3:2 (1991): iii–xviii.

D'Emilio, John. *Sexual Politics, Sexual Communities: The Making of a Homosexual Minority in the United States, 1940–1970.* Chicago and London: University of Chicago Press, 1983.

D'Emilio, John and Estelle Freedman. *Intimate Matters: A History of Sexuality in America.* New York: Harper and Row, 1988.

Dhairyam, Sagri. " 'Artifacts for Survival': Remapping the Contours of Poetry with Audre Lorde." *Feminist Studies* 18:2 (Summer 1992): 229–56.

—— " 'A House of Difference': To Construct a Lesbian Poet." Diss. University of Illinois, 1993.

—— "Racing the Lesbian, Dodging White Critics." In Laura Doan, ed., *The Lesbian Postmodern,* 25–46. New York: Columbia University Press, 1994.

Di Stefano, Christine. "Dilemmas of Difference: Feminism, Modernity, and Post-modernism." In Linda J. Nicholson, ed., *Feminism/Postmodernism*, 63–82. New York and London: Routledge, 1990.

Doan, Laura, ed. *The Lesbian Postmodern.* New York: Columbia University Press, 1994.

— "Preface." In Laura Doan, ed., *The Lesbian Postmodern*, ix–xi. New York: Columbia University Press, 1994.

Douglas, Carol Anne. "I'll Take the Low Road: A Look at Contemporary Feminist Theory." *off our backs* 23:2 (February 1993): 16–17.

— *Love and Politics: Radical Feminist and Lesbian Theories.* San Francisco: Ism, 1990.

Duberman, Martin. *Stonewall.* New York: Plume, 1994 [1993].

Du Bois, Shirley Graham. "Kwame Krumah: African Liberator." *Freedomways* 12:3 (1972): 197–206.

Duggan, Lisa. "Scholars and Sense." *Village Voice Literary Supplement,* June 1992, 27.

Dykes for an Amerikan Revolution. "Lesbian Feminist Declaration of 1976." New York: Lesbian Herstory Archives.

Emery, Kim. "Teaching Writing and the Lesbian Subject." MLA convention, New York City, December 29, 1992.

Erkkila, Betsy. "Dickinson and Rich: Toward a Theory of Female Poetic Influence." *American Literature: A Journal of Literary History, Criticism, and Bibliography* 56:4 (December 1984): 541–59.

Eshleman, Clayton. "Poems as a Mirror Image of Self." Review of Judy Grahn, *The Work of a Common Woman. Los Angeles Times Book Review*, January 20, 1985, 4.

Espinoza, Dionne. "Women of Color and Identity Politics: Translating Theory, *Haciendo Teoría.*" In Sandra Kumamoto Stanley, ed., *Other Sisterhoods: Literary Theory and U.S. Women of Color,* 44–62. Urbana: University of Illinois Press, 1998.

Estrin, Barbara L. "Space-Off and Voice-Over: Adrienne Rich and Wallace Stevens." *Women's Studies* 25 (1995): 23–46.

Evans, Sara. *Personal Politics: The Roots of Women's Liberation in the Civil Rights Movement and the New Left.* New York: Vintage, 1979.

Evans, Sara and Harry Boyte. *Free Spaces: The Sources of Democratic Change in America.* Chicago: University of Chicago Press, 1992.

Faderman, Lillian. "Afterword." In Dana Heller, ed., *Cross Purposes: Lesbians, Feminists, and the Limits of Alliance,* 221–29. Bloomington: Indiana University Press, 1997.

— "The Morbidification of Love Between Women by Nineteenth-Century Sexologists." *Journal of Homosexuality* 4:1 (Autumn 1978): 309–32.

— *Odd Girls and Twilight Lovers: A History of Lesbian Life in Twentieth-Century America.* New York: Columbia University Press, 1991.

— "Preface." In Lillian Faderman, "Love Between Women in Drag." Unpublished manuscript. 1994.

— *Surpassing the Love of Men: Romantic Friendship and Love between Women from the Renaissance to the Present.* New York: William Morrow, 1981.

Farwell, Marilyn. *Heterosexual Plots and Lesbian Narratives.* New York and London: New York University Press, 1996.

— "Toward a Definition of the Lesbian Literary Imagination." 1988. In Susan J. Wolfe and Julia Penelope, eds., *Sexual Practice, Textual Theory: Lesbian Cultural Criticism,* 66–84. Cambridge and Oxford: Blackwell, 1993.

Felman, Jyl Lynn. "I Am Your Sister/Soy Tu Hermana." *Lambda Book Report.* 2:8 (January/February 1991): 16–17.

Felstiner, John. "Judy Grahn." In Marilyn Yalom, *Women Writers of the West Coast: Speaking of Their Lives and Careers,* 93–101. Santa Barbara: Capra, 1983.

Fernández, Charles. "Undocumented Aliens in Queer Nation." *Out/Look* 12 (1991): 20–23.

Findlay, Heather. "Forum: The Question of Lesbian Separatism." Review of Sheila Jeffreys, *The Lesbian Heresy. Lesbian Review of Books* 1:2 (Winter 1994–1995): 3.

Flier advertising Pat Parker reading poetry at Harvard University, September 7, 1985. New York: Lesbian Herstory Archives.

Folayan, Ayofemi. "Gifts of a Mentor." *Gay Community News* (September 3–9, 1989): 9.

— "I Am Your Sister: A Tale of Two Conferences." *off our backs* 20:11 (December 1990): 1–2.

Folayan, Ayofemi S. and Stephanie Byrd. "Pat Parker (1944–1989)." In Sandra Pollack and Denise D. Knight, eds., *Contemporary Lesbian Writers of the United States,* 415–19. Wesport, Conn. and London: Greenwood, 1993.

Ford, Donis W. Review of Pat Parker, *Jonestown and Other Madness. Calyx: A Journal of Art and Literature by Women* 10:1 (Summer 1986): 83–84.

Foster, Jeannette. *Sex Variant Women in Literature.* Tallahassee: Naiad, 1985 [1956].

Foster, Thomas. " 'The Very House of Difference': Gender as 'Embattled' Standpoint." *Genders* 8 (Summer 1990): 17–37.

Fowlkes, Diane L. "Moving from Feminist Identity Politics to Coalition Politics Through a Feminist Materialist Standpoint of Intersubjectivity in Gloria Anzaldúa's *Borderlands/La Frontera: The New Mestiza.*" *Hypatia* 12:2 (Spring 1997): 105–24.

Fraser, Nancy and Linda J. Nicholson. "Social Criticism Without Philosophy: An Encounter Between Feminism and Postmodernism." In Linda J. Nicholson, ed., *Feminism/Postmodernism,* 19–38. New York and London: Routledge, 1990.

Freedman, Estelle. "Missing Links." Review of Lillian Faderman, *Odd Girls and Twilight Lovers. Women's Review of Books* 9:1 (October 1991): 15–17.

Friedman, Susan Stanford. " 'I Go Where I Love': An Intertextual Study of H.D. and Adrienne Rich." *Signs* 9:2 (Winter 1983): 228–45.

— "Reply to Rich." *Signs* 9:2 (Winter 1983): 738–40.

Fuss, Diana. *Essentially Speaking: Feminism, Nature, and Difference.* New York and London: Routledge, 1989.

Fuss, Diana, ed. *Inside/Out: Lesbian Theories, Gay Theories.* New York and London: Routledge, 1991.

Gallop, Jane. *Around 1981: Academic Feminist Literary Theory.* New York and London: Routledge, 1992.

Garber, Linda. "Giving Voice to the Gay and Lesbian Experience: Founders of Bay Area Feminist Movement to Speak." *Stanford Daily,* February 28, 1989, 6.

Garrison, Lisa. "Tribunal Benefit 'Like a Patchwork Quilt.'" *Majority Report,* February 7–February 21, 1976, 15.

Gentile, Mary. "Adrienne Rich and Separatism: The Language of Multiple Realities." *Maenad* 2:2 (Winter 1982): 136–46.

Gibbs, Joan and Sara Bennett, eds. *Top Ranking: A Collection of Articles on Racism and Classism in the Lesbian Community.* Brooklyn: February 3rd Press, 1980.

Gilbert, Sandra and Susan Gubar. *The Madwoman in the Attic: The Woman Writer and the Nineteenth-Century Literary Imagination.* New Haven: Yale University Press, 1979.

Goldsby, Jackie. "Queen for 307 Days: Looking B[l]ack at Vanessa Williams and the Sex Wars." In Arlene Stein, ed., *Sisters, Sexperts, Queers: Beyond the Lesbian Nation,* 110–28. New York: Plume, 1993.

Gomez, Jewelle. "The First Everything." *Gay Community News,* September 3–9, 1989, 9.

— "Imagine a Lesbian . . . a Black Lesbian . . ." *Trivia* 12 (Spring 1988): 45–60.

Grahn, Judy. *Another Mother Tongue: Gay Words, Gay Worlds.* Boston: Beacon, 1984.

— *The Common Woman.* Self-published, 1969.

— "Drawing in Nets." In James McCorkle, ed., *Conversant Essays: Contemporary Poets on Poetry,* 101–3. Detroit: Wayne State University Press, 1990.

— *Edward the Dyke and Other Poems.* Oakland: Women's Press Collective, 1971.

— *The Highest Apple: Sappho and the Lesbian Poetic Tradition.* San Francisco: Spinsters Ink, 1985.

— "Introduction." In Pat Parker, *Movement in Black: The Collected Poetry of Pat Parker, 1961–1978,* 11–15. 1978. Trumansburg, N.Y.: Crossing, 1983.

— "Introduction: Murdering the King's English." In Judy Grahn, ed., *True to Life Adventure Stories,* 6–14. Vol. 1. Oakland: Diana, 1978.

— *The Queen of Swords.* Boston: Beacon, 1987.

— *Really Reading Gertrude Stein: A Selected Anthology with Essays by Judy Grahn.* Freedom, Calif.: Crossing, 1989.

— "Red and Black with Fish in the Middle (A Discussion of Political Decisions Involved in the Common Woman Poems)." In Linda Koolish, ed., *A Whole New Poetry Beginning Here: Contemporary American Women Poets,* 538–60. Vol. 2. Stanford University, 1981.

— *She Who*. Oakland: Diana, 1977.

— *A Woman Is Talking to Death*. Oakland: Diana, 1977.

— *The Work of a Common Woman*. Trumansburg, N.Y.: Crossing, 1978.

Gregg, Debbie. "A Pioneer in Feminist Health Care." *Gay Community News* 17:8 (September 3–9, 1989): 9, 12.

Grier, Barbara [Gene Damon]. *The Lesbian in Literature*. Tallahassee: Naiad, 1981 [1967].

Guy-Sheftall, Beverly and Robin Kilson. "New Directions: A Conversation with Beverly Guy-Sheftall and Robin Kilson." *Women's Review of Books* 15:5 (February 1998): 30–31.

Halberstam, Judith. "Forum: The Question of Lesbian Separatism." Review of Sheila Jeffreys, *The Lesbian Heresy*. *Lesbian Review of Books* 1:2 (Winter 1994–1995): 4–6.

— "Queering Lesbian Studies." In Bonnie Zimmerman and Toni A. H. McNaron, eds., *The New Lesbian Studies: Into the Twenty-First Century*, 256–61. New York: Feminist Press at the City University of New York, 1996.

Hall, Lisa Kahaleole Chang. "Bitches in Solitude: Identity Politics and the Lesbian Community." In Arlene Stein, ed., *Sisters, Sexperts, Queers: Beyond the Lesbian Nation*, 218–29. New York: Plume, 1993.

Hall, Radclyffe. *The Well of Loneliness*. New York: Avon, 1981 [1928].

Hall, Stuart. "Minimal Selves." In Houston A. Baker, Jr., Manthia Diawara, and Ruth H. Lindeborg, ed., *Black British Cultural Studies: A Reader*, 114–19. Chicago and London: University of Chicago Press.

Hammond, Karla. "Audre Lorde: Interview." *Denver Quarterly* 16:1 (Spring 1981): 10–27.

— "An Interview with Audre Lorde." *American Poetry Review* 9:2 (March/April 1980): 18–21.

Hammonds, Evelyn. "Black (W)holes and the Geometry of Black Female Sexuality." *differences* 6:2/3 (1994): 126–45.

Haraway, Donna. "A Manifesto for Cyborgs: Science, Technology, and Socialist Feminism in the 1980s." 1985. In Linda J. Nicholson, ed., *Feminism/Postmodernism*, 190–233. New York and London: Routledge, 1990.

Harper, Phillip Brian, Anne McClintock, José Esteban Muñoz, and Trish Rosen, eds., "Queer Transexions of Race, Nation, and Gender: An Introduction." *Social Text* 52–53 (Fall/Winter 1997).

Harris, Bertha. "Introduction." In Bertha Harris, *Lover*, xvii–lxxviii. New York and London: New York University Press, 1993.

Hedley, Jane. "Nepantilist Poetics: Narrative and Cultural Identity in the Mixed-Language Writings of Irena Klepfisz and Gloria Anzaldúa." *Narrative* 4:1 (January 1996): 36–54.

— "Surviving to Speak New Language: Mary Daly and Adrienne Rich." *Hypatia* 7:2 (Spring 1992): 40–62.

Heller, Dana, ed. *Cross Purposes: Lesbians, Feminists, and the Limits of Alliance.* Bloomington: Indiana University Press, 1997.

Hennessy, Rosemary. "Queer Theory: A Review of the *differences* Special Issue and Wittig's *The Straight Mind.*" *Signs* 18:4 (Summer 1993): 964–73.

Hernton, Calvin. "The Sexual Mountain and Black Women Writers." 1984. In Joanne M. Braxton and Andrée Nicola McLaughlin, eds., *Wild Women in the Whirlwind: Afra-American Culture and the Contemporary Literary Renaissance,* 195–212. New Brunswick, N.J.: Rutgers University Press, 1990.

Herskovits, Melville J. *Dahomey: An Ancient West African Kingdom.* Vols. 1–2. Evanston: Norwestern University Press, 1967 [1938].

Herzog, Anne. "Adrienne Rich and the Discourse of Decolonization." *Centennial Review* 33:3 (Summer 1989): 258–77.

Hogeland, Lisa. "Feminism in the 1970s." In Lisa Hogeland, "Re-Visionary Heteroglossia," 124–73. Diss. Stanford University, 1991.

Holland, Sharon P. "(White) Lesbian Studies." In Bonnie Zimmerman and Toni A. H. McNaron, eds., *The New Lesbian Studies: Into the Twenty-First Century,* 247–55. New York: Feminist Press at the City University of New York, 1996.

Homans, Margaret. "Despecularizing Feminist Literary Theory." Feminist Criticism and (Re)Formations of Literary History Panel. MLA convention, San Diego, December 1994.

hooks, bell. "Postmodern Blackness." In bell hooks, *Yearning: Race, Gender, and Cultural Politics.* Boston: South End, 1990.

Hull, Gloria T. "Living on the Line: Audre Lorde and *Our Dead Behind Us.*" In Cheryl A. Wall, ed., *Changing Our Own Words: Essays on Criticism, Theory, and Writing by Black Women,* 150–72. New Brunswick, N.J. and London: Rutgers University Press, 1989.

Hull, Gloria T., Patricia Bell Scott, and Barbara Smith, eds. *All the Women Are White, All the Blacks Are Men, But Some of Us Are Brave: Black Women's Studies.* New York: Feminist Press at the City University of New York, 1982.

Hutcheon, Linda. *A Poetics of Postmodernism: History, Theory, Fiction.* New York and London: Routledge, 1988.

Ikas, Karin. "Interview with Gloria Anzaldúa." In Gloria Anzaldúa, *Borderlands/La Frontera: The New Mestiza,* 227–46. 2d ed. San Francisco: Aunt Lute, 1999.

"In Memoriam: Pat Parker (1944–1986)." *Black American Literature Forum* 23:3 (Fall 1989).

"An Interview: Audre Lorde and Adrienne Rich." In Audre Lorde, *Sister Outsider: Essays and Speeches,* 81–109. Freedom, Calif.: Crossing, 1984.

Isaacs, D. S. Review of Pat Parker, *Jonestown and Other Madness. Choice* 23:3 (November 1985): 450.

Isabell, Sharon. *Yesterday's Lessons.* Oakland: Women's Press Collective, 1974.

Jaggar, Alison M. *Feminist Politics and Human Nature.* Totowa, N.J.: Rowman and Allanheld, 1983.

JanMohamed, Abdul and David Lloyd. "Introduction: Toward a Theory of Minority Discourse." *Cultural Critique* 6 (Spring 1987): 5–12.

Jeffreys, Sheila. *The Lesbian Heresy: A Feminist Perspective on the Lesbian Sexual Revolution.* North Melbourne: Spinifex, 1993.

— "The Queer Disappearance of Lesbians: Sexuality in the Academy." *Women's Studies International Forum* 17:5 (1994): 459–72.

Johnson, Shelli. Promotional letter for Pat Parker's performance, February 1, 1982. New York: Lesbian Herstory Archives.

Joseph, Gloria I. "A Personal and Political Sketch of Audre Lorde." Program, "I Am Your Sister: Forging Global Connections Across Differences," 19–25. October 5–8, 1990.

"Judy Grahn" (biographical note). In Carl Morse and Joan Larkin, eds. *Gay and Lesbian Poetry in Our Time,* 140. New York: St. Martin's, 1988.

Karp, Sheema Hamdani. "Adrienne Cecile Rich." In Lina Mainiero, ed., *American Women Writers from Colonial Times to the Present: A Critical Reference Guide,* 462–64. Vol. 3. New York: Ungar, 1981.

Kaup, Monika. "Crossing Borders: An Aesthetic Practice in Writings by Gloria Anzaldúa." In Winfried Siemerling and Katrin Schwenk, eds., *Pluralism and the Limits of Authenticity in North American Literatures,* 100–11. Iowa City: University of Iowa Press, 1996.

Kaye/Kantrowitz, Melanie. "Crossover Dreams." Review of Gloria Anzaldúa, *Borderlands/La Frontera.* 1988. In Melanie Kaye/Kantrowitz, *The Issue Is Power: Essays on Women, Jews, Violence, and Resistance,* 237–39. San Francisco: Aunt Lute, 1992.

— "Culture Making: Lesbian Classics in the Year 2000?" *Sinister Wisdom* 13 (Spring 1980): 23–34.

Keating, AnaLouise. "Making 'our shattered faces whole': The Black Goddess and Audre Lorde's Revision of Patriarchal Myth." *Frontiers* 13:1 (1992): 20–33.

— "Myth Smashers, Myth Makers: (Re)Visionary Techniques in the Works of Paula Gunn Allen, Gloria Anzaldúa, and Audre Lorde." In Emmanuel S. Nelson, ed., *Critical Essays: Gay and Lesbian Writers of Color,* 73–95. New York: Haworth, 1993.

— "Writing, Politics, and las Lesberadas: *Platicando con* Gloria Anzaldúa." *Frontiers* 14:1 (Fall 1993): 105–30.

Keating, AnaLouise, ed. *Gloria E. Anzaldúa: Interviews/Entrevistas.* New York and London: Routledge, 2000.

Kennedy, Elizabeth Lapovsky and Madeline D. Davis. *Boots of Leather, Slippers of Gold: The History of a Lesbian Community.* New York and London: Routledge, 1993.

Kim, Willyce. Interview. October 28, 1992.

Kinney, Jeanne. Review of Judy Grahn, *The Work of a Common Woman. Best Sellers* 40:3 (June 1980): 108.

Kinsman, Clare D., ed. "Bullins, Ed." *Contemporary Authors,* 89–91. Vols. 49–52. Detroit: Gale, 1975.

Koolish, Lynda. "A Whole New Poetry Beginning Here: Contemporary American Women Poets." Vols. 1–2. Stanford University, 1981.

Kowalewski, Jean. "Edward the Dyke; Parker the Poet." Review of Judy Grahn, *The Work of a Common Woman*, and Pat Parker, *Movement in Black*. *Body Politic* 64 (June/July 1980): 36.

Kranich, Kimberlie A. "Catalysts for Transforming Ourselves and the World: U.S. Women of Color Periodicals, 1968–1988." National Women's Studies Association Conference, Towson State University, June 1989. New York: Lesbian Herstory Archives.

Kristeva, Julia. *Semiotikè: Recherches pour une sémanalyse.* Paris: Seuil, 1969.

Kushner, Tony. "Last Word: The Lawyer, the Poet." *Advocate* 734 (May 27, 1997): 104.

Lamos, Colleen. "Sexuality Versus Gender: A Kind of Mistake?" In Dana Heller, ed., *Cross Purposes: Lesbians, Feminists, and the Limits of Alliance*, 85–94. Bloomington: Indiana University Press, 1997.

Larkin, Joan. "Taking Risks: Underground Poets from the West Coast—Alta, Judy Grahn, Susan Griffin." *Ms.* 3:11 (May 1975): 90–93.

Lesbian Concentrate: A Lesbianthology of Songs and Poems. Los Angeles: Olivia Records, 1977.

"The *Lesbian Poetry* Reading." Program, Boston, May 9, 1981 or 1982. New York: Lesbian Herstory Archives.

Leyva, Yolanda Chávez. "Breaking the Silence: Putting Latina Lesbian History at the Center." In Bonnie Zimmerman and Toni A. H. McNaron, eds., *The New Lesbian Studies: Into the Twenty-First Century*, 145–52. New York: Feminist Press at the City University of New York, 1996.

A Litany for Survival. Dir. Michelle Parkerson and Ada Gay Griffin. Third World Newsreel, 1995.

Lorde, Audre. "Age, Race, Class, and Sex: Women Redefining Difference." 1980. In Audre Lorde, *Sister Outsider: Essays and Speeches*, 114–23. Freedom, Calif.: Crossing, 1984.

—— *The Black Unicorn.* New York: Norton, 1978.

—— *The Cancer Journals.* San Francisco: Spinster's Ink, 1980.

—— *Chosen Poems: Old and New.* Norton, 1982.

—— *Coal.* New York: Norton, 1976.

—— "Foreword." 1978. In Pat Parker, *Movement in Black: The Collected Poetry of Pat Parker, 1961–1978*, 32–33. Ithaca, N.Y.: Firebrand, 1999.

—— "An Interview: Audre Lorde and Adrienne Rich." 1979. In Audre Lorde, *Sister Outsider: Essays and Speeches*, 81–109. Freedom, Calif.: Crossing, 1984.

—— "Eye to Eye: Black Women, Hatred, and Anger." In Audre Lorde, *Sister Outsider: Essays and Speeches*, 145–75. Freedom, Calif.: Crossing, 1984.

—— "Man Child: A Black Lesbian Feminist's Response." 1979. In Audre Lorde, *Sister Outsider: Essays and Speeches*, 72–80. Freedom, Calif.: Crossing, 1984.

— "The Master's Tools Will Never Dismantle the Master's House." 1979. In Audre Lorde, *Sister Outsider: Essays and Speeches,* 110–13. Freedom, Calif.: Crossing, 1984.

— "An Open Letter to Mary Daly." 1979. In Audre Lorde, *Sister Outsider: Essays and Speeches,* 66–71. Freedom, Calif.: Crossing, 1984.

— "Poetry Is Not a Luxury." 1977. In Audre Lorde, *Sister Outsider: Essays and Speeches,* 36–39. Freedom, Calif.: Crossing, 1984.

— *Sister Outsider: Essays and Speeches.* Freedom, Calif.: Crossing, 1984.

— "The Transformation of Silence Into Language and Action." 1977. In Audre Lorde, *Sister Outsider: Essays and Speeches,* 40–44. Freedom, Calif.: Crossing, 1984.

— "The Uses of Anger: Women Respond to Racism." 1981. In Audre Lorde, *Sister Outsider: Essays and Speeches,* 124–33. Freedom, Calif.: Crossing, 1984.

— "Uses of the Erotic: The Erotic as Power." 1978. In Audre Lorde, *Sister Outsider: Essays and Speeches,* 53–59. Freedom, Calif.: Crossing, 1984.

— *Zami: A New Spelling of My Name.* Trumansburg, N.Y.: Crossing, 1982.

Lorde, Audre and Susan Leigh Star. "Interview with Audre Lorde." In Robin Ruth Linden, Darlene R. Pagano, Diana E. H. Russell, and Susan Leigh Star, eds., *Against Sadomasochism: A Radical Feminist Analysis,* 66–71. San Francisco: Frog in the Well, 1982.

Louÿs, Pierre. *The Songs of Bilitis.* New York: Capricorn, 1932.

Lugones, María. "On *Borderlands/La Frontera:* An Interpretive Essay." *Hypatia* 7:4 (Fall 1992): 31–37.

Lunde, Diane. "Judy Grahn." In Sandra Pollack and Denise D. Knight, eds., *Contemporary Lesbian Writers of the United States,* 237–43. Wesport, Conn. and London: Greenwood, 1993.

McCorkle, James. *The Still Performance: Writing, Self, and Interconnection in Five Postmodern American Poets.* Charlottesville: University Press of Virginia, 1992.

McDaniel, Judith. *Reconstituting the World: The Poetry and Vision of Adrienne Rich.* Argyle, N.Y.: Spinsters, 1978.

McDowell, Deborah E. "New Directions for Black Feminist Criticism." 1980. In Elaine Showalter, ed., *The New Feminist Criticism: Essays on Women, Literature, and Theory,* 186–99. New York: Pantheon, 1985.

McLaurin-Allen, Irma. "Audre Lorde." In Trudier Harris and Thadious M. Davis, eds., *Afro-American Poets Since 1955,* 217–22. Detroit: Bruccoli Clark, 1985.

McNaron, Toni A. H. and Bonnie Zimmerman. "Introduction." In Bonnie Zimmerman and Toni A. H. McNaron, eds., *The New Lesbian Studies: Into the Twenty-First Century,* xiii–xix. New York: Feminist Press at the City University of New York, 1996.

McPherson, Diane. "Adrienne Rich." In Sandra Pollack and Denise D. Knight, eds., *Contemporary Lesbian Writers of the United States,* 433–45. Wesport, Conn. and London: Greenwood, 1993.

Malinowitz, Harriet. "Lesbian Studies and Postmodern Queer Thoery." In Bonnie Zimmerman and Toni A. H. McNaron, eds., *The New Lesbian Studies: Into the Twenty-First Century,* 262–68. New York: Feminist Press at the City University of New York, 1996.

Marcus, Jane. "Still Practice, A/Wrested Alphabet: Toward a Feminist Aesthetic." In Shari Benstock, ed., *Feminist Issues in Literary Scholarship,* 79–97. Bloomington: Indiana University Press, 1987.

Marks, Elaine. "Lesbian Intertextuality." In Susan Wolfe and Julia Penelope, eds., *Sexual Practice, Textual Theory,* 271–90. Oxford and Cambridge, Mass.: Blackwell, 1993.

Martin, Biddy. "Sexual Practice and Changing Lesbian Identities." In Michèle Barrett and Anne Phillips, eds., *Destabilizing Theory: Contemporary Feminist Debates,* 93–119. Stanford: Stanford University Press, 1992.

Martin, Wendy. "Another View of the 'City Upon a Hill': The Prophetic Vision of Adrienne Rich." In Susan Merrill Squier, ed., *Women Writers and the City: Essays in Feminist Literary Criticism,* 249–64. Knoxville: University of Tennessee Press, 1984.

Martin, Del and Phyllis Lyon. *Lesbian/Woman.* New York: Bantam, 1972.

Martinez, Inez. "The Poetry of Judy Grahn." *Margins* 23 (August 1975): 48–50.

Meese, Elizabeth. *(Ex)tensions: Re-figuring Feminist Criticism.* Urbana: University of Illinois Press, 1990.

Miller, Mev. "Forum: The Question of Lesbian Separatism." Review of Sheila Jeffreys, *The Lesbian Heresy. Lesbian Review of Books* 1:2 (Winter 1994–1995): 4.

Millett, Kate. *Sexual Politics.* 1969. New York: Ballantine, 1989.

Modleski, Tania. "The White Negress and the Heavy-Duty Dyke." In Dana Heller, ed., *Cross Purposes: Lesbians, Feminists, and the Limits of Alliance,* 64–82. Bloomington: Indiana University Press, 1997.

Mohr, Richard. "When Men Kiss Men." Review of Eve Kosofsky Sedgwick, *Tendencies. Lambda Book Report* 4:2 (January/February 1994): 24–25.

Montefiore, Jan. *Feminism and Poetry: Language, Experience, Identity in Women's Writing.* London and New York: Pandora, 1987.

Moraga, Cherríe. *The Last Generation.* Boston: South End, 1993.

Moraga, Cherríe and Gloria Anzaldúa, eds. *This Bridge Called My Back: Writings By Radical Women of Color.* New York: Kitchen Table, 1983 [1981].

Morgan, Robin. "Introduction: The Women's Revolution." In Robin Morgan, ed., *Sisterhood Is Powerful: An Anthology of Writings from the Women's Liberation Movement,* xv–xlvi. New York: Vintage, 1970.

Morgan, Thaïs. "The Space of Intertextuality." In Patrick O'Donnell and Robert Con Davis, eds., *Intertextuality and Contemporary American Fiction,* 239–79. Baltimore and London: Johns Hopkins University Press, 1989.

Morse, Carl and Joan Larkin, eds. *Gay and Lesbian Poetry in Our Time.* New York: St. Martin's, 1988.

— "Introduction: A Conversation with Carl Morse and Joan Larkin." In Carl Morse and Joan Larkin, eds. *Gay and Lesbian Poetry in Our Time*, xv–xxvi. New York: St. Martin's, 1988.

Morton, Donald. "Birth of the Cyberqueer." *PMLA* 110:3 (May 1995): 369–81.

— "The Politics of Queer Theory in the (Post)Modern Moment." *Genders* 17 (Fall 1993): 121–50.

Munt, Sally, ed. *New Lesbian Criticism: Literary and Cultural Readings*. New York: Columbia University Press, 1992.

Myrsiades, Kostas and Linda Myrsiades, eds. *Race-ing Representation: Voice, History, and Sexuality*. Lanham, Md.: Rowman and Littlefield, 1998.

Nestle, Joan. "A Place for All of Us: *Lesbian Poetry Anthology*." 1981. Review of Elly Bulkin and Joan Larkin, eds., *Lesbian Poetry: An Anthology*. New York: Lesbian Herstory Archives.

"A New Book of Lesbian Poetry by Pat Parker." *Furies* (June–July 1972): 4.

Nicholson, Linda J., ed. *Feminism/Postmodernism*. New York and London: Routledge, 1990.

Nkrumah, Kwame. "On the Coup in Ghana." *The Black Scholar* (May 1972): 23–26.

"A Note to the Reader." In Carl Morse and Joan Larkin, eds., *Gay and Lesbian Poetry in Our Time*, xxvii. New York: St. Martin's, 1988.

Oktenberg, Adrian. "A Quartet of Voices." Review of Pat Parker, *Jonestown and Other Madness. Women's Review of Books* 3 (April 1986): 17–19.

Ongiri, Amy Abugo. "We Are Family: Miscegenation, Black Nationalism, Black Masculinity, and the Black Gay Cultural Imagination." In Kostas Myrsiades and Linda Myrsiades, eds. *Race-ing Representation: Voice, History, and Sexuality*, 231–46. Lanham, Md.: Rowman and Littlefield, 1998.

Ostriker, Alicia. *Stealing the Language: The Emergence of Women's Poetry in America*. Boston: Beacon, 1986.

— *Writing Like a Woman*. Ann Arbor: University of Michigan Press, 1983.

Parker, Pat. *Child of Myself*. 2d ed. Oakland: Women's Press Collective, 1972.

— *Jonestown and Other Madness*. Ithaca: Firebrand, 1985.

— *Movement in Black: The Collected Poetry of Pat Parker, 1961–1978*. Ithaca: Firebrand, 1999 [1978].

— *Movement in Black: The Collected Poetry of Pat Parker, 1961–1978*. Trumansburg, N.Y.: Crossing, 1983 [1978].

— *Pit Stop*. Oakland: Women's Press Collective, 1973.

— "Revolution: It's Not Neat or Pretty or Quick." 1980. In Cherríe Moraga and Gloria Anzaldúa, eds., *This Bridge Called My Back: Writings by Radical Women of Color*, 238–42. New York: Kitchen Table, 1983.

— "Where Will You Be?" In Barbara Smith, ed., *Home Girls: A Black Feminist Anthology*, 209–13. New York: Kitchen Table, 1983.

— *Womanslaughter*. Oakland: Diana, 1978.

— "Womanslaughter" [excerpts]. 1974. In Diana E. H. Russell and Nicole Van de

Ven, eds., *Crimes Against Women: Proceedings of the International Tribunal,* 147–50. East Palo Alto: Frog in the Well, 1984.

Pellegrini, Ann. "Women on Top, Boys on the Side, But Some of Us Are Brave: Blackness, Lesbianism, and the Visible." In Kostas Myrsiades and Linda Myrsiades, eds., *Race-ing Representation: Voice, History, and Sexuality,* 247–63. Lanham, Md.: Rowman and Littlefield, 1998.

— *Performance Anxieties: Staging Psychoanalysis, Staging Race.* New York and London: Routledge, 1997.

Pérez-Torres, Rafael. *Movements in Chicano Poetry: Against Myths, Against Margins.* New York: Cambridge University Press, 1995.

Perry, Donna. "Interview with Gloria Anzaldúa." In Donna Perry, *Backtalk: Women Writers Speak Out,* 19–42. New Brunswick, N.J.: Rutgers University Press, 1993.

Peters, Colette. "'Whatever Happens, This Is': Lesbian Speech-Act Theory and Adrienne Rich's 'Twenty-One Love Poems.'" *English Studies in Canada* 21:2 (June 1995): 189–205.

Phelan, Shane. "(Be)Coming Out: Lesbian Identity and Politics." *Signs* 18:4 (Summer 1993): 765–90.

— *Getting Specific: Postmodern Lesbian Politics.* Minneapolis and London: University of Minnesota Press, 1994.

— *Identity Politics: Lesbian Feminism and the Limits of Community.* Philadelphia: Temple University Press, 1989.

Phelan, Shane, ed. *Playing with Fire: Queer Politics, Queer Theories.* New York and London: Routledge, 1997.

"A Poetry Reading Workshop from Open Lines." Advertisement. New York City. 1985. New York: Lesbian Herstory Archives.

Pollack, Sandra and Denise D. Knight, eds. *Contemporary Lesbian Writers of the United States.* Wesport, Conn. and London: Greenwood, 1993.

Preminger, Alex, ed. *Princeton Encyclopedia of Poetry and Poetics.* Enlarged ed. Princeton: Princeton University Press, 1974.

Price, Deborah. "Patchwork" (Lillian Faderman). *Belles Lettres* 6 (Summer 1994): 62–64.

Provost, Kara. "Becoming Afrekete: The Trickster in the Work of Audre Lorde." *MELUS* 20:4 (Winter 1995): 45–59.

Radicalesbians. "The Woman-Identified Woman." 1970. In Anne Koedt, Ellen Levine, and Anita Rapone, eds., *Radical Feminism,* 240–45. New York: Quadrangle, 1973.

Raiskin, Judith. "Inverts and Hybrids: Lesbian Rewritings of Sexual and Racial Identities." In Laura Doan, ed., *The Lesbian Postmodern,* 156–72. New York: Columbia University Press, 1994.

Ramírez, Arthur. Review of Gloria Anzaldúa, *Borderlands/La Frontera. Americas Review* 17:3–4 (Fall-Winter 1989): 185–87.

Ramos, Colleen. "Letter to the Editor." *LGSN* 20:3 (November 1993): 3.

Ramos, Juanita, ed. *Compañeras: Latina Lesbians*. New York: Latina Lesbian History Project, 1987.

Randall, Dudley, ed. *The Black Poets*. New York, Bantam, 1971.

Reagon, Bernice Johnson. "Coalition Politics: Turning the Century." 1981. In Barbara Smith, ed., *Home Girls: A Black Feminist Anthology*, 356–68. New York: Kitchen Table, 1983.

Retallack, Joan. ":Rethinking:Literary: Feminism: (Three Essays Onto Shaky Grounds)." In Lynn Keller and Cristanne Miller, eds., *Feminist Measures: Soundings in Poetry and Theory*, 344–77. Ann Arbor: University of Michigan Press.

Reuman, Ann E. " 'Wild Tongues Can't Be Tamed': Gloria Anzaldúa's (R)evolution of Voice." In Deidre Lashgari, ed., *Violence, Silence, and Anger: Women's Writing as Transgression*, 305–19. Charlottesville: University Press of Virginia, 1995.

Review of Audre Lorde, *The Black Unicorn.Kirkus Reviews*, October 1, 1978, 1129.

Review of Audre Lorde, *Chosen Poems: Old and New. Publisher's Weekly* 221:20 (May 14, 1982): 214.

Rich, Adrienne. "Blood, Bread, and Poetry: The Location of the Poet." 1983. In Adrienne Rich, *Blood, Bread, and Poetry: Selected Prose, 1979–1985*, 167–87. New York: Norton, 1986.

— *Blood, Bread, and Poetry: Selected Prose, 1979–1985*. New York: Norton, 1986.

— "Comment on Friedman's ' "I Go Where I Love": An Intertextual Study of H.D. and Adrienne Rich.' " *Signs* 9:2 (Winter 1983): 733–38.

— "Compulsory Heterosexuality and Lesbian Existence." 1980. In Adrienne Rich, *Blood, Bread, and Poetry: Selected Prose, 1979–1985*, 23–75. New York: Norton, 1986.

— "Conditions for Work." 1976. In Adrienne Rich, *On Lies, Secrets, and Silence: Selected Prose, 1966–1978*, 203–214. New York: Norton, 1979.

— "Disloyal to Civilization: Feminism, Racism, Gynephobia." 1978. In Adrienne Rich, *On Lies, Secrets, and Silence: Selected Prose, 1966–1978*, 275–310. New York: Norton, 1979.

— *The Dream of a Common Language: Poems, 1974–1977*. New York: Norton, 1978.

— "The Fact of a Doorframe." 1974. In Adrienne Rich, *The Fact of a Doorframe: Poems Selected and New, 1950–1984*. New York: Norton, 1984.

— "It Is the Lesbian in Us . . . 1976. In Adrienne Rich, *On Lies, Secrets, and Silence: Selected Prose, 1966–1978*, 199–202. New York: Norton, 1979.

— "The Meaning of Our Love for Women Is What We Have Constantly to Expand." 1977. In Adrienne Rich, *On Lies, Secrets, and Silence: Selected Prose, 1966–1978*, 223–30. New York: Norton, 1979.

— "Motherhood: The Contemporary Emergency and the Quantum Leap." 1978. In Adrienne Rich, *On Lies, Secrets, and Silence: Selected Prose, 1966–1978*, 259–74. New York: Norton, 1979.

— *Necessities of Life*. New York: Norton, 1966.

— "North American Time." In Adrienne Rich, *Your Native Land, Your Life,* 33–36. New York: Norton, 1986.

— *On Lies, Secrets, and Silence: Selected Prose, 1966–1978*. New York: Norton, 1979.

— "Power and Danger: The Work of a Common Woman by Judy Grahn." 1977. In Judy Grahn, *The Work of a Common Woman,* 7–21. Trumansburg, N.Y.: Crossing, 1978.

— *Poems: Selected and New, 1950–1974*. New York: Norton, 1975.

— *Sources*. Woodside, Calif.: Heyeck, 1983.

— "Split at the Root: An Essay on Jewish Identity." 1982. In Adrienne Rich, *Blood, Bread, and Poetry: Selected Prose, 1979–1985,* 100–23. New York: Norton, 1986.

— "Teaching Language in Open Admissions." 1972. In Adrienne Rich, *On Lies, Secrets, and Silence: Selected Prose, 1966–1978,* 51–68. New York: Norton, 1979.

— "Toward a Woman-Centered University." 1973–74. In Adrienne Rich, *On Lies, Secrets, and Silence: Selected Prose, 1966–1978,* 125–56. New York: Norton, 1979.

— *What Is Found There: Notebooks on Poetry and Politics*. New York: Norton, 1993.

— "When We Dead Awaken: Writing as Re-Vision." 1971. In Adrienne Rich, *On Lies, Secrets, and Silence: Selected Prose, 1966–1978,* 35–49. New York: Norton, 1979.

Riffaterre, Michael. "Intertextual Representation: On Mimesis as Interpretive Discourse." *Critical Inquiry* 11:1 (1984): 141–62.

Roof, Judith. *A Lure of Knowledge: Lesbian Sexuality and Theory*. New York: Columbia University Press, 1991.

RR. Review of Pat Parker, *Jonestown and Other Madness.Library Journal* 110:12 (July 1985): 77.

Rule, Jane. *Lesbian Images*. 1975. New York: Pocket, 1976.

Runzo, Sandra. "Intimacy, Complicity, and the Imagination: Adrienne Rich's *Twenty-One Love Poems*." *Genders* 16 (Spring 1993): 61–79.

Rupp, Leila. "Finding the Lesbians in Lesbian History: Reflections on Female Same-Sex Sexuality in the Western World." In Bonnie Zimmerman and Toni A. H. McNaron, eds., *The New Lesbian Studies: Into the Twenty-First Century,* 153–59. New York: Feminist Press at the City University of New York, 1996.

Rushin, Kate. "Pat Parker: Creating Room to Speak and Grow." Interview. *Sojourner* 11 (October 1985): 28–9.

Rushing, Andrea Benton. "A Creative Use of African Sources." Review of Audre Lorde, *The Black Unicorn.Obsidian* 5:3 (Winter 1979): 114–16.

Rycenga, Jennifer. "Multiple Lesbian Identities. Review of Arlene Stein, ed., *Sisters, Sexperts, Queers.Lesbian Review of Books* 1:2 (Winter 1994–95): 22.

Salaam, Kalamu ya and Jerry W. Ward Jr. "Sayings, Sermons, Tall Tales, and Lies— Contemporary Black Poetry." *African American Review* 27:1 (Spring 1993): 117–18.

Saldívar-Hull, Sonia. "Introduction to the Second Edition." In Gloria Anzaldúa, *Borderlands/La Frontera: The New Mestiza,* 1–15. 2d ed. San Francisco: Aunt Lute, 1999.

Sandoval, Chela. "Mestizaje as Method: Feminists-of-Color Challenge the Canon." In Carla Trujillo, *Living Chicana Theory*, 352–70. Berkeley: Third Woman, 1998.

— "U.S. Third World Feminism: The Theory and Method of Oppositional Consciousness in the Postmodern World." *Genders* 10 (Spring 1991): 1–24.

Schenck, Celeste. *Mourning and Panegyric: The Poetics of Pastoral Ceremony.* University Park: Pennsylvania State University Press, 1988.

Schulman, Sarah. "Revisiting the Sex Wars." Review of Arlene Stein, ed., *Sisters, Sexperts, Queers.Lambda Book Report* 3:11 (July/August 1993): 24–25.

Seajay, Carol. "The Women-in-Print Movement, Some Beginnings: An Interview with Judy Grahn." Part 1. *Feminist Bookstore News* 13:1 (May/June 1990): 19–25.

— "The Women-in-Print Movement, Some Beginnings: An Interview with Judy Grahn." Part 2. *Feminist Bookstore News* 13, Summer Supplement (August 1990): 53–61.

— "The Women-in-Print Movement, Some Beginnings: An Interview with Judy Grahn." Part 3. *Feminist Bookstore News* 13:3 (September/October 1990): 35–43.

Sedgwick, Eve Kosofsky. *Epistemology of the Closet.* Berkeley and Los Angeles: University of California Press, 1990.

— *Tendencies.* Durham: Duke University Press, 1993.

Seibles, Timothy. "A Quilt in Shades of Black: The Black Aesthetic in Twentieth-Century African American Poetry." In Jack Myers and David Wojahn, eds., *A Profile of Twentieth-Century American Poetry*, 158–89. Carbondale and Edwardsville: Southern Illinois University Press, 1991.

SGJ. Review of Pat Parker, *Jonestown and Other Madness. New Pages* 10 (1986): 24–5.

Shakur, Assata. *Assata.* Westport, Conn.: Hill, 1987.

Shariat, Fahamisha. Review of Audre Lorde, *The Black Unicorn.Conditions: Five, The Black Women's Issue* 2:2 (Autumn 1979): 173–76.

Showalter, Elaine, ed. *The New Feminist Criticism: Essays on Women, Literature, and Theory.* New York: Pantheon, 1985.

Siconolfi, Michael T. Review of Audre Lorde, *The Black Unicorn.Best Sellers* 38:10 (January 1979): 327.

Sinister Wisdom 43/44 (Summer 1991). "The 15th Anniversary Retrospective."

Smith, Barbara, ed. *Home Girls: A Black Feminist Anthology.* New York: Kitchen Table, 1983.

— "Naming the Unnameable: The Poetry of Pat Parker." *Conditions: Three* 1:3 (Spring 1978): 99–103.

— "Queer Politics: Where's the Revolution?" *Nation* (July 5, 1993): 12–16.

— "Toward a Black Feminist Criticism." 1977. In Gloria T. Hull, Patricia Bell Scott, and Barbara Smith, eds., *All the Women Are White, All the Blacks Are Men, But Some of Us Are Brave: Black Women's Studies*, 157–75. New York: Feminist Press at the City University of New York, 1982.

Smith, David Lionel. "The Black Arts Movement and Its Critics." *American Literary History* 3:1 (Spring 1991): 93–110.

Sorrel, Lorraine and Sue Sojourner. "Interview: Lesbian Poetry." *off our backs* 11:8 (August-September 1981): 20–1.

South, Cris. Review of Pat Parker, *Movement in Black*. *Feminary: A Feminist Journal for the South* 10:3 (1980): 69–74.

SP. Review of Judy Grahn, *The Work of a Common Woman*. *Booklist* 77:1 (September 1, 1980): 25.

Spelman, Elizabeth. *Inessential Woman: Problems of Exclusion in Feminist Thought*. Boston: Beacon, 1988.

Stanley, Sandra Kumamoto, ed. *Other Sisterhoods: Literary Theory and U.S. Women of Color*. Urbana: University of Illinois Press, 1998.

Stato, Joanne. "I Am Your Sister: Tribute to Audre Lorde." *off our backs* 20:11 (December 1990): 2–5+.

— "Pat Parker, 1944–1989." *off our backs* (August-September 1989): 1, 31.

Steakley, James. *The Homosexual Emancipation Movement in Germany*. New York: Arno, 1975.

Stein, Arlene. *Sex and Sensibility: Stories of a Lesbian Generation*. Berkeley: University of California Press, 1997.

— "Sisters and Queers: The Decentering of Lesbian Feminism." *Socialist Review* 22:1 (January-March 1992): 33–55.

Stein, Arlene, ed. *Sisters, Sexperts, Queers: Beyond the Lesbian Nation*. New York: Plume, 1993.

Stenson, Linnea A. Review of Lillian Faderman, *Odd Girls and Twilight Lovers: A History of Lesbian Life in Twentieth-Century America. Discourse* 15:1 (Fall 1992): 182–86.

Stepto, R. B. "The Phenomenal Woman and the Severed Daughter." Review of Maya Angelou, *And Still I Rise*, and Audre Lorde, *The Black Unicorn. Parnassus* 8:1 (Fall/Winter 1979): 312–20.

Stimpson, Catharine R. "Adrienne Rich and Lesbian/Feminist Poetry." In Catharine R. Stimpson, *Where the Meanings Are: Feminism and Cultural Spaces*, 140–54. New York and London: Methuen, 1988.

sudi mae. "We Have to Be Our Own Spark: An Interview with 'Gente' Third-World Lesbian Softball Team." *Tide* 3:9 (July 1974): 6–7, 25.

Suleiman, Susan Rubin. *Subversive Intent: Gender, Politics, and the Avant-Garde*. Cambridge and London: Harvard University Press, 1990.

Swanson, Diana L. "Subverting Closure: Compulsory Heterosexuality and Compulsory Endings in Middle-Class British Women's Novels." In Susan J. Wolfe and Julia Penelope, eds., *Sexual Practice, Textual Theory: Lesbian Cultural Criticism*, 150–63. Cambridge and Oxford: Blackwell, 1993.

Tallen, Bette. "Forum: The Question of Lesbian Separatism." Review of Sheila Jeffreys, *The Lesbian Heresy*. *Lesbian Review of Books* 1:2 (Winter 1994–1995): 6.

Taylor, Verta and Leila J. Rupp. "Women's Culture and Lesbian Feminist Activism: A Reconsideration of Cultural Feminism." *Signs* 19:1 (Autumn 1993): 32–61.

"The Ten Most Influential Women and Men in Gay and Lesbian Literature in the Past Decade." *Lambda Book Report* 2:9 (March/April 1991): 11.

"Tribute to Pat Parker." *Calyx: A Journal of Art and Literature by Women* 12:1 (Summer 1989): 90–94.

Trujillo, Carla, ed. *Chicana Lesbians: The Girls Our Mothers Warned Us About.* Berkeley: Third Woman, 1991.

— *Living Chicana Theory.* Berkeley: Third Woman, 1998.

Vance, Carole S., ed. *Pleasure and Danger: Exploring Female Sexuality.* Boston: Routledge and Kegan Paul, 1984.

"The Varied Voices of Black Women." Concert/reading program, New York City, November 7, 1978. New York: Lesbian Herstory Archives.

Wakeling, Louise Katherine, Margaret Bradstock, and Mary Fallon. "Poetry Doesn't Sell." *Connexions* 13 (Summer 1984): 27–27.

Warner, Michael. "From Queer to Eternity: An Army of Theorists Cannot Fail." *Village Voice Literary Supplement,* June 1992, 18–19.

Warner, Michael, ed. *Fear of a Queer Planet: Queer Politics and Social Theory.* Minneapolis and London: University of Minnesota Press, 1993.

Wescott, Pamela. "Judy Grahn: Pursuing the Work We Want." *Gay Community News* 14:37 (April 5, 1987): 8–9.

Weston, Kath. "Theory, Theory, Who's Got the Theory?" In Kath Weston, *Long Slow Burn: Sexuality and Social Science,* 143–46. New York and London: Routledge, 1998.

"Where Will You Be? A Tribute to Pat Parker." Program, New York City, September 15, 1989. New York: Lesbian Herstory Archives.

Whisman, Vera. "Identity Crises: Who Is a Lesbian, Anyway?" In Arlene Stein, ed., *Sisters, Sexperts, Queers: Beyond the Lesbian Nation,* 47–60. New York: Plume, 1993.

Wiegman, Robyn. "Introduction: Mapping the Lesbian Postmodern." In Laura Doan, ed., *The Lesbian Postmodern,* 1–20. New York: Columbia University Press, 1994.

Wilson, Anna. "Audre Lorde and the African-American Tradition: When the Family Is Not Enough." In Sally Munt, ed., *New Lesbian Criticism: Literary and Cultural Readings,* 75–93. New York: Columbia University Press, 1992.

Wittig, Monique. *The Lesbian Body.* Trans. David Le Vay. New York: Avon, 1978.

— *The Straight Mind and Other Essays.* Boston: Beacon, 1992.

Wolfe, Maxine. "Interview with Roma Guy, Director of the Capital Campaign for the San Francisco Women's Building and One of Its Founders." February 18, 1993. New York: Lesbian Herstory Archives.

Wolfe, Susan J. and Julia Penelope, eds., *Sexual Practice, Textual Theory: Lesbian Cultural Criticism.* Cambridge and Oxford: Blackwell, 1993.

Woman to Woman: A Book of Poems and Drawings by Women. 2d ed. Oakland: Women's Press Collective, 1974.

Wood, Deborah. "Interview with Audre Lorde." In Juliette Bowles, ed., *In the Memory and Spirit of Frances, Zora, and Lorraine: Essays and Interviews on Black Women and Writing,* 11–22. Howard University: Institute for the Arts and Humanities, 1979.

Woodwoman, Libby. "Pat Parker Talks About Her Life and Her Work." *Margins* 23 (August 1975): 60–61.

Worsham, Fabian Clements. "The Poetics of Matrilineage: Mothers and Daughters in the Poetry of African American Women, 1965–1985." In Elizabeth Brown-Guillory, ed., *Women of Color: Mother-Daughter Relationships in Twentieth-Century Literature,* 117–31. Austin: University of Texas Press, 1996.

Wright, Jay. "Desire's Design, Vision's Resonance: Black Poetry's Ritual and Historical Voice." *Callaloo* 10:1 (Winter 1987): 13–28.

Yarbro-Bejarano, Yvonne. "Gloria Anzaldúa's *Borderlands/La Frontera:* Cultural Studies, 'Difference,' and the Non-Unitary Subject." *Cultural Critique* (Fall 1994): 5–28.

Yorke, Liz. "Constructing a Lesbian Poetic for Survival: Broumas, Rukeyser, H.D., Rich, Lorde." In Joseph Bristow, ed., *Sexual Sameness, Textual Difference: On Lesbian and Gay Writing,* 187–209. New York and London: Routledge, 1992.

—— *Impertinent Voices: Subversive Strategies in Contemporary Women's Poetry.* New York and London: Routledge, 1991.

—— "Primary Intensities: Lesbian Poetry and the Reading of Difference." In Liz Yorke, *Impertinent Voices: Subversive Strategies in Contemporary Women's Poetry,* 157–202. New York and London: Routledge, 1991.

Zimmerman, Bonnie. " 'Confessions' of a Lesbian Feminist." In Dana Heller, ed., *Cross Purposes: Lesbians, Feminists, and the Limits of Alliance,* 157–68. Bloomington: Indiana University Press, 1997.

—— "History, Canons, and the Question of Citation." Feminist Criticism and (Re)Formations of Literary History Panel. MLA convention, San Diego, December 1994.

—— "Lesbians Like This and That: Some Notes on Lesbian Criticism for the Nineties." In Sally Munt, ed., *New Lesbian Criticism: Literary and Cultural Readings,* 1–15. Columbia University Press, 1992.

—— "Placing Lesbians." In Bonnie Zimmerman and Toni A. H. McNaron, eds., *The New Lesbian Studies: Into the Twenty-First Century,* 269–75. New York: Feminist Press at the City University of New York, 1996.

—— "What Has Never Been: An Overview of Lesbian Feminist Criticism." 1981. In Elaine Showalter, ed., *The New Feminist Criticism: Essays on Women, Literature, and Theory,* 200–24. New York: Pantheon, 1985.

Zimmerman, Bonnie and Toni A. H. McNaron, eds. *The New Lesbian Studies: Into the Twenty-First Century.* New York: Feminist Press at the City University of New York, 1996.

Index